BLACK WOMEN'S PATHWAYS TO EXECUTIVE ACADEMIC LEADERSHIP

BLACK WOMEN'S PATHWAYS TO EXECUTIVE ACADEMIC LEADERSHIP

LESSONS FROM LIVED EXPERIENCES

Edited by

Crystal R. Chambers, JD, PhD

BLACK WOMEN'S PATHWAYS TO EXECUTIVE ACADEMIC LEADERSHIP:
LESSONS FROM LIVED EXPERIENCES

ISBN: 978-1-942774-93-8

Printed in the United States of America.

Mailing/Submissions:
Universal Write Publications, LLC
421 8th avenue, Suite 86
New York, NY 10116

Website: UWPBooks.com

This book has been partially supported with a financial grant from SAGE Publishing.

"When and where I enter...
then and there the whole
Negro race enters with me."

– ANNA JULIA COOPER

Contents

About the Editor

Dr. Crystal R. Chambers is a 2018 Carnegie Fellow and Professor of Educational Leadership at East Carolina University. Additional honors include the American Association of Higher Education Black Caucus Doctoral Student Award (2005), a 2013 Chancellor's Leadership Academy Fellowship, a 2016 East Carolina University Women of Distinction Award, and 2021 Fellow of the UNC System Executive Leadership Institute. Her areas of expertise are centered on issues of race and gender in higher education and include college choice, faculty advancement, and doctoral education. She is the author of over 30 peer-reviewed articles and book chapters. In addition to this volume she is an editor and author of several book volumes such as *Law and Social Justice in Higher Education* (Routledge, 2016) and *African American Rural Education* (Emerald, 2020).

List of Tables and Figures

Foreword

Crystal Chambers' *Black Women's Pathways to Executive Academic Leadership: Lessons From Lived Experiences* is an insightful and inspirational work for women of color who are pursuing careers in senior-level administrative positions in higher education. This volume is written through the lenses of successful Black women who have occupied seats at the executive table.

Despite observations in the workplace that demonstrate women face challenges different from men, they are not compensated at the rate of men for the comparable experience, education, and effort. Women are still receiving "first woman" appointments in the workplace—the clarion call has been issued for empowered women to serve in seats of power in the academe and beyond.

I met Crystal Chambers over 15 years ago when she was serving as a junior faculty member at a university in North Carolina. Over the years, she has evolved into a scholar who doesn't accept mediocrity, dares to question, and has a direct approach to addressing issues which has garnered her respect in the academe. Dr. Chambers has expertise in law and policy in higher education, race, gender, and intersectionality, which allows her to frame this volume with keen insight. She is a respected author, researcher, and educator.

Throughout my career, I have prepared for opportunities that would lead to a seat at the table. My journey has had steps that included positions as a lecturer and academic advisor, an assistant vice provost at a university, and the ranks from assistant vice president for Academic and Student Affairs to Vice President for Academic and Student Affairs at the University of North Carolina System Office, all of which played a role in preparing me to serve as the chancellor of Elizabeth City State University (NC).

Each step of the way, I was fortunate to have mentors and sponsors who helped me navigate my way to the table and equipped me with leadership nuggets that would help me remain there. *Black Women's Pathways to Executive Academic Leadership: Lessons From Lived Experiences* is a must read for women who are seeking authentic insight into senior leadership in higher education. Research literature shows how Black women are underrepresented as leaders at the helm of higher education institutions. However, the readers will benefit from the lived experiences of successful Black women whose pathways led them to the helm.

This volume showcases pathways of Black women who are senior executives at varied institution types—community colleges, four-year predominantly White and historically Black public institutions. Chambers introduces the book with insightful demographics of Black women who have traversed pathways of executive leadership in higher education. The authors of the various chapters not only explore the challenges these executives faced, but also share how these challenges were met and what institutions can do to be intentional in preparing women to navigate leadership challenges and successfully lead higher education institutions.

I highly recommend *Black Women's Pathways to Executive Academic Leadership: Lessons From Lived Experiences* to women who aspire to have a seat at the higher education executive table. There is rich insight that flows up from a spring of experiences that will enrich the reader. The book is not just for Black women. It is also a good read for those who can influence positive change that will remove the unnecessary irritants that hinder women in pursuit of leading America's colleges and universities.

Some people will assert that leadership is more about influence than about a title or position. There are people without the title who have far-reaching influence. Unfortunately, there are people with the title who have little influence. However, the day has come for those with the influence to be rewarded with the position and the pay.

It is your time! It is my time! It is our time! Ladies, we can do this! Former Supreme Court Justice Ruth Bader Ginsberg said, "Women belong in places where decisions are being made. It shouldn't be that women are the exception."

How do we get there?

In the words of Shirley Chisolm, the first African American woman in Congress and the first woman and African American to seek the nomination for president of the United States, "If they don't give you a seat at the table, bring a folding chair."

Karrie G. Dixon, Chancellor
Elizabeth City State University (NC)

Dr. Karrie Dixon is the 12th senior executive officer and 7th chancellor of Elizabeth City State University. Dr. Dixon has served as a senior administrator in the University of North Carolina System since 2008, previously serving as the Vice President for Academic and Student Affairs at the University of North Carolina System Office, where she guided policy and practice for academic and student affairs across the 17 campus systems, the senior executive student affairs officer for the UNC System, assistant Vice provost and adjunct assistant professor at North Carolina State University. Dr. Dixon serves on the Southern Association of Colleges and Schools Commission on Colleges (SACSCOC) Board of Trustees, the Board of Directors of the American Association of State Colleges and Universities (AASCU), and the Association of Governing Boards (AGB) Council of Presidents. In 2020, Dr. Dixon was named by the HBCU Campaign Fund, as one of "The Ten Most Dominant HBCU Leaders of 2020." In that same year she was named to the newly formed national Women in Aviation Advisory board (WIAAB) by the U.S. Department of Transportation Secretary, Elaine L. Chao, and in 2019 she was awarded *The Old North State Award*, one of the highest honors granted by the State of North Carolina by Governor Roy Cooper, among other accolades.

Introduction to the Volume

In their 2009 volume *Answering the Call: African American Women in Higher Education Leadership* (Stylus, LLC), Beverly L. Bower and Mimi Wolverton assert that while the leadership industry is lush in its production of literature, there is little that focuses on the leadership experiences of Black women. This work follows a tradition wherein Black women tell their own stories and readers are left to draw themes across the volume in order to take directions for their own leadership and career pathways (see, e.g., *Sisters of the Academy: Emergent Black Women Scholars in Higher Education* [2001, Stylus], *Black Women in the Academy: Promises and Perils* [1997, University Press of Florida], and *Journeys of Social Justice: Women of Color Presidents in the Academy* [2019, Peter Lang]). In *Pathways to Higher Education Administration for African American Women* (2012, Stylus), conversations regarding the cultivation of leadership skills and navigation of pathways are topically driven but situated solely within the four-year institutional sector and it is written from a scholarly perspective. The current volume bridges these traditions by presenting the stories of women who are senior executives in community colleges, historically Black, and historically White institutions. Moreover, it provides an updated take on Black women's leadership in academe at a time when there is increasing focus on Black women in leadership roles more generally (see e.g., *Lead from the Outside: How to Build your Future and Make Real Change* [2018, Henry Holt & Co.], *How Exceptional Black Women Lead* [2017, Incite Publishing], *Your Next Level Life: 7 Rules of Power, Confidence, and Opportunity for Black Women in America* [2019, Mango], and *The Memo: What Women of Color Need to Know to Secure a Seat at the Table* [2019, Seal Press]).

In the present volume, the authors bring to light the pathways of Black women senior executives at community colleges, four-year historically White, and historically Black public institutions. Here, the authors explore the challenges these women faced, often being the first or only within their leadership circles, how these challenges were met, and how institutions can systematically address hurdles within leadership pathways that not only address the specific challenges of Black women, but more generally and intentionally grow a diverse pool of leaders who are prepared and supported to lead U.S. higher education into the future. This content is research based, derived from studies centered on the leadership pathways of Black women across these higher education contexts.

The volume begins with a foreword by Dr. Karrie Dixon, Chancellor of Elizabeth City State University. After years of underinvestment and leadership instability, Dr. Dixon has become a beacon of light for students, parents, faculty, and staff, as demonstrated through an increase in student enrollments by one-third and an improvement in campus climate, moving from the bottom of the University of North Carolina System to the top, all within a four-year period. After Dr. Dixon's words of wisdom, I provide an overview of the challenges and trajectories of Black women academic leaders in Chapter 1. This chapter closes with a guide for readers through a reflective exercise for their academic leadership journey.

The volume from here is divided into three parts. In Part I—The Community College Context, Dr. Katrina Arnold explores Black women's pursuits of the presidency in the associates degree granting institutional context. In Chapter 2 she examines themes emerging during her research with Black women executive leaders in contexts such as maintaining a strong support system, work-life balance, and spirituality. Here the participants in her study discuss their passion for leading and the paths they had to take to accomplish their goals. In Chapter 3, Dr. Arnold turns toward a discussion of the future for community colleges. Here she examines the demographics of academic executive leadership and shares recommendations for how boards of trustees can attract more Black women to the community college presidencies.

In Part II—The Historically White Institutional Context, Dr. Tamika Williams explores the leadership challenges of Black women in historically White four-year colleges and universities. In Chapter 4 she focuses on the access Black women have toward leadership roles in higher education, using the glass ceiling and glass cliff theoretical frames to understand leadership opportunities for Black women serving in the capacity of provost. The leaders in her study share about the programs that supported their transition to the role, negotiation strategies, and how their experiences were compared to other provosts. In Chapter 5, Dr. Williams more closely examines themes of "survival" within a system wherein Black women leaders are few and far between. She describes barriers to leadership as discussed by participants in her study, and the maneuvers to overcome them. Finally, she discusses the internal challenges Black women in her study experienced: self-doubts, motivations, and how a position of power brings an obligation to "pay it forward."

In Part III—The Historically Black Institutional Context, Dr. Nichole Lewis explores Black women leaders at historically Black institutions. In Chapter 6, she explores the experiences and interactions with the organizational cultures of the historically Black colleges and universities (HBCUs) in which participants in her study served, and the impact of prevailing climate, hidden organizational challenges that Black women Presidents faced in leading their institutions through crises. Participants in this study describe their outsider perspective and what adjustments were made in order to fulfill job duties at private and public HBCUs. The chapter also contains an exploration of the local media and its influence on Black women's leadership. In Chapter 7, Dr. Lewis focuses on the personal commitments Black women leaders made and the responsibility of leading while being Black and a woman. She dives into challenges participants faced and the strategies taken to maintain and preserve the mission of HBCUs and discusses the notion of legacy, knowing when to move to the next career stage at the end of the presidency.

The volume concludes with an afterword by Dr. Kassie Freeman, President of the African Diaspora Consortium. Dr. Freeman's leadership journey took her through an Assistant Professorship of Higher Education at Peabody College, Vanderbilt, tenure, promotion, and service as Dean and Professor at Dillard University, and the Vice President for Academic and Student Affairs for the Southern University and A&M College System. Here, she shares reflections on intergenerational mentorship and sponsorship of aspiring Black women leaders.

Interspersed between the chapters are African proverbs on leadership, which provide further opportunity for a reflective practice. Resources in the Appendix should also prove useful for current and aspiring leaders.

The timing of this volume is particularly apropos. Retirements and resignations, the great resignation fueled by the coronavirus pandemic, and culture wars have each contributed to leadership change in academe. Taking heed of present trends, we hope that through this volume, leaders are inspired to provide opportunities for Black women to serve our institutions through formal leadership.

A NOTE ON TERMINOLOGY

The use of the term Black in this volume is inclusive of all peoples of Black African heritages. The term BIPOC (Black Indigenous Peoples of Color) is used to collectively identify people not of European heritages and usually is used in conjunction with aggregated nationally collected data. This term is used sparingly (Grady, 2020) as this volume is focused on the experiences of Black women, although leaders of other minoritized and marginalized heritages may benefit from the wisdom within. The authors acknowledge that there is a difference between sex (a biological construct) and gender (a sociological construct). Neither construct is binary. All data are reported in terms of gender, although because of institutional and federal reporting guidelines, much of the data collected are on the basis of sex. Participants within studies were selected because they identified as Black and as a woman. Future work should incorporate the experiences of more leaders beyond the binary. For a fuller discussion on the complexity in reporting demographic data for use in organizational change see "Beyond the Kumbaya: A reflective case study of one university's diversity, equity, and inclusion journey" (Chambers et al., 2023).

The institutional types in this study included open access, traditionally known as community colleges, historically Black colleges and universities (HBCUs), and historically White institutions (HWIs). The historical reference to both acknowledges the changing demographics of students both sets of institutions contemporarily serve. The term minority serving institution (MSI) refers to a collection of institutions including HBCUs, predominantly Black institutions (PBIs), Hispanic serving institutions (HSIs), tribal colleges, Native American serving non-tribal institutions

(NASNTI), and Asian American and Native American Pacific Islander-serving institutions (AANAPISIs) among others. With few exceptions beyond HBCUs, most of these institutions were not founded to serve minoritized communities, although increasingly many endeavor to do so (Palmer et al., 2018). We use the term minoritized in acknowledgment that many marginalized communities and demographic populations collectively are in the global majority. Colonial-settler histories divide world populations into minority and majority groups, with limited attention to the role of conquest, continued power, and dominance. As such, the use of minority in this volume is solely in conjunction with the MSI term defined federally in the Higher Education Act (HEA).

The names of leadership positions vary between and within postsecondary educational institutions. For shorthand, the term campus president is used in this volume. It includes those campus-level leaders whose titles may be that of president, chancellor, principal, and the like. This terminology is used regardless of institutional type (college or university) or scope of service—associates, baccalaureate, master's, or doctoral institution. The term academic executive leadership refers to leadership positions within the academic organizational structure of campus at the level of dean/director and above. Future work should consider the role of academic executive leadership at the level of university systems.

SPECIAL THANKS

I would like to extend special thanks to my leadership coach, Jeanne Duncan (Center for Creative Leadership), for helping me rekindle the voice of my leader within. I would also like to thank Lynn Duffy (Senior Associate Vice President of Leadership Development and Talent Acquisition, University of North Carolina System) for her push and consistent posing of hard questions and Drs. Gailda Davis (American Council for Education) and Virginia Hardy for their mentorship. I would like to acknowledge the support of my Chancellors, Drs. Phillip Rogers and Ron Mitchelson as well as East Carolina University's (ECU) Chief of Staff, Dr. Christopher Locklear. And I am especially grateful for the sound advice and sounding boards of Drs. Mary Farwell and Kristen Myers of ECUs NSF ADVANCE Adaptation Grant THRIVE@ECU (thrive.ecu.edu).

REFERENCES

Bower, B. L., & Wolverton, M. (2009). *Answering the call: African American women in higher education leadership*. Stylus Publishing, LLC.

Chambers, C. R., King, B., Myers, K. A., Millea, M., & Klein, A. (2023). Beyond the Kumbaya: A reflective case study of one university's diversity, equity, and inclusion journey. *The Journal of Research Administration*. https://www.srainternational.org/blogs/srai-jra2/2023/06/30/beyond-the-kumbaya-a-reflective-case-study-of-one

Grady, C. (2020, June 30). Why the term "BIPOC" is so complicated, explained by linguists. *Vox*. https://www.vox.com/2020/6/30/21300294/bipoc-what-does-it-mean-critical-race-linguistics-jonathan-rosa-deandra-miles-hercules

Palmer, R. T., Maramba, D. C., Arroyo, A. T., Allen, T. O., Boykin, T. F., & Lee, J. M. (2018). *Effective Leadership at Minority-Serving Institutions*. Routledge.

CHAPTER 1

Executive Academic Leadership Pathways: An Overview

ABSTRACT

In this chapter I discuss traditional and nontraditional pathways to senior executive academic leadership. By executive I mean senior-level formal leadership positions leading to college and university presidencies: academic deanships, provostships, and the presidency. From here, I discuss the demographics of campus presidencies, the underrepresentation of Black women as presidents, and the challenges they face along the pipeline. For Black women, academic executive leadership is more than a position, but a calling. Given the challenges of the presidency, I will then guide you through a reflective practice for your leadership journey.

INTRODUCTION

Contemporarily, Black women in the United States are touted as the most educated demographic (Katz, 2020; Snyder et al., 2019). Yet, they remain significantly underrepresented throughout academe, especially at the level of senior executive academic leadership. Many institutions are touting their firsts while others are yet to have one Black woman in their leadership circles. Yet, as articulated by Anna Julia Cooper, a historic figure in Black women's educational leadership, "when and where I enter … then and there the whole Negro race enters with me" (1886/1998, p. 63). Cooper's words continue to ring true but are more expansive of just Black women. Through other mothering and empathetic, communal approaches to human resources and student development, Black women use their leadership positionality to build others within their orbit (León & Thomas, 2016; Okoli et al., 2020; Washington Lockett et al., 2018). Their span of care extends to faculty and staff and especially to students. Given that traditionally aged college students are now more racially, ethnically, and socioeconomically diverse (Snyder et al., 2019), leadership that can foster the academic, social, emotional, and civic development of students across the board is highly valuable (Long, 2002; Teece & Falconi, 2018). In this chapter I discuss traditional and nontraditional pathways to executive academic leadership. By executive I mean senior-level formal leadership positions leading to campus presidencies: academic deanships, provostships, and the presidency. From here, I discuss the demographics of campus presidencies, the underrepresentation of Black women as presidents, and the challenges they face along the pipeline. For Black women, academic executive leadership is more than a position, but a calling. Given the challenges of the presidency, I will then guide you through a reflective practice for your leadership journey.

PATHWAYS TO EXECUTIVE ACADEMIC LEADERSHIP

There are pathways to executive academic leadership that are more traveled and some whose travelers are fewer but are increasing. In this section, I first discuss the traditional pathway through the faculty ranks and into middle and executive leadership roles. This includes a discussion of interim appointments. I then discuss nontraditional pathways and the potential to broaden access to academic executive leadership through insider nontraditional paths and outsider nontraditional paths, adding a cautionary note on the broadening of paths to outsiders while overlooking underutilized leaders within. This includes many Black women in formal and informal college and university leadership roles.

Advancing Through the Faculty Ranks

In their classic, *Leadership and Ambiguity: The American College Presidency*, Cohen and March (1974, 1986) discuss traditional pathways to college presidency and the challenges that lie therein. The traditional academic leadership pathway in postsecondary institutions begins with a newly hired tenure-track professor who after their probationary term (often a six-year up for tenure or out) is promoted to the associate professor level and tenured. Promotion is determined by faculty productivity in teaching/advising, research/scholarship/creative activity, and service to the college/university and their profession. Standards regarding the quantity of expected scholarly works, quality metrics, and the relative weight of teaching in evaluations vary by institutional type: community/open college, liberal arts, master's comprehensive, and research institutions. Pathways by service focus—predominantly White, historically Black, or other minority-serving institution—are similar. Not all institutions have tenure rights, tenure being a property right in one's faculty position. In addition, ranks vary across institutions. A common professorial rank schema may begin with the rank of an instructor (typically nontenure track) or an assistant professor (tenure track) at an entry level, with subsequent advancement opportunities to the associate level, followed by promotion to full (see Figure 1.1). Some institutions provide opportunities for nontenure-track faculty to advance in rank, using titles such as teaching assistant, teaching associate, and master teaching professor. At some institutions, rank is flat with the key differentiation being between full- and part-time faculty statuses. Given the amount of variation between institutions, it is important for faculty to become familiar with institutional structure and promotion standards.

The standard term to describe criteria for promotion and/or tenure is probably too strong a term as organizational units (departments, schools, colleges) have varying guidelines as well as unpublished rules of thumb. Expectations vary not only between but within institutions. Institutions endeavoring to be more equitable and inclusive while promoting and supporting a diverse faculty should work toward making the invisible visible. Yet, as these hidden expectations can impinge on one's career trajectory, it is important for individual faculty to gain familiarity with the unwritten rules in order to be successful in achieving promotion and tenure (Matthew, 2016).

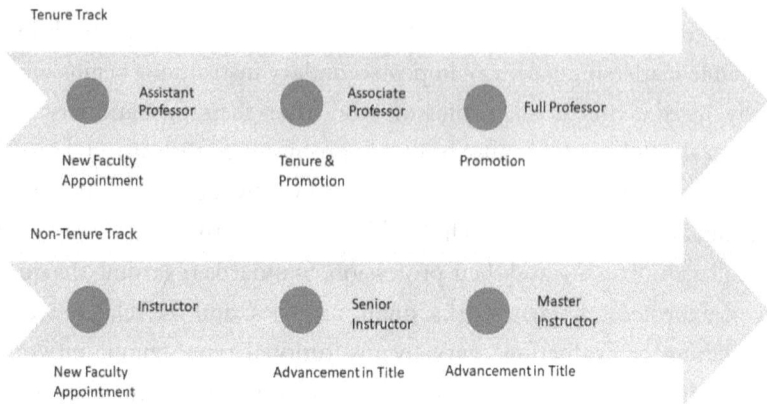

Figure 1.1   Faculty Ranks

Consideration for promotion and tenure typically begins at the level of department or school units. Promotion and tenure committees at that unit level use institutional guidelines to determine whether a faculty member has met formal written criteria available in codes, bylaws, manuals, or other relevant human resource documents for faculty. Committee faculty also review informal criteria, institutional norms, and departmental fit. Whether they are legally permitted to do so is a question of law. The practice, however, is standard and thus institutions pursuing inclusive excellence should work toward greater clarity and transparency.

Promotion and tenure committees are composed of faculty within that organizational unit and in the case of tenure, there are often rules specifying that only tenured faculty serve in this capacity. Guidelines regarding the number of publications produced annually or meeting a certain metric on student evaluations, more nuanced appraisals of faculty work including the quality of publications, quality of the journals, and impact introduce ambiguity into the process. This is especially true when promotion and tenure committee members are unfamiliar with the specific area of study, which is often the case for Black women faculty among other marginalized faculty groups. Bias in student evaluations of teaching, navigating stereotypes, microaggressions, and disproportionate institutional service including student mentorship and advising can impinge on Black women's propensity toward tenure (Carter & Craig, 2022; Corbin et al., 2018; Croom, 2017; Croom & Patton, 2011; Harley, 2008).

Once a faculty member achieves tenure and promotion to an associate level, the next step on the traditional academic leadership pathway is a promotion to full. I provide a depiction of traditional and nontraditional pathways to the presidency in Figure 1.2. Although criteria for tenure and promotion tend to be vague and subject to interpretation, guidance on promotion to full tends to have even less specification. Croom (2017) confirms the observations of prior scholars that considerations for promotion to full are subjective, tied to status and perceptions of collegiality and institutional loyalty, and based on seniority with considerations of merit grounded in bias. Yet, achievement of promotion to full is critical for faculty on academic leadership pathways because it positions one to be considered for formal leadership opportunities. At many institutions, achieving the rank of full is a prerequisite for positions such as the department chair, director, or dean. At other institutions, where associate professors are permitted to assume these roles, those taking this path can become saddled with department service obligations and may be unable to execute scholarship at a level deemed commensurate for full. While some institutions will balance service and leadership with scholarship, many will not. And just as in the case of tenure, deliberation on promotion to full for many Black women occurs within closed confidential meetings by individuals who are often not familiar with one's scholarly work, advising, and mentoring, among other institutional and professional contributions.

Formal Leadership Pathways (Traditional)

Leadership can be defined as "a social process that involves relationships of influence, learning, and exchange" (Bolman & Gallos, 2011, p. 10). As such the essence of leadership is influence. Thus, faculty and other actors in academe need not occupy formal leadership positions but can lead others through their research, teaching, and service. "Leadership in place is having the opportunity, the ability, and the courage to sense the need for leadership in the moment, then seizing the opportunity" (Wergin, 2007, p. 224). In this vein

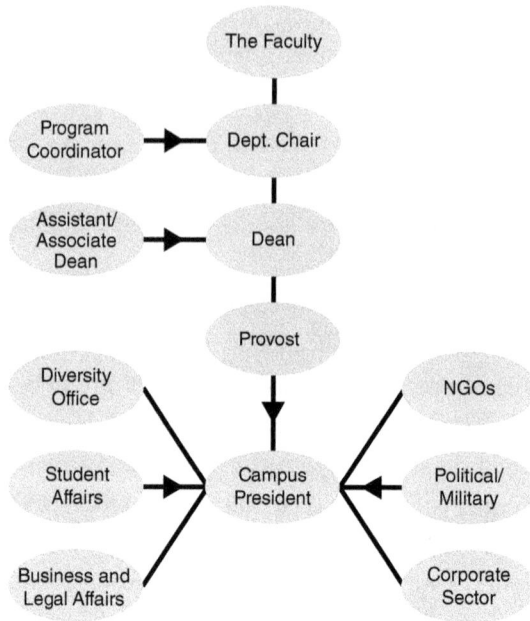

Figure 1.2   Traditional and Nontraditional Pathways to the Campus Presidency

> Leaders in place have no expectation that their leadership will lead to long-term changes in their professional roles. They see a need for leadership: they step forward and respond; and then they step back. (p. 224)

Historically, Ginsberg (2011) concedes the excellence faculty exemplified as academic managers as "essentially working in their spare time [they] helped to build a number of the world's premier institutions of higher education" (p. 2). However, given the complexity of challenges faced by higher education, regulatory regimes, the largess of institutional size, scope, and competing attentive publics, formal leadership roles and functions are vital. These functions cannot be attended solely on a part-time basis; yet, the alarm Ginsberg heralds regarding professional managerialism has merit. "The purpose of the university was [and still is] the promotion of education and research" (2011, p. 2). Thus, leadership and managerial position is not an end unto itself but is subservient to "the larger goals of higher education and society" (Bolman & Gallos, 2011, p. 220).

The essence of leadership may be influence; however, formal positions tend to carry additional authority and responsibilities wherefrom one can advance institutional mission for the greater good. Formal leadership opportunities expand for faculty at the rank of full, with the pinnacle of campus leadership being the college/university president or chancellor. Formal titles vary across institutions and therefore it is important to become familiar with individual institutional organization charts.

From promotion to full, the next step may be an appointment as a department chair or department head, as it is called in some places, an assistant or an associate dean appointment which is more centrally located within one's college or school, or a directorship of a school or center. Terminology varies considerably between and within institutions. Appointment to the department chair typically is the most direct pathway to the provost, the senior executive leader for academic affairs.[1] Department chairs are responsible for academic program development and delivery, faculty development and evaluation, as well as budgeting and resource allocation within a department. They often also work as part of a team of leaders within a college. Department chair roles are challenging as they carry a lot of responsibility without a lot of direct authority to ensure collaborative engagement among faculty toward common departmental goals. It is also the ultimate middle management position wherein chairs are squeezed between upper administrative directives and faculty demands, with little professional development in navigating the role (Zahneis, 2022). Toward this end, department chairs and other mid-career leaders must be provided with professional development and support so that they can best execute their work. They are the first in line for cultivating a healthy academic workplace. They support the people who directly connect with students and thus shape an environment for teaching and learning.

At this point, I would be remiss not to mention the intermediate leadership role of program coordinator/program director. These faculty are

---

[1]Note the exclusion of the term "chief academic officer." The term chief is from the French word "chef" and was conferred not only to Indigenous leadership in the Americas, but also to denote Indigenous men in the same way that African American men were called "boy." According to Cornel Pewewardy (2021), Vice Chair of the Comanche Nation and Professor Emeritus of Indigenous Nations Studies, Portland State University, "Whether intentional or not, this language communicates hostile, derogatory, and negative racial, gender, sexual orientation, and religious insults" (p. 30). Thus, in solidarity I urge for the abandonment of the term in academe and beyond. For those who push back and say that the term is one of honor, the distinction is not honorable if it demeans others.

often responsible for academic program development, scheduling, taking the lead on staffing courses and assessment among other program-related duties. Faculty in these roles have direct responsibility for the program but no supervisory authority over other faculty. Thus, program coordinators must work with department chairs and cultivate positive relationships with other faculty within the department to garner influential authority. After all, influence is leadership, formal positionality aside. One can advance from the program coordination to a department chair; however, that step typically is not necessary. That said, the program coordinator role is one where a person can distinguish themselves in leadership, service, and commitment.

Academic director roles are similar to department chair positions and are typically associated with a school. Center directorships usually involve the facilitation of services within the institution, to the community or service region, or implementation of a research project. Assistant and associate deanships are typically service roles, where a person serves to facilitate the research of other faculty, is responsible for enrollment management or student services, faculty professional development, evaluation, assessment, or serves as a college-level diversity officer among other potential roles and responsibilities. These positions vary by and within institutions and can include centralized academic units such as the graduate school. Assistant and associate deans have even less access to professional development, resources, or research literature to help guide their work (Preston & Floyd, 2016; Sayler et al., 2019). For an aspirant campus president, assistant and associate deanships pose a challenge in that they can be an end unto themselves. For those who seek to serve in this capacity, this is a good thing. But for those aspiring to further service, it is important not to stay in these roles for too long, else one's service may be perceived as indispensable and one's positionality seen as tied to that role.

The next step in the academic leadership ladder is that of a dean. Deans are the senior executive leaders for a college or school. Department chair, director, and assistant/associate dean positions can serve as preceptors to the deanship. Deans are responsible for the academic, programmatic, managerial, and fiscal workings of a college or school. They are responsible for articulating a mission and vision, preferably codeveloped with the faculty, as well as are often the hiring authority enabled to negotiate salary and employment packages with faculty and staff candidates. Their offices are responsible for enrollment management, student services, assessment, diversity, equity, and inclusion, budget and resource allocations within a college, facilities, compliance with federal, state, and local laws as well as institutional policy, student success, employee advancement, alumni affairs, and development among others. Typically, within a dean's suite, these roles would be divided and shared among assistant and associate deans. Deans have the budgetary authority to direct the college's mission and vision. This is in contrast to department chairs whose budgets are largely operational (although chairs can always ask deans to fund mission-aligned, evidence-supported initiatives). Deans are most like campus presidents in that they are the face of their unit, the way a president is the face of a college or university. They also increasingly play lead roles in friend-raising and fundraising to support college programming (Nielsen, 2013).

Historically, the role of the provost is the next step to the presidency. However, as these roles differentiated over time, campus presidents (sometimes called chancellors or principals) fill an outward-facing role, principally interacting with the general public, political bodies, alumni, and donors. By contrast, the provost is the senior executive academic leader on campus, responsible for all academic units including centers, support, and activity units, in addition to faculty affairs. As denoted in this volume by Dr. Tamika Williams (Chapters 4 and 5), the provost is second-in-command, representing the campus president in their absence. Achievement of the rank of full is typically a prerequisite for the provost, more so than other aforementioned leadership roles. As described by Nielsen (2013), the top three jobs of the provost are strategic planning, personnel management, and budgets. Toward this end, provosts lead strategic planning and implementation; strategically direct the budget; authorize faculty hires and certify promotion and tenure decisions; are diversity, equity, and inclusion leaders; work with faculty senates or in some states, unions, to shape policies and practices within academic affairs; support and provide direction for research, scholarly activities, civic engagement, institutional research and assessment; and work with student affairs to provide academic student support services among other responsibilities. Like the deanship, provosts share duties among a suite of assistant, associate, and/or vice provosts to execute these duties. Amid the COVID-19 pandemic, culture wars, climate, and surmounting crises, provosts are increasingly tasked to lead institutional responses, to assure multiple even fractured attentive publics, while ensuring the institution carries out business as close to usual as possible. The faculty often look up to provosts as a model of faculty excellence in teaching, scholarly activities, and service. A good provost is able to do so, as they master what Nielsen (2013, p. 306) describes as a series of balancing acts:

- Increase the quality of the student body BUT retain accessibility to underrepresented populations.
- Make the curriculum relevant to tomorrow's needs BUT respect the essential role of faculty in curricular matters.
- Encourage innovation BUT retain our historic strengths.
- Address the professional preparation of students BUT encourage broad appreciation of the humanities and arts.
- Infuse the campus with modern technology BUT maintain the personal touch that students love and parents expect.
- [and within state systems] Become a global university BUT advance the state's economic development.

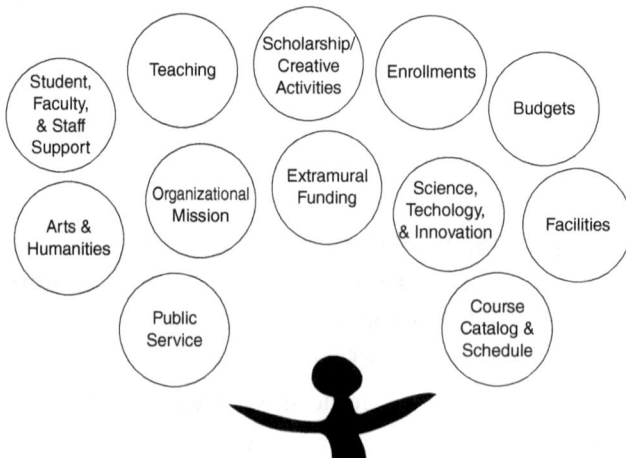

Figure 1.3   The Provost's Balancing Act

A Note on Interim Appointments

Interim appointments in academia are common and can occur with any formal academic leadership position. Interim appointments arise when a leader vacates a position during a contractual term and someone, typically a campus insider, is selected to fill the role of that position until a new permanent appointment is made, usually after a formal hiring search. The power of interims may vary based upon their sphere of influence and informal power, and whether they are tasked with leading their unit as opposed to being caretakers requested to manage until a new appointment is made. Sometimes interim positions are a trial leadership opportunity, whereby assessments regarding the individual's leadership capacity and direction are made for that particular leadership position, or perhaps another. At other times, the interim is chosen specifically because they either do not want to be considered for the permanent leadership position or the organization is not considering them for a permanent role.

Evidence from Canada suggests that women are more likely to advance in their career through interim appointments (Lavigne, 2020). The concern is that for BIPOC (Black, Indigenous, People of Color) advancement through leadership ranks becomes more challenging the higher up the leadership ladder. Lavigne (2020) calls this upward cumulative attrition and conjectures that these women "are judged more severely when occupying positions of leadership. They get their chance, but they cannot capitalize on it and are unable to move further" (p. 1955). He emphasizes that while BIPOC women may access leadership positions, their success requires greater perseverance for further promotion. This stands to reason as the advantages to taking an interim appointment are experiential and can help broaden one's perspective while the disadvantages are significant including significantly increased administrative work without training, perceptions of being not qualified for a permanent position, workload emphases on tasks (administrivia) over strategic change, a short "honeymoon" period, inadequate time to cultivate buy-in for decisions or to make a distinctive impress on the unit (Huff & Neubrander, 2015). As Black women are more likely to be misperceived, misinterpreted, and penalized for missteps, it is crucial to ponder the following questions (among others) before taking on an interim appointment:

- Why am I being asked to serve in this capacity?
- Can I be considered for the real role if I decide I am interested?

- How long will the assignment last?
- Will I be expected to do this job in addition to my regular role?
- Will I be taken seriously?
- How will I make my mark?
- How will it feel to go back to my previous role? (Valliancourt, 2018)

These questions can help one navigate the role for which they are being sought after (a contender for the permanent position, a disrupter to prepare for future change, or a caretaker to keep things afloat in the interim), work expectations, potential for achievement, and one's work life future. As a Black woman, negotiating these questions can help one determine if this role is glorified service (Griffin et al., 2013; Harley, 2008) or a true leadership opportunity.

Nontraditional Pathways

Increasingly, institutional boards and leaders involved with the selection of a campus president are increasingly turning to leaders from nontraditional backgrounds. As boards of trustees and other leaders key in selecting new presidents consider "*What strengths do we need in a leader given who we are and what we need to accomplish now?*" they are looking to sectors beyond academe to select those at promise for success when "the need for great leadership and leaders in higher education today is acute" (Beardsley, 2017, p. 38, *emphasis in the original*). Within the liberal arts sector, nearly a third of campus presidents are coming through nontraditional pathways. As Beardsley notes, however, trends within liberal arts institutions are often harbingering change in higher education writ large.

Pathways for nontraditional leadership are divergent. For simplicity, here we can divide these into insider and outsider nontraditional paths. In life, however, individuals may swirl between academic and nonacademic, for-profit and not-for-profit sectors, and so the delineation is not necessarily so clear.

In the case of insider nontraditional pathways, individuals may come through alternative college/university divisions. This may include pathways through student affairs, diversity and equity offices, university advancement, as well as financial and business affairs among others.

See resources on nontraditional pathways to the presidency below. In her dissertation about the Black women's nontraditional pathways to the presidency, Polk-Johnson (2019) finds that Black women from nontraditional pathways experience the same challenges as women from traditional pathways, just without the tenure process. Her work emphasizes the role of agency when blazing new paths, generally or specifically within a particular higher education institution. This includes education and preparation, finding mentors and advocates, seeking role models and role modeling themselves, as well as using self-awareness and strategy to drive success.

In the case of outsider nontraditional pathways, leaders typically are selected from corporate, nonacademic, nonprofit (such as hospitals or nongovernmental organizations [NGOs]), or political sectors and the military (Heuvel, 2017; see Figure 1.3). When considering some of the most pressing challenges facing higher education are related to institutional finance, the draw to presidents with corporate backgrounds and civic influences is prescient with many boards. Presidents from these backgrounds have networks that assist with fundraising and "friend-raising" as well as support legislative and executive governmental relations that can translate into resources for the campus (Ivory, 2017). Moreover, as "you have a large sum of essential activity that a true academic doesn't want to get his hands dirty with" (Donald Hess, *quoted in* Beardsley, 2017, p. 56), insider and outsider nontraditional pathways have the potential to align nonacademic skills with institutional needs. The logic behind the support for nontraditional presidencies is that academics can focus on teaching and scholarship while leaders and administrators can focus on steering the organization. While the validity of this logic is unclear, this skill alignment perspective is supported by the Association of Governing Boards of Universities and Colleges (AGB, 2016). Advancing an enterprise approach to leadership, MacTaggart (2017) draws from leadership characteristics such as "tough-minded realism, sophisticated interpersonal skills, and courage" to establish an institutional vision, develop strategies, garner resources, and add competitive value. While this approach does not/should not discredit academic leaders from the traditional ranks, it does broaden the pool of potential leaders.

Any leader pursuing nontraditional leadership pathways to be successful will need to earn buy-in from the faculty (Ivory, 2017). Faculty will need to be convinced of the nontraditional president's commitment to the academic core, student success, and shared governance. The latter may be most challenging for corporate executives unused to quasi-legislative constituents evaluating and questioning both their actions and intentions. Building a strong relationship with the faculty and having a relationship that is consultative, where insights and perspectives can be shared, can be mutually beneficial. Through honest, transparent brokering, nontraditional presidents can present faculty with the truth of institutional challenges faced fiscally and organizationally while cultivating an opportunity for faculty to cocreate solutions that support the academic core. This honest appraisal can in turn help faculty to see the difficult challenges presidents face and lend their support for institutional change (Delabbio & Palmer, 2009; Zemsky, 2009). There may also be positive benefits to faculty morale, lessons both traditional and nontraditional leaders can take.

Most studies of nontraditional presidencies are agnostic to whether traditional or nontraditional presidents are more successful in terms of student outcomes, fiscal sustainability, and institutional prestige. However, there is evidence that expertise in fields such as law and finance is helpful, and service in the public sector is most helpful in preparing one to navigate institutional culture and the regulatory environment. Nielson (2013) reflects

> How many times have you heard: "If I ran my business the way you guys run the university, I'd be out of business in a week." ... And if we ran the university the way they run their business, we'd be in jail in a week. (p. 143)

As such it is important for all leaders to respect the regulatory environments of their respective industries. Thus, while there is the business of higher education, higher education is not a business.

Distorted Opportunities, Perhaps?

For women, the broadening of pathways to the presidency may be a mixed blessing. On the one hand, limited opportunities for women in formal leadership roles via traditional pathways can be attributed to lower percentages of women in senior faculty roles, which in turn implicates lower numbers of women in middle management (department chair, director, and associate dean roles) and subsequently executive-level academic positions (Rodriguez-Farrar & Jack, 2022). By being able to capitalize on insider nontraditional paths, particularly from those with greater women's representation such as student affairs and diversity offices, the pool of women generally, Black women specifically, with leadership potential expands significantly. On the other hand, outsider leadership pathways are dominated by White men who through privileged networks are coming through corporate, political, and NGO pathways, potentially displacing qualified leaders from within academe (Birnbaum & Umbach, 2001).

Woollen (2016) found that participants in her study of nontraditional women presidents from both insider and outsider pathways attributed their successes to an entrepreneurial spirit that they translated from other sectors and their ability to develop relationships with multiple stakeholders. Thus, skepticism regarding the qualifications of both insider and outsider nontraditional presidents can be overcome through an understanding of academic cultures and relationship building. For Black women presidents, traditional or nontraditional, racism and sexism, and interactions thereof can be significant obstacles in entering the presidency (Polk-Johnson, 2019). Mentorship, external professional networks, and attention to one's leader within were avenues participants in the Polk-Johnson study pursued to overcome these challenges.

THE CAMPUS PRESIDENCY

In a 2022 *Chronicle of Higher Education* advice column, Clarion University of Pennsylvania President Emerita Karen M. Whitney describes four stages of the campus presidency: aspiring, acquiring, attending, and adjourning. To her point, in this volume we have attended the aspiring stage wherein one develops leadership experiences in preparation to become a campus president. Hereto, attention to leadership skill development is significantly important. In this section, I discuss professional development opportunities for aspirant campus presidents. And as I close this chapter, I invite you to think about the acquisition stage, when you consider your knowledge, skills, abilities, and dispositions and match them with institutional type and professional fit (Whitney, 2022). Chapters 2 through 5 expound on the aspiring stage and explore the acquiring stage. Chapters 6 and 7 will discuss attending to the role of the presidency, in essence being a campus president, and knowing when to seal one's legacy, leaving in a position of strength.

The scope of the campus presidency is vast. Campus presidents are the face of the college or university to which an institution's academic success with students, administrative efficacy, and scholarly prestige can be intricately tied. Responsibility includes executive oversight of the faculty and staff; budget and finances; federal, state, and local law and regulatory compliance; enrollment, retention, and graduation rates; program and curriculum advances; and external relations (alumni, donors, legislators, governing boards, etc.).

While much of the preparation for the presidency comes through prior leadership experiences, there are formal leadership programs designed to assist aspiring presidents. See Table 1.1 for a list of national programs.

Experiences coming into the presidency may diverge but there is a clear consensus on the role of terminal degrees, particularly doctorates. According to the 2022 American Council on Education (ACE) Survey of College and University Presidents, 84% held a doctoral-level degree, doctorates of philosophy from a wide array of social science and humanities disciplines, or EdDs (doctorate of education). This preference for doctoral attainment may be attributed to the traditional pathway through the presidency and the requirement of terminal degrees to be able to teach as a tenured or tenure-track faculty member in many academic programs (Cooney & Martin, 2021). Among other notable professional terminal degrees are the JD (law degree), MBA (master's in business), and MD (medical doctorate). In 2022, 9.4% of the Presidents held such professional degrees. An additional 6.1% of presidents held other master's degrees (Melidona et al., 2023).

Table 1.1 Professional Development for Current and Aspiring Campus Presidents

Organization	Program	Target Audience
American Association of Community Colleges (AACC)	Presidents Academy Summer Institute	Current Community/Open Access College Presidents
American Association of State Colleges and Universities (ASCU)	Executive Leadership Academy	Senior Cabinet Executives with Presidential Aspirations State Colleges & Universities
	New Presidents Academy	New Presidents State Colleges & Universities
	Millennium Leadership Initiative	Aspiring Presidents from Historically Underrepresented Backgrounds
American Council on Education (ACE)	Institute for New Presidents	Interim and New Presidents with less than 2 Years' Experience
	ACE Fellows Program for Rising Administrators	Aspiring Presidents
Association of Catholic Colleges and Universities (ACCU)	Institute for New Presidents of Catholic Colleges & Universities	New and Interim Presidents Catholic Colleges & Universities
Council for Christian Colleges and Universities (CCCU)	2020 New Presidents Institute	New Presidents Christian Colleges & Universities
Council for Independent Colleges (CIC)	New Presidents Program	Current Presidents
Harvard Graduate School of Education (HGSE)	Harvard Seminar for Presidential Leadership	Current Presidents
	Seminar for New Presidents	First-time College and University Presidents
Higher Education Leadership Foundation (HELF)	Leadership Institute	Aspiring HBCU Presidents
Hispanic Association of Colleges and Universities (HACU)	La Academia de Liderazgo	Aspiring HSI Presidents
The Aspen Institute	Aspen New Presidents Fellowship Program	Community College Presidents with No More than 5 Years of Experience

Adapted with permission from Cooney and Martin (2021).

Having a doctorate can be especially helpful for nontraditional presidents (insiders or outsiders) in garnering credibility with faculty and trustee boards. At community colleges, while doctoral degrees historically were not requirements, there is evidence that they are important to advancement within these institutions and help gain presidential candidates an invitation to the interview process (Artis & Bartel, 2021; Cooney & Martin, 2021; McNair, 2015).

Preparation for the presidency can be broad based; however, some skills are essential:

- Listening
- Effective communication across administrative and academic cultures
- Sound decision-making
- Cultivating and connecting networks
- Professional ethics
- Team development
- Strategic planning
- Supervisory oversight
- Emotional intelligence

to name but a few (Ruben et al., 2021). It is a juggling act. A successful academic leader engages the

> Skills of a good *analyst* and *social architect* who can craft a high-functioning institution where all the parts contribute to the whole, a *political leader* who can forge necessary alliances and partnerships in service of the mission, a *prophet* and an *artist* who can envision a better college or university and inspire others to heed its call, and a *servant* to both the institution and to the larger goals of higher education and society. (Bolman & Gallos, 2011, p. 221, *emphases in the original*)

Increasingly, new leaders see themselves as operational and financial strategists with complementary experts in academic and student affairs serving within an executive cabinet (Cooney & Martin, 2021). The challenge, therefore, is to effectively manage the business of education without squelching academe's heart through managerialism.

Given the number and complexity of skills and dispositions in leadership literature, Ruben (2006) distilled five leadership competency clusters:

- *Positional competencies* regard field-specific knowledge, skills, and abilities (KSAs);
- *Personal competencies* include values, ethics, integrity, intelligence, and dispositions;
- *Organizational competencies* refer to administrative capacity including goal setting, strategic planning, strategic management, crisis management, and goal attainment;
- *Communication competencies* reference effective interpersonal, group, organizational, and external relationship building; and
- *Analytic competencies* regard reflective practice, problem-solving, stakeholder, organizational and situational analytics, and learning from past practices. (Ruben et al., 2021)

Here competencies refer to things that leaders know and do. The leadership competencies scorecard can be used to assess one's knowledge and skills as well as to identify areas for growth (Ruben, 2006, 2012). It can also be used within group and organizational settings (Ruben, 2019). By developing these competencies, leaders develop the capacity relevant toward meeting the needs, expectations, and sensitivities of divergent stakeholders, respond to interdependently connected wicked problems, within the culturally divided setting and bring them together to forward higher education opportunities for today and tomorrow (Gigliotti, 2019). And yet, all of this is at the essence of Black women's ways of being:

> i used to dream radical dreams
>
> Of blowing everyone away with my perceptive powers of correct analysis i even used to think I'd be the one to stop the riot and negotiate the peace
>
> then I awoke and dug that if i dreamed natural dreams of being a natural woman doing what a woman does when she's natural i would have a revolution. (Giovanni, 1974/1996, p. 79)

BECOMING A CAMPUS PRESIDENT WHILE BEING BLACK AND A WOMAN

In 2014, Gwendolyn Boyd became the first woman president in Alabama State University's then 147-year history. Her contract garnered national attention as it included a clause that stated "For so long as Dr. Boyd is president and a single person, she shall not be allowed to cohabitate in the president's residence with a person with whom she has a romantic relation" (*quoted in* Jacobs, 2014, para. 3).

With the exception of that language, her contract was deemed pretty standard in terms of provision of a campus residence, vehicle, and salary (Rivard, 2014), albeit $25,000 less than her predecessor, Joseph Silver (Belanger, 2014). "I can read. I read my contract thoroughly, I knew what I was signing, and I have no issue with it at all" she told the Associated Press (AP, 2014, para. 5).

The board asserted that the rationale for that language stemmed from the increasing scrutiny paid to the daily lives of campus presidents. Nevertheless, no such clause existed in the contract of Judy Bonner who was serving as the President of the University of Alabama at the time of Boyd's appointment. Bonner, too, was a single woman but White. In fact, commentators at the time were not aware of similar contractual obligations at any other institution, and it was perceived of as illegal, in contravention of Supreme Court precedents and Title VII of the Civil Rights Act of 1964. In addition, there were questions about how such a contractual term could be enforced: "Would you go marching into a president's home and say, 'Stop that, get your hands off him or her!'" (Cotton, *quoted in* Rivard, 2014, para. 17). The fact that it appeared in Dr. Boyd's contract harkens to racialized stereotypes of Black women as "morally obtuse" and "openly licentious" (Giddings, 2006, p. 31). That Dr. Boyd, an Engineer and 33-year veteran of the academy (Johns Hopkins University), would not understand how to comport herself within academic norms is incredulous, mounting scandals regarding inappropriate relationships in academe notwithstanding. As underscored by President Emerita of Bennett College, Julianne Malveaux, "I would dare anyone to show me a single man's contract that said anything like that" (*quoted in* Elliott, 2014, para. 18). Nevertheless, Malveaux reflects that presidential appointments present "opportunities and challenges to serve" and therefore "that probably outweighed any of the nonsense of this contract" (*quoted in* Elliott, 2014, para. 22).

That Boyd was fired within two years spoke to greater leadership challenges given the rapid succession of presidential appointments during that period. The reason proffered was a lack of confidence from the board. However, the conditions in which she accepted leadership speak more of institutional challenges than her leadership abilities. Consistent with Lavigne's (2020) findings, Black women are more likely to be penalized and offered less leeway to fully demonstrate leadership capabilities. The fact that Alabama State is a historically Black institution should not be remised. Most colleges and universities in the United States are shaped by White dominance and patriarchy (Watkins, 2001). Efforts to decolonize and liberate higher education are (mostly) laudable (Stein & Andreotti, 2016); yet, such a transitional process will be decades, if not a century, in the making.

THE NEED FOR BLACK WOMEN IN HIGHER EDUCATION LEADERSHIP—NOW

Higher education institutions need competent leaders now. The 2023 edition of the *American College President*'s survey documents a growing number of newer presidents. Although in 2006, the average president had served 8.5 years at the time of the survey, by 2022, that figure reduced to 5.9 years. In addition, presidential turnover is more frequent: "Not only are presidents newer to their positions than those in previous surveys, over half (55 percent) planned to step down from their current roles within the next five years" (Melidona et al., 2023, p. 14). The COVID-19 pandemic compounded by ongoing racial, climate change, political, and culture war crises contributed to this increase in turnover (Burns, 2021; Rodriguez-Farrar & Jack, 2022). Yet, women generally, Black women specifically, are an underutilized human capital asset well suited toward navigating complexity under opaque conditions.

From a pool of 3,955 presidents, data from the 2023 edition of the *American College President*'s survey reveal that twice as many men than women presently serve as college presidents. Approximately 25% of presidents are BIPOC with about 10% of presidents being women of color. Among minority serving institutions (MSIs), men of color are nearly twice as likely to lead historically and predominantly Black institutions as compared to women of color (Melidona et al., 2023). Thus, the gender trend for women of color is replicated among MSIs.[2]

Data from the College and University Professional Association for Human Resources (CUPA-HR) confirm similar trends. Out of a smaller sample of 811 institutions, 31.6% of presidents in 2021–2022 were women, and 84% of those women were White. According to CUPA-HR, 3% of presidents in their sample are Black women, and 5.5% are Black men (College and University Professional Association for Human Resources [CUPA-HR], 2022; see Figure 1.4). Data from the 2022 ACE Presidential Survey include more Black presidents, with Black women serving in 5.4% of institutions and Black men in an additional 8.2%. Nevertheless, 15% of all students are Black women (Snyder et al., 2019) and women generally have outpaced men in college enrollments since 1979 (Giddings, 2006; Melidona et al., 2023; Rodriguez-Farrar & Jack, 2022).

Beyond overall numbers, there are gender-based differences in presidential service by institutional type. Men are more than twice as likely to lead doctoral institutions, at 70.9% as compared to 29.1% of campus presidencies. From this start, representation by gender is inversely proportional to institutional type, with women most likely to lead at associate's, baccalaureate, and special focus institutions. Although nearly 60% of women serve at public institutions, men are nearly evenly split between service at public and private colleges and universities (Gluckman, 2017). As such, men generally, White men particularly, are more likely to serve at the helm of the most prestigious institutions. Women generally, Black women particularly, are more likely to serve at broadly accessible institutions with a local and/or regional reach, often absent national prestige.

---

[2]It should be noted that there are more women of color than men of color serving at the helm of Hispanic Serving Institutions (HSIs). The majority of HSI presidents are White, nearly equally split by gender. White women were more likely to serve as the president at Asian American and Native American Pacific Islander-Serving Institutions (AANAPISI). White men were more likely to serve as presidents at Native American-Serving Nontribal Institutions (NASNTI), but at Tribal Colleges and Universities (TCU), men of color are more likely to be presidents. As the differential patterns here may in some cases be attributed to smaller sample sizes, further investigation in trends among MSI presidencies is warranted.

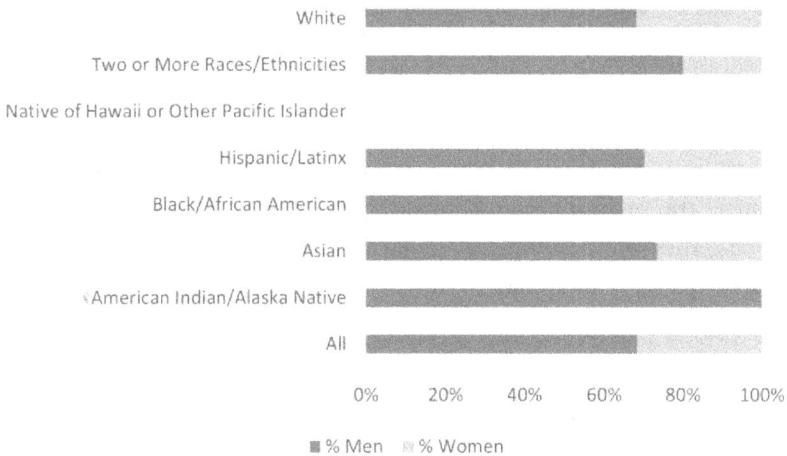

Figure 1.4   Campus and System Presidents by Race/Ethnicity and Gender (*N*=811). Data from CUPA-HR (2022)

In parallel with trends in Canada (Lavigne, 2020), women presidents in the United States are significantly more likely than men to come through traditional academic leadership pathways (Melidona et al., 2023). In a prior ACE survey, it was found that nearly 35% of women presidents served as a provost or senior executive academic officer before assuming the role of a president. The same survey found that more than 65% of women of color served as provosts or other senior campus executives before assuming the presidency (Gagliardi et al., 2017). More recently, it was found that Black women, more so than their White and Hispanic counterparts, come through campus insider nontraditional pathways to presidential leadership: Student affairs, auxiliary services, and finance were but a few examples (Melidona et al., 2023). On the one hand, this demonstrates the depth of experience Black women have when assuming the presidency. On the other hand, these narrowed pathways often funnel out women with the KSAs to serve. It may be the case that broadening insider nontraditional pathways are helping some, as Black women from student affairs, diversity offices, and business and legal affairs are charting realistic pathways to the presidency. Yet, for outsider nontraditional paths, women are at a distinct disadvantage given the male dominance and attendant networks in corporate and political spheres.

As for women on the traditional path, they are more likely to stop their career progression at the provost's office (Rodriguez-Farrar &

Jack, 2022). While the reasons for doing so may be unclear, the sheer delay in making a distinctive impact at each level of the leadership ladder may be pushing women to serve at the later stages of their career, that is, at preretirement. Women may also be delayed in career progression due to caregiving and other family obligations. While women are maintaining professional networks through caregiving periods, they are nevertheless penalized in the achievement of senior leadership roles (Woollen, 2016).

Age is not a barrier for men ascending to the presidency, but it may be the case that given their on-campus leadership experiences, women may be identified for presidential leadership development earlier than what is typical. The average president is 60 years old, with 55% of presidents considering retirement within five years (Melidona et al., 2023). At a traditional retirement age of 65, the span from the development of presidential aspirations to retirement is about 15 years. On average, presidents report developing presidential aspirations at 44.9 and assuming their first presidency 6.8 years later, at age 51.7. Women generally and women of color develop these aspirations slightly later, at ages 46.9 and 45.7, respectively. Women on average receive their first presidential appointment at 52.8. Women of color receive their first appointments closer to the average age, at 51.6 (Melidona et al., 2023). More research on age, gender, and the presidency is needed to understand these findings, and address whether the presidential traditional path is delaying women's trajectories given their higher levels of academic service. Could women be identified for presidencies/presidential leadership development earlier given their prior campus leadership experiences?

Despite an experiential advantage, few Black women are heirs apparent, identified as leadership successors even as the overwhelmingly White and male baby boomer generation continues their journeys toward retirement. Instead, they face barriers such as exclusion from informal networks, sponsorship, and limited support to succeed as leaders (Jackson & Harris, 2007; Seltzer, 2018).

The narrowed leadership paths of Black women are particularly unfortunate given the need for leaders who understand the experiences of racially and ethnically diverse student bodies, who can identify barriers that mask merit, and who can garner the support to make campuses welcoming and inclusive spaces for all. Nearly 40% of Black women from ages 18 to 24 are enrolled in a postsecondary institution, this compares to 44% of White women and 31% of Black men (National Center for Education Statistics [NCES], 2019). There is some evidence that trends are changing. One-third of presidents hired in 2021–2022 were Black. Analysts note that there are more qualified Black leadership aspirants, many of whom have taken advantage of professional leadership development programs. The challenge of diverse leadership is no longer in the pipeline (Lederman, 2022).

To have leadership that is not only better reflective of student bodies but also brings in essential leadership qualities to support diverse student populations and lead public higher education in precarious times, it is important to eradicate unnecessary barriers to leadership and enable access. Colleges and universities cannot wait. The time to hire more equitably is now (Rodriguez-Farrar & Jack, 2022).

ANSWERING THE CALL TO LEAD

A lot of people think you can be a president of just any institution, but it doesn't really work that way. First of all, institutions find you, you don't find them. Second, you can only be a president of an institution that you truly love because it's such a demanding role.

It's a 24/7 job. … You are in many ways married to the institution. When I was inaugurated at Spelman, it was like a wedding, all the pomp and circumstance, and vows. Cornel West says that you can't lead the people unless you love the people, and I think you can't lead the institution unless you love the institution. You have to be passionate. A sense of calling helps generate the stamina, energy, and resilience you need to do the job. To be effective, you have to be totally committed. (Tatum, *quoted in* Bower & Wolverton, 2009, p. 78)

In their volume, on African American women's campus presidential leadership, Bower and Wolverton advance the concept of the six C's of leadership: caring, confidence, competence, communication, credibility, and calling. Of these, they identify a sense of calling as the driving force behind the successes of the seven Black women leaders in their study: Debra Austin (University of Florida System), Lois Carson (San Bernardino Community College Board of Trustees), Marvalene Hughes (California State University, Stanislaus & Dillard University), Yolanda Moses (City College of New York), Beverly Tatum (Spelman College), Jerry Sue Thorton (Cuyahoga Community College), and Belle S. Wheelan (Southern Association of Colleges & Schools, Commission on Colleges). Beyond enthusiasm and passion, calling implicates a sense of purpose and meaning. It is that sense of calling which spurred Dr. Boyd to sign a contract with Alabama State, a contract that unconscionably was invalidating of her personhood. That calling enabled her to work toward the removal of Alabama State's accreditation warning despite continued challenges from the board. Dr. Boyd now engages with the AGB as an executive-level search consultant. Her caring, confidence, competence, communication, and credibility will continue to propel her relevance in the field. Her calling and the prescient need for six C's leaders would be the driving force behind a future presidency.

But what propels you? Presidential leadership is more than a position. Aspirant academic executive leaders will face declining public resources for higher education; defrayed maintenance and dilapidating physical plants; fewer 18 to 24-year-olds from traditional backgrounds leading to the need for creative recruitment strategies and captivating educational experiences; a need to broaden campus cultures to be welcoming and inclusive; the culture wars with fake theories about White replacement fueling racial resentments; Black and Brown death by vigilantes, police, and illness; assaults on the bodies of women and femme men borne out of toxic masculinity in insular pockets of campus culture; the need to broaden understanding and acceptance of nonbinary genders as well as variances in dis/ability; reducing campus carbon footprints and cleanup in the wake of "natural" disasters fueled by climate change; and keeping up with the pace with ongoing technological innovations, among other challenges.

As you consider career pathways in academia, particularly the pathway to the president, beyond concern and passion, consider your calling—your vocation and purpose for leading. Ponder the following questions:

1. Why do I want to lead? What are the issues/concerns that beckon me to leadership?
2. Am I prepared to lead? Do I have the KSAs to shape the direction of a campus community?
3. What are my strengths?
4. What do I need to learn more about?
5. From where can I get professional development, leadership coaching, and mentorship?
6. Do I have a network of support?
7. What are my values? When I need to make tough decisions, what principles guide my choices?
8. Am I prepared to do it alone?

Leadership can be an arduous, lonely business (Soares et al., 2018). Purpose and principles will steer a good leader.

KEY TAKEAWAYS

- There are multiple pathways to the campus presidency.
- If that is your aspiration, be prepared and be confident in who you are and in your purpose.

KEYWORDS

Pathways to the presidency; traditional pathways; nontraditional insider pathways; nontraditional outsider pathways; leadership competencies; presidential demographics; reflective practice

REFERENCES

Artis, L., & Bartel, S. (2021). Filling the leadership pipeline: A qualitative study examining leadership development practices and challenges facing community college presidents in Illinois. *Community College Journal of Research and Practice*, 45(9), 674–686.

Association of Governing Boards of Universities and Colleges (AGB). (2016). *Shared governance: Is ok good enough?* https://agb.org/reports-2/shared-governance-is-ok-good-enough/

Associated Press (AP). (2014, January 14). Alabama State bars president from campus cohabitation. *Tuscaloosa News.com*. https://www.tuscaloosanews.com/story/news/2014/01/15/alabama-state-bars-president-from-campus-cohabitation/29917414007/

Beardsley, S. C. (2017). *Higher calling: The rise of nontraditional leaders in academia*. University of Virginia Press.

Belanger, C. (2014, January 8). New Alabama State University president to get $1,000-per-month vehicle allowance, up to $10,000 for moving expenses. *Advance Local*. https://www.al.com/wire/2014/01/alabama_state_to_pay_new_presi.html

Birnbaum, R., & Umbach, P. D. (2001). Scholar, steward, spanner, stranger: The four career paths of college presidents. *The Review of Higher Education*, 24(3), 203–217.

Bolman, L. G. & Gallos, J. V. (2011). *Reframing academic leadership*. Jossey-Bass.

Bower, B. L., & Wolverton, M. (2009). *Answering the call: African American women in higher education leadership*. Stylus Publishing, LLC.

Burns, H. (2021, September 23). *College president turnover sees an uptick in 2021. What's driving the churn?* https://www.bizjournals.com/bizjournals/news/2021/09/23/college-president-turnover-2021.html

Carter, T. J., & Craig, M. O. (2022). It could be us: Black faculty as "threats" on the path to tenure. *Race and Justice*, 12(3), 569–587. https://doi.org/10.1177/21533687221087366

Cohen, M., & March, J. (1974). *Leadership and ambiguity: The American college presidency*. McGraw Hill.

Cohen, M., & March, J. (1986). *Leadership and ambiguity: The American college president* (2nd ed.). The Harvard Business School Press.

Cooney, M. A., & Martin, Q., III. (2021). Pathways to the presidency. In M. T. Miller & G. D. Gearhart (Eds.), *Handbook of research on the changing role of college and university leadership* (pp. 18–35). IGI Global.

Cooper, A. J. (1886/1998). Womanhood: A vital element in the regeneration and progress of a race. In C. L. Lemert & E. Bhan (Eds.), *The voice of Anna Julia Cooper* (pp. 53–71). Rowman & Littlefield.

Corbin, N. A., Smith, W. A., & Garcia, J. R. (2018). Trapped between justified anger and being the strong Black woman: Black college women coping with racial battle fatigue at historically and predominantly White institutions. *International Journal of Qualitative Studies in Education*, 31(7), 626–643.

Croom, N. N. (2017). Promotion beyond tenure: Unpacking racism and sexism in the experiences of Black womyn professors. *The Review of Higher Education*, 40(4), 557–583.

Croom, N. N., & Patton, L. (2011). The miner's canary: A critical race perspective on the representation of Black women full professors. *Negro Educational Review*, *62–63*(1–4), 13–39.

College and University Professional Association for Human Resources (CUPA-HR). (2022). *CUPA-HR 2021-22 Administrators in Higher Education Survey*. www.cupahr.org/surveys

Delabbio, D., & Palmer, L. (2009). A 360° view of non-traditional university presidents. *Academic Leadership: The Online Journal, 7*(1), https://scholars.fhsu.edu/alj/vol7/iss1/2

Elliott, D. (2014, January 17). No 'cohabitation' for Alabama State's first female president.*NPR*.https://www.npr.org/sections/codeswitch/2014/01/17/263484808/no-cohabitation-for-alabama-states-first-female-president

Gagliardi, J. S., Espinosa, L. E., Turk, J. M., & Taylor, M. (2017). *American college president study 2017*. American Council on Education.

Giddings, P. J. (2006). *When and where I enter: The impact of Black women on race and sex in America*. Amistad.

Gigliotti, R. A. (Ed.). (2019). An introduction to competencies and competency-based leadership. In R. A. Gigliotti (Ed.), *Competencies for effective leadership: A framework for assessment, education, and research* (pp. 1–16). Emerald Publishing Limited.

Ginsberg, B. (2011). *The fall of the faculty*. Oxford University Press.

Giovanni, N. (1974/1996). Revolutionary dreams. In N. Giovanni (Ed.), *The selected poems of Nikki Giovanni* (p. 79). William Morrow and Company, Inc.

Gluckman, N. (2017, May 15). What should a college president do in year one? *The Chronicle of Higher Education*. https://www.chronicle.com/article/What-Should-a-College/240074

Griffin, K. A., Bennett, J. C., & Harris, J. (2013). Marginalizing merit?: Gender differences in Black faculty D/discourses on tenure, advancement, and professional success. *The Review of Higher Education*, *36*(4), 489–512.

Harley, D. A. (2008). Maids of academe: African American women faculty at predominately white institutions. *Journal of African American Studies*, *12*(1), 19–36.

Heuvel, S. (2017). Understanding a new type of higher education leader: A call to arms to study nontraditional college presidents. *International Leadership Journal*, *9*(2), 80–84.

Huff, M. T., & Neubrander, J. (2015). Interim administrators in higher education: A national study. *Journal of Academic Administration in Higher Education*, *11*(1), 9–15.

Ivory, J. (2017). *A review of nontraditional presidents in higher education: Benefits and challenges of change agents in colleges and universities* [Doctoral Dissertation, Benedictine University, Lisle, IL].

Jackson, S., & Harris, S. (2007). African American female college and university presidents: Experiences and perceptions of barriers to the presidency. *Journal of Women in Leadership*, 5(2), 119–137.

Jacobs, P. (2014, January 10). Alabama State University's new single president is forbidden by her contract from having 'lovers' stay overnight. *Business Insider*. https://www.businessinsider.com/gwendolyn-boyd-forbidden-by-her-contract-from-having-lovers-stay-overnight-2014-1

Katz, N. (2020, January 28). Black women are the most educated group in the U.S. *Thought.Co.* https://www.thoughtco.com/black-women-most-educated-group-us-4048763

Lavigne, E. (2020). The demographics and career paths of Canadian university deans: Gender, race, experience, and provenance. *Studies in Higher Education*, 45(9), 1949–1960.

Lederman, D. (2022, February 14). Diversity on the rise among college presidents. *Inside Higher Ed* https://www.insidehighered.com/news/2022/02/14/colleges-have-hired-more-minority-presidents-amid-racial-reckoning

León, R., & Thomas, N. D. (2016). Critical race theory and the cultivation, mentorship and retention of Black women faculty. *American International Journal of Humanities and Social Science*, 2(1), 1–16.

Long, S. E. (2002). *The new student politics: The wingspread statement on student civic engagement.* A report prepared for Campus Compact.

MacTaggart, T. (2017). *The 21st century presidency: A call to enterprise.* https://agb.org/reports-2/the-21st-century-presidency-a-call-to-enterprise-leadership-2/

McNair, D. E. (2015). Deliberate disequilibrium: Preparing for a community college presidency. *Community College Review*, 43(1), 72–88.

Matthew, P. A. (Ed.). (2016). *Written/unwritten: Diversity and the hidden truths of tenure.* UNC Press Books.

Melidona, D., Cecil, B. G., Cassell, A., & Chessman, H. M. (2023). *The American college president: 2023 edition.* American Council on Education. https://www.acenet.edu/Documents/American-College-President-IX-2023.pdf

National Center for Education Statistics (NCES). (2019). *U.S. Department of Commerce, Census Bureau, Current Population Survey (CPS), October, 1970 through 2017 (Table No. 302.60).* https://nces.ed.gov/programs/digest/d18/tables/dt18_302.60.asp

Nielsen, L. A. (2013). *Provost: Experiences, reflections and advice from a former "number two" on campus.* Stylus Publishing, LLC.

Okoli, G. N., Moore, T. A., Thomas, S. L., & Allen, T. T. (2020). Minority women in educational leadership. In R. Papa (Ed.), *Handbook on promoting social justice in education* (pp. 1711–1727). Springer.

Pewewardy, C. (2021). Why we can't ignore the "chief" in chief diversity officer. *Multicultural Education, 28*(3/4), 28–31.

Polk-Johnson, C. R. (2019). *Nontraditional pathways to the college presidency: Journeys of African American women* [Doctoral dissertation, Capella University, Minneapolis, MN].

Preston, D., & Floyd, A. (2016). Supporting the role of associate dean in universities: An alternative approach to management development. *Higher Education Quarterly, 70*(3), 264–280.

Rivard, R. (2014, January 10). President's home or prison? *Inside Higher Ed.* https://www.insidehighered.com/news/2014/01/10/alabama-university-limits-presidents-love-life

Rodriguez-Farrar, H., & Jack, L. H. (2022). Pathways to the presidency: An analysis of the gender gap at American four-year colleges and universities. In B. Cozza & C. Parnther (Eds.), *Voices from women leaders on success in higher education* (pp. 15–29). Routledge.

Ruben, B. D. (2006). *What leaders need to know and do: A leadership competencies scorecard.* National Association of College and University and Business Officers.

Ruben, B. D. (2012). *Leadership competencies scorecard 2.0.* Rutgers Center for Organizational Leadership. https://ol.rutgers.edu/research-development/leadership-competencies-scorecard/

Ruben, B. D. (2019). An overview of the leadership competency framework. In R. A. Gigliotti (Ed.), *Competencies for effective leadership* (pp. 19–28). Emerald Publishing Limited.

Ruben, B. D., De Lisi, R., & Gigliotti, R. A. (2021). *A guide for leaders in higher education: Concepts, competencies, and tools.* Stylus Publishing, LLC.

Sayler, M. F., Pedersen, J., Smith, M. C., & Cutright, M. (2019). Hidden leaders: Results of the national study of associate deans. *Studies in Higher Education, 44*(7), 1119–1129.

Seltzer, R. (2018, February 16). For college presidents, is 70 the new 50? *Inside Higher Education.* https://www.insidehighered.com/news/2018/02/16/colleges-keep-hiring-experienced-presidents-even-their-60s-and-70s

Snyder, T. D., de Brey, C., and Dillow, S. A. (2019). Postsecondary education. *Digest of education statistics 2017* (NCES 2018-070) (379-629). National Center for Education Statistics, Institute of Education Sciences, U.S. Department of Education.

Soares, L., Gagliardi, J. S., Wilkinson, P. J., & Hughes, S. L. (2018). *Innovative leadership: Insights from the American College president study 2017.* American Council on Education. https://www.acenet.edu/Documents/Innovative-Leadership-Insights-from-the-ACPS-2017.pdf

Stein, S., & Andreotti, V. D. O. (2016). Decolonization and higher education. In M. Peters (Ed.), *Encyclopedia of educational philosophy and theory* (pp. 1–6). Springer. https://doi.org/10.1007/978-981-287-532-7_479-1

Teece, D. J., & Falconi, S. (2018, November 20). What the 'American College President' needs today. *Inside Higher Education.* https://www.insidehighered.com/advice/2018/11/20/todays-presidents-should-focus-their-colleges-dynamic-capabilities-and-ecological

Valliancourt, A. M. (2018, May 14). Are you sure you want that interim job? *The Chronicle of Higher Education.* https://www.chronicle.com/article/are-you-sure-you-want-that-interim-job/Washington Lockett, A., Gasman, M., & Nguyen, T. H. (2018). Senior level administrators and HBCUs: The role of support for Black women's success in STEM. *Education Sciences, 8*(2), 48. https://doi.org/10.3390/educsci8020048

Watkins, W. H. (2001). *The White architects of Black education: Ideology and power in America, 1865–1954.* Teachers College Press.

Wergin, J. (2007). *Leadership in place: How academic professionals can find their leadership voice.* Ankor Publishing.

Whitney, K. M. (2022, August 24). The 4 stages of a presidential lifecycle. *The Chronicle of Higher Education.* https://www.chronicle.com/article/the-4-stages-of-a-presidential-life-cycle

Woollen, S. A. (2016). The road less traveled: Career trajectories of six women presidents in higher education. *Advancing Women in Leadership, 36,* 1–10.

Zahneis, M. (2022, February 4). The faculty job (almost) no one wants. *The Chronicle of Higher Education.* https://www.chronicle.com/article/the-faculty-job-almost-no-one-wants

Zemsky, R. (2009). *Making reform work: The case for transforming American higher education.* Rutgers University Press.

PART I

The Community College Context

By Dr. Katrina Arnold

Dr. Katrina Ramsey Arnold (she/her/hers) serves as the Senior Director of Developmental Education and Academic Support at Pitt Community College (PCC) in Winterville, NC. In addition to this role, Dr. Arnold has served as Co-Chair of Achieving the Dream at PCC and has been active on various campus committees. Dr. Arnold holds three degrees from East Carolina University: A bachelor of arts in political science, a master of arts in adult education, and a doctorate of education in educational leadership—higher education administration. Dr. Arnold's research interests include community college leadership, Black women leaders and their experiences as administrators at community colleges and supporting racially minoritized students at community colleges. Dr. Arnold is active in her local community and serves on the Corporate Board of the Boys & Girls Club of the Coastal Plain and the East Carolina University Women's Roundtable Board. She is also a member of Alpha Kappa Alpha Sorority, Inc. and the Greenville-Pitt County area section of the National Council of Negro Women. Dr. Arnold currently resides in Pitt County, NC, with her husband and daughter.

"You learn how to cut down trees by cutting them down."

—Congolese proverb

CHAPTER 2

Black Women and Their Pursuit to the Community College Presidency

ABSTRACT

This chapter discusses Black women and their pursuit to the community college presidency, the barriers faced during this pursuit, and how they overcome those barriers to achieve senior-level administrative positions at the community college level. A brief historical background of women's leadership in community colleges as well as how race and gender have contributed to the barriers faced during the career advancement of Black women community college leaders is included. Through a phenomenological approach and the use of Critical Race Feminism, the chapter examines and focuses on themes that emerged during interviews of Black women community college administrators. These women shared their passion for leading and the paths taken to accomplish their goals.

INTRODUCTION

Educational and career opportunities for women in higher education and society in large have not always been comparable to men. According to del Mar Alonso-Almeida (2014), the number of women in the workforce is increasing although the rate is not comparable to the population they represent. Thus, although women hold more than 50% of administrative titles within community colleges, representation among the presidency and senior academic leadership is not similarly comparable (Phillippe, 2016).

Women have responded to the shifts in the economy and the workforce by enrolling in higher education institutions, and community colleges have played a significant role in this increase (St. Rose & Hill, 2013). In addition, many women are continuing their education by receiving graduate and advanced degrees. As a result, women are obtaining degrees and credentials that are necessary to achieve top-level positions. Presently, women occupy approximately 28% of all presidencies at community colleges and 21% of senior academic leadership positions that include dean, vice president of academic affairs, and provost. As the prime pathway to the community college presidency is through positions such as provost and senior academic affairs administrator, the future of women leading community colleges is promising because many women are serving as senior-level administrators. A significant change in leadership structure and culture also occurs when women community college leaders constitute about 40% within a state (Eddy & Khwaja, 2019).

Several researchers acknowledge the barriers that make it difficult for Black women to experience success in higher education (Grant & Simmons, 2008). So, while the future of Black women in senior-level administrative positions is promising, the journey to those positions can be quite tumultuous. As a result of the challenges faced by Black women in their pursuit of the community college presidency, it is important to understand both the details of these challenges and how to overcome them. This chapter will highlight and examine the themes that emerged from interviews of Black women who serve in executive leadership roles at community colleges. A particular focus is given to the experiences of these women and strategies utilized to advance and overcome challenges and barriers to achieve executive leadership positions at community colleges.

LITERATURE REVIEW

The Growth of Women's Leadership in Community Colleges

According to Stephenson (2001), the 1960s were faced with unparalleled growth of community colleges nationally. At the same time, many community colleges became open to women in positions of leadership. While this was not necessarily the case for all institutions that identified themselves as community colleges, those that did not accept women in leadership positions would ultimately be forced to do so because of the demographics of the institutions (Stephenson, 2001). Furthermore, as a matter of symbol, the quest for Title IX revealed issues related to gender in higher education in 1972. This ultimately allowed the underrepresentation of women in higher education leadership to become a significant focus of study. During the 30 years after the passing of Title IX, the number of male higher education administrators increased by 10% and the number of female administrators increased by 147% (Opp & Gosetti, 2002). The fact that women in leadership positions at community colleges are largely accepted and more and more women succeed in securing these positions each year is extremely positive. However, it will be several decades before the number of female leaders at community colleges match the number of women students and employees on college campuses (Giannini, 2001). Thus, in spite of the fact that community colleges are comprised of a diverse student body that includes a large number of women and people of color, the makeup of the administration at these institutions does not necessarily mirror this diversity. However, the community college sector fares better than others in this regard (Phillippe, 2016).

When compared to four-year higher education institutions, community colleges enroll and employ a higher number of women. However, there is an underrepresentation of women in senior-level administrative roles within community colleges (VanDerLinden, 2004). This is especially interesting since community colleges are frequently regarded as having the ability to be more supportive to the career pathways of women. While this support is quite apparent as women continue to attain greater representation within community colleges when compared to other institutions, their advancement is at a much slower pace than their male counterparts (Eddy, 2008).

The slow advancement of women administrators in community colleges is especially true for women of color. Even as the presence of Black women in higher education increases, they continue to be underrepresented in leadership positions (Agosto & Karanxha, 2011–2012). Eddy (2018) notes that a survey by the American Council on Education confirms that 80% of community college presidents are White and 36% of community college presidents are women. Additionally, when race and gender are considered, men of color make up the majority of leaders who are non-White at 12.9%. Women of color fall behind at 7.4% (Eddy, 2018). This evidence illustrates the fact that women of color have progressed at a slow rate in their attempts to obtain positions as higher education administrators.

Cook (2012) explains that BIPOC women and men are raised to believe that hard work and education will ultimately lead them to successful careers and lives. This belief is coupled with the idea that race and gender are not factors in this pursuit for success. Although there is truth in the idea that hard work and education will lead to success, many racially minoritized individuals eventually learn that their race and even their gender can significantly impact their ability to climb the career ladder or break the infamous glass ceiling (Cook, 2012). Additionally, while higher education is viewed as being essential for economic progression and success, it is not immune from the inequalities that pollute the rest of society (Harris & Gonzalez, 2012).

Barriers to Black Women Leadership in Community Colleges

Black women are not often at the forefront as institutional change agents and are frequently viewed through stereotypical contexts such as "Mammy," "Sapphire," "Jezebel," and "Superwoman" (Patton & Haynes, 2018). Further, the symbolism associated with Black women's work is quite heavy in that it includes various forms of oppression such as racism, sexism, and classism (Patton & Haynes, 2018). Women administrators in higher education face these barriers and others as they attempt to advance professionally. These barriers often discourage Black women administrators from becoming effective, fulfilled, and successful members of the academy. According to Opp and Gosetti (2002), earlier literature proposes that the underrepresentation of women administrators in higher education was a result of personal aspects such as minimal self-confidence, a lack of required credentials, and the inability to relocate. As a result of these issues, it is important to analyze the particular barriers that women face within the academy. More specifically, it is vital to express that the issues faced by Black women at predominantly White institutions are unique when compared to Black men and their White female counterparts.

Race

According to Harvey (1999), for most administrative positions in higher education institutions, the review of candidates consists of an assessment of qualifications, accomplishments, educational background, and professional training. In addition, personal style and mannerisms are assessed to determine whether or not an individual will be able to perform specific job responsibilities in an effective manner. While these qualities assist some individuals in climbing the career ladder, others are often overlooked and disqualified for certain positions even when they possess the required qualities to perform the duties of that position. The one disqualifying factor for many of these individuals is race. The history of racial discrimination in the United States has resulted in Blacks not receiving comparable consideration for positions, particularly positions of power and authority in colleges and universities that are predominantly White (Harvey, 1999).

Jackson and Daniels (2007) note that there were practically no Blacks working in administrative positions at predominantly White institutions prior to the civil rights movement. The only administrative opportunities for Blacks during that time were at historically Black colleges and universities. Subsequently, the demands of Black students, civil rights legislation, and affirmative action encouraged predominantly White institutions to increase Black representation in administrative areas. While this was promising, many Black administrators were only given responsibility, not authority. Therefore, many of their decisions were questioned and they were limited to what they actually could do in their positions (Jackson & Daniels, 2007).

Like their White counterparts, Blacks desire administrative positions at the highest level; however, the largest representation of Blacks tend to be in areas that are not favorably seen as pathways to the top (Harvey, 1999). The reason for this is that White males have filled these positions for many years, making it difficult for Black and Brown individuals to become essential parts of college and university administrative staffs (Jackson & Daniels, 2007). For instance, a larger proportion of Blacks seem to be located in the areas of student affairs, minority affairs, and affirmative action. While top administrative positions such as dean and vice president exist in these areas, they do not traditionally lead to presidencies like the top positions in academic and financial affairs do. Nevertheless, there are cases where Black administrators have beaten the odds and advanced into top administrative positions that have been traditionally held by their White counterparts only to find that they must encounter personal slights, aggravation, and insults all because of the color of their skin (Harvey, 1999).

A study conducted by Rolle et al. (2000) revealed that Black administrators working in a predominantly White environment must familiarize themselves with the culture of the environment in order to be successful. The burden of comprehending and dealing with institutional and personal racism is a common experience of Black administrators in higher education. These administrators must develop skills that allow them to manage working in a hostile environment and survive in an atmosphere that is filled with institutional racism. It is important to note that race is a key concept that structures the Black administrator in higher education institutions that are predominantly White. Issues of race often appear during the hiring process and the overall structuring of the positions that Black administrators hold. The issue of institutional racism provides a need for Black administrators to understand their roles in both Black and White environments. Further, this necessity is coupled with the understanding of how to become an effective leader in a predominantly White atmosphere (Rolle et al., 2000).

Gender

Shifts in gender roles in higher education have been present in American culture during recent years. There have been an increasing number of women attending and obtaining degrees from higher education institutions, which has resulted in those women being educationally prepared for career advancement. While this is true, women are still considerably underrepresented in senior administrative positions at higher education institutions. There has been a misconception of women leaders in higher education because of several appointments of women as leaders of prestigious institutions over the past few years (Longman & Lafreniere, 2012).

External barriers also exist in the form of devaluation, responsibilities of home and family, role models and networks, and systemic partiality. Many women encounter these obstacles that ultimately limit their career mobility. For instance, in many cases, women are offered lower salaries and are not provided with much room to negotiate. In contrast, men experience more flexibility and have the ability to obtain their desired positions and salaries. Women are also faced with the challenge of balancing the roles of mother and wife with their professional roles. Although men do have familial responsibilities, women are more likely to take on the bulk of these responsibilities. This, in turn, makes it difficult for women to succeed and stay on an ideal career track within the academy because they often have to step away to handle familial duties (Cook, 2010).

The barrier of role models and networks in the lives of women seeking higher-level positions in higher education is also significant since individuals tend to gravitate to those they are most like. Because there are not a large number of women who have successfully navigated and achieved career success within the academy, women desiring to obtain that status find it difficult to meet other women who have these experiences and can provide them with the support they need. In addition, many women often prefer to work with men, making it tougher for women to obtain much needed information and establish career networks. Certain systemic biases and stereotypes such as the idea that Black women are committed to caring for others can discourage these women from attempting to obtain positions of power because they have a difficult time visualizing themselves in those positions. Moreover, others may have difficulty imagining Black women in certain roles as a result of the stereotypes society places on them (Patton & Haynes, 2018).

THEORETICAL FRAMEWORK

Critical race feminism (CRF) provides a foundation to explain the experiences of Black women. CRF is an extension of critical race theory

(CRT), but its focus is centered on the experiences of women of color (Pratt-Clarke, 2010. This is essential to this study due to its emphasis on the experiences of Black women administrators who are in positions within the pipeline to the community college presidency. According to Childers-McKee and Hytten (2015), CRF broadens the scope of CRT by exploring the "social phenomena of people doubly marginalized by both race and gender" (p. 395). Unlike other theories, the utilization of CRF allows one to view the experiences of Black women as being distinct in relation to the experiences of White women and Black men (Berry, 2010). Black women experience oppression and marginalization that is twofold, and it is important to be able to analyze their unique experiences.

For the purpose of this study, CRF adds a more intersectional and gendered perspective than CRT. CRF underscores the significance of intersectionality and multiple identities when analyzing the various challenges that Black women community college administrators experience as they navigate the community college presidency pipeline (Childers-McKee & Hytten, 2015). In this study, CRF provides a basis for evaluating the narratives of Black women community college administrators.

An influx of scholarly attention emerged at the end of the 20th century regarding the legal status of women of color. During this period, scholars in both the areas of civil rights and CRT attempted to incorporate the experiences of women of color into law and legal scholarship. Intersectionality, with roots in both Black feminism and CRT, was introduced by Kimberlé Crenshaw to address the marginalization of Black women within antidiscrimination law, as well as in feminist and antiracist theory and politics (Carbado et al., 2013). Crenshaw's perspective about the way a commitment to all women can obscure the particular struggles of certain women provides a unique view of the issues that exist within feminism (Harris, 2011). Intersectionality deals with the incapability of organizational structures to improve discrimination due to social dynamics (Crenshaw, 1989). It speaks to the interaction of race, gender, and other aspects while indicating the means in which racism, sexism, and other forms of oppression function concurrently (Junior, 2015). Crenshaw (1989) discusses the fact that Black women are often "caught at the intersections of race and gender discrimination law and left without an effective remedy" due to the fact that the law may not understand the differences in issues between Black women versus Black men and Black women versus White women (p. ix).

While the concept of intersectionality was an outcome of this effort, CRF extended its notion of the experiences of Black women by concentrating on how race, gender, and class interrelate for women of color who are burrowed in an organization characterized by White patriarchy and racial oppression (Wiggins, 2001). Further, CRF emerged as an attempt within the legal area of higher education to highlight the legal issues of a specific group of individuals that consist of BIPOC women of a low socioeconomic status (Wing, 2003).

As Black women continue to experience issues and barriers related to the intersection of race, class, and gender, it is necessary to be able to identify a framework to study the multifaceted effects of these characteristics on women of color. CRF offers a legal framework to examine the intricate effects of race, class, and gender on women of color. The focus of traditional legal scholarship is challenged by CRF. This traditional scholarship involves analyzing a legal case based on the outcomes of previous related cases, determining and investigating the differences of each analysis based on the distinctive facts of the cases, and applying both the constitutional and legal interpretations that are reflected in previous decisions to the new facts (Pratt-Clarke, 2010). Because this method infrequently discusses the operation of authority, structures of domination, or social justice engagement, it is unlikely for transformative change to occur because an unaccompanied legal approach to a complex social problem will hardly ever result in a complete understanding of the issue. As a result of this limitation and the fact that the law has been designed to only permit minimal and marginal change and progress, CRF materialized as an obligatory lens to examine the experiences of women of color (Pratt-Clarke, 2010).

The decision to use the term CRF to provide an emphasis on women of color was a sensible one as it specifies the connection to critical legal studies, CRT, and feminist law (Wing, 2003). It offers an unremorseful analysis of the intersection of race, class, and gender within the legal domain and the wide-ranging experiences of women of color. As a result, the principles of CRF are separate from those of CRT, but the two occasionally intersect (Evans-Winters & Esposito, 2010). This is

due to the fact that CRF builds on the concepts of CRT. The roles, experiences, and stories of women of color in the legal arena become the
focal point of analysis in CRF. This focus includes the numerous identities of women and how their experiences are a product of those
individualities. In all, CRF can be described as a field of study that
encompasses a number of related areas that include critical legal studies, CRT, gender studies, race and ethnic studies, and communications
studies (Pratt-Clarke, 2010).

For quite some time now, scholars in the field of education have explored
CRT and the method in which theories related to race explain the social
structure and existence of racism in educational institutions (Parker,
1998). As a branch of CRT, CRF has also found its place in education.
For example, Evans-Winters and Esposito (2010) explain that CRF is
valuable to the examination and the construction of theories that are
linked to educational issues affecting Black females in a variety of ways.
First, as a theoretical lens, CRF indicates that the experiences and viewpoints of women of color are not the same as what is experienced by men
of color and White women. In addition, the focus of CRF is on the lives
of women of color and the numerous forms of discrimination they face
as a result of the intersection of race, class, and gender within a structure
that is characterized by White male patriarchy and racial persecution.
Furthermore, CRF affirms the various individualities and cognizance of
women of color; it is multifaceted in scope; and it appeals to theories and
practices that study gender and racial oppression concurrently (Evans-
Winters & Esposito, 2010).

METHODOLOGY

This study is qualitative in nature and utilizes a phenomenological
approach. In a qualitative study, the researcher makes claims based on
the perspectives and multiple meanings of the experiences of individuals,
meanings that are socially and historically formed, all with an intent on
creating a theory or pattern (Creswell, 2003). According to Smith (2013),
phenomenology is the study of "phenomena" and the way things are
experienced by individuals. Further, these experiences are from a

first-person point of view. Creswell (2003) notes that in qualitative research, the investigator collects open-ended, evolving data with the key intent on developing themes from the data.

To explore the experiences of Black women in positions within the community college presidential pipeline, a phenomenological approach to collect data is necessary. This approach allows for the use of open-ended interview questions to discover the lived experiences of the research participants.

Semi-structured interview questions guided the one-on-one interviews with five women who are senior leaders at community colleges that are located within the regions established by the National Council on Black American Affairs (NCBAA). In addition to the one-on-one interviews, resumes and curricula vitae were collected from study participants in order to gather additional information on education and career background. Further, 20 resumes and curricula vitae also were collected from willing members of the NCBAA and National Council of Instructional Administrators who either did not qualify for one-on-one interviews because they do not meet the criteria or those who did not wish to participate in the interview process. This allowed for a resume-mapping process that helped to understand the paths taken by individuals working in executive leadership positions at community colleges. In addition, this resume-mapping process contributed to the analysis of the interview data by allowing for a comparison and contrast of education/career paths of interview participants and of those individuals who only submitted resumes and curricula vitae. Results from the resume-mapping process are included in Chapter 3.

Participants selected for this study are Grace, who serves as Vice President of Student Services at a community college in the southern region; Hope, who serves as Campus President at a community college in the north central region; Serenity, who serves as Campus President at a community college in the north central region; Faith, who serves as the Vice President of Workforce Development at a community college in the southern region; and Destiny, who serves as the Campus President at a community college in the northeast region. Names utilized in this study are pseudonyms.

Table 2.1 Participants

Pseudonym	Title	Institution size (number of students)	Location
Grace	Vice President of Student Services	30,000–60,000	Southern region
Hope	Campus President	60,000+	North central region
Serenity	Campus President	15,000–30,000	North central region
Faith	Vice President of Workforce Development	0–5,000	Southern region
Destiny	Campus President	60,000+	Northeast region

Data collected from the one-on-one interviews and supporting materials were analyzed to identify emergent themes. Emergent themes were (1) maintaining a strong support system; (2) work-life balance; (3) spirituality; and (4) overcoming barriers related to race and gender. These themes provide more insight into the lives of Black female community college administrators and their experiences while working in positions within the pathway to the community college presidency.

FINDINGS

Maintaining a Strong Support System: Who Can I Depend On?

Maintaining a strong support system was highlighted as an important aspect of reaching one's career goals in the field of community college administration. All five participants noted that a strong support system that includes family, friends, and mentors has been influential during their career journeys.

Serenity identifies her support system in three distinct groups: mentors, her kitchen cabinet, and coaches. She notes that her early career consisted of colleagues, supervisors, and individuals with experience in the field of higher education. Serenity's mentors, kitchen cabinet, and coaches are all different people in her life. She reflected on three mentors during her career. Two were Black men and one was a White man. They provided her with the support and nurturing she needed. This was especially important to Serenity as an administrator at predominantly White colleges. They talked to her about aspirations, career goals, and they identified her mistakes during her journey and provided her with advice on how to handle those mistakes. Serenity's kitchen cabinet provides her with the type of support that only close friends and family can. Her husband, for example, does not work in higher education, but she is able to go to him for advice about things she is experiencing as a community college campus president. She explains:

> My husband was a businessman and he's now retired. Before I send an email because somebody makes me angry, I can call him up and say, "Listen to this. What do you think about this?" He'll say, "Don't send that email." He's not in higher education, but he's a great supporter of me.

Serenity's coaches emerged during the latter part of her career. As she has gained more experience and became an executive-level community college leader, her mentors have become more of coaches to her. They are individuals who have similar current experiences and have risen through the ranks just like Serenity.

Faith describes her group of supporters as her cheerleaders. She feels it is important to surround yourself with people who will support you and have your back no matter what. Her family, her minister, and her girlfriends have been that constant support system for Faith. She also credits her mentors for constant support during her career journey. She is extremely grateful for the support, but she does acknowledge that it can become stressful when you have to navigate different groups in order to reach your goals. Faith explains:

> It's lovely to be able to just get right to the core of it with my professional girlfriends' circle and then on the other side, being able to go to my other mentors and express to them my interest in that position and if they'd be willing to make a call or send an email on my behalf. That combination of things seems to have served me fairly well, but again, it adds more stress having to work these multiple channels.

Grace also has the support of her family. Her husband has especially been her rock as he has relocated in order for her to pursue a job opportunity. He travels with her for business purposes and accompanies her to community events. Grace is also able to confide in him about issues she may be dealing with at work. He offers a perspective that is both critical and understanding. She reflects on the importance of sharing her day with her husband:

> I go home and I share my day with my husband, unless I just can't tell him because of confidentiality. I do this because your family is the one who loves you the most and they're going to support you the most, so those are the least people that you should isolate. So I say, "Well, what do you think about this?" I find that to be helpful during this journey.

Grace has also had a number of mentors who have been influential throughout her career. Most of her mentors have been college presidents, even early in her career. Interestingly, all the college presidents who have served as mentors to Grace have been men. She notes that women have never been elected to serve as a mentor to her. She feels that this may be due to the competitive nature of some women. She shared the following thoughts:

> Some women don't like to see other women succeed, and I don't know if that's a gender thing or a race thing or whatever, but that has been my experience. I guess the reason women may have felt that way is, as I was coming up the success ladder, it was during the time when not too many women had opportunities that we have today. I guess because of this, they were competitive against me. They probably weren't about to let a young, up-and-coming woman take their position.

Grace hopes things have changed and more women are stepping up to mentor women who are on the path to leading community colleges.

Hope and Destiny also acknowledge their family as being strong supporters during their career journeys. Destiny adds that her current chancellor is her strongest mentor. She credits several other mentors in her life, but her chancellor believed in her and gave her a chance. Hope explains that while her peer group has become very small since she has become a campus president, she is thankful for the small group of peers, her family, and professional mentors who have continued to have her back.

Work-Life Balance: How Do I Balance It All?

All five women interviewed noted that balancing family life and career responsibilities is sometimes a challenge. Destiny reflected on a period when she separated from her husband and the separation eventually led to a divorce. She had just begun a full-time position and it was difficult because she was the "present parent" to her daughter. As the parent who is present, she was the one who was there all the time to care for her daughter. Destiny notes that family and friends were extremely instrumental in assisting her with her daughter as she climbed the ladder to her current leadership position. Serenity also credited family as being extremely supportive during the time she became a single parent. This occurred during a time in her life where she was a bit overwhelmed with the work she was doing. She eventually decided to pursue jobs closer to her parents' home in another state and ultimately obtained a position in the area. This provided Serenity and her daughter with support and allowed Serenity to continue working because her parents were there to assist her with her daughter. Hope also explained the significance of her family and friends in helping her balance multiple responsibilities:

> Because of the time that I have put into my work, I have to have a lot of support related to helping me with my children. I have two children. You want them to have a full experience and you do not want your job to stop them from exploring, and learning, and developing as children. So, I have a lot of family that help me. I have family members that help me with the kids' pick up. I have family members that help me with keeping the kids when I have things that I need to do on the weekends that are related to work. As a working mother, having a family structure where people are willing to support you is invaluable.

Faith described being a single mother of a young son and the caretaker of her parents. She has to constantly juggle those responsibilities with the demands of her career. She notes that she has to take her roles as a mother and a caretaker into consideration when making decisions about her career. As someone who is open to career advancement, she also understands that to accept a new position, it would have to work within the constraints of her life. With that, she understands and is content with the possibility of not being able to advance if a position is not a good fit with her responsibilities as a mother and a caretaker. She explains:

> When we talk three or five years from now, maybe I will not be a president as a result of some of those constraints that I put on myself. That is how it is right now. You have to remember as a woman, I think we always have a greater level of responsibility for things outside of our work that men do not.

Faith also discussed the differences she sees between mothers and fathers. At the community college where she currently works, she has noticed several male employees in leadership positions being praised for taking a day off to care for a sick child. This has been very interesting for Faith, a mother of a son who suffers from asthma. There have been times when she had to care for her son during asthma attacks that even required a visit to the emergency room. She reflects:

> I don't remember any kudos for me being out with my son who had asthma attacks and he was in the emergency room. I don't remember one bit of kudos. The assumption is that as women, as mothers, of course, that's your job. However, when men do it, "Oh, that's outstanding. You took care of your son."

Several of the women interviewed also discussed how their careers have impacted their romantic relationships. Three out of the five women interviewed have been divorced. It is difficult to balance the demands of life as a woman and relationships often are affected. Destiny reflected on a time when she was married and had a commuting relationship due to career responsibilities. The distance jeopardized the relationship and it ultimately ended in divorce. Serenity, who is celebrating 22 years of marriage with her third husband, admits that moving around so much in her career journey has been hard on her relationships.

While attempting to maintain work-life balance as a woman in an executive leadership position at a community college, Faith acknowledges that you cannot do everything. This is sometimes difficult for women to grasp because they are accustomed to being "all things to all people." Faith explains:

If you are trying to do everything, the reality is that you cannot do every-thing at the highest level. You've got to, at some point, accept that, and this is a quote from somebody and I cannot remember who said it, but that your best is different every single day based on a whole range of fac-tors. When I've been up all night giving my son breathing treatments every four hours while he sleeps, well then, my best that next day at work is not going to be the same best that it would be if I'd gotten a full night's rest. Those are the trade-offs we make.

All five women interviewed for the purpose of this research spoke of the issues related to being wives, mothers, and caretakers while simultane-ously working as community college leaders. Depending on the support of others to assist in childcare, the difference between how mothers and fathers are viewed, and the impact of career on romantic relationships are all significant components of work-life balance. So, how do you balance it all? According to five women who experience juggling multiple roles every day, you rely on those closest to you to help because you are only one person. While planning, prioritizing, and making sure you include your work and family demands on your daily agenda, you must realize that there will be days when something will not get done or you are not at your best. That is okay! Faith explains, "I think that's just part of what it means to be a woman in a leadership position. You are constantly jug-gling and balancing, but you do so in a way that allows you to meet the needs of yourself as a working woman in a leadership position as well as the needs of those around you."

Spirituality: What Keeps Me Grounded?

Staying grounded and maintaining the ability to make it through difficult situations can be challenging for Black women in community college leadership positions. Three of the women interviewed discussed their spirituality and the existence of a faith system. Their Christian values and faith keep them going when they feel as if they can't take another step. Serving in an executive leadership role at a community college can be very demanding. The demands of the job coupled with all of life's responsibilities can be challenging. Destiny, Faith, and Grace all agree that spirituality is essential in helping one reach their goals and overcome obstacles that are encountered along the way.

Destiny is extremely involved in the African Methodist Episcopal (AME) Zion Church. She serves on the board and actively represents her church in the community. Destiny credits the AME Zion church as being a huge support to her as she has navigated her career and life. She notes, "I depend a lot on my spirituality." For Destiny, her faith is her balance. When she is confronted with challenges in her personal life or in her career, she relies on her faith to pull her through.

Faith believes that having an internal core of values is necessary when pursuing leadership positions. This, coupled with a faith system helps to create a balance that is necessary in this journey. Many days as an executive community college administrator are difficult, therefore it requires a tremendous amount of strength and determination. Her faith in God is essential in getting her through those days that are especially difficult. Faith believes that her faith system has greatly impacted her career success and her ability to juggle her other responsibilities.

Not only does Grace have an advanced degree in higher education, she also holds a master's of divinity. She prays and reads her bible daily because she sees it as an investment. In turn, that investment creates a balance and allows you to be both mentally and emotionally stable. Grace believes in the power of prayer. She always seeks God for understanding and asks Him to lead her down the appropriate path. This is how she stays grounded and is able to overcome obstacles she encounters as an administrator. Grace does not believe in worrying. She trusts God to take care of her needs.

THE BARRIERS: HOW DO I HANDLE ISSUES RELATED TO MY RACE AND GENDER?

Four of the women interviewed discussed issues related to race and gender during their career journeys. Faith has the ability to analyze and separate the obstacles she has encountered into three categories: race, gender, and being the outsider. She explained how her experiences differed in each of these areas. As for race, Faith has learned that as a person of color, it is her responsibility to be extremely conscious when discussions arise regarding the implementation of new policies. She always questions these potential policies to determine whether they will harm specific groups of students such as students of color or first-generation college students. She also has to be strategic about how she phrases those questions to other administrators so that they are not viewed negatively. As a woman, Faith does not want to be viewed as "mothering." It is important for her employees and colleagues to view her as a leader and a supervisor, not as a wife and a mother. Preventing these roles from mixing when she is in the workplace has been instrumental in her success as an executive leader. Faith also notes that her experiences have revealed that sometimes it has nothing to do with race or gender and everything has to do with the fact that she is an outsider. Working in a small rural community where she was not raised has been a challenge at times. She explains, "What I find is that there's a moment and it's mostly because I'm an outsider. What I'm learning is that it has less to do with my race and my color than the fact that I'm not a known quantity."

Faith and Hope both note that as Black women, your response to certain questions and situations can ultimately affect how you are viewed by others. For example, Faith reflected on attending a meeting when she first began her position as vice president. While meeting various individuals at the meeting, including an older White woman who was an elected official, Faith recalls turning around to speak to someone when she felt her head being pulled. She quickly turned around and the elected official stated, "I'm sorry, I couldn't help myself. I just wanted to feel them." Faith's hair is styled in locks and the woman had taken it upon herself to satisfy her curiosity by touching them. Faith reflects:

> Twenty years ago, I would have probably cursed her out and been very unhappy, but I'm a little more mature now and I realize that elected officials hold the purse strings to our funding. How I respond will determine what our relationship is like and how she perceives the college. Unfortunately, my response in that setting has to be, "No problem putting your hands in my hair" with a smile and then just moving on. To this day, I interact with this woman and she gives me a hug and she's very happy to see me. She probably doesn't even recall that incident. When I talk to my male counterparts, they don't tell me about being inappropriately touched, they don't talk about those kinds of things.

Hope has been strategic in how she delivers information and responds to issues. She explains that many Black women have raw passion and it is often viewed negatively. It is extremely important to be kind, respectful, and empathetic when sharing information with others. "There are expectations on who you are and how you should act as a Black woman and what they expect from you," shares Hope. As a result, Hope is very conscious of her demeanor.

Three of the women interviewed noted that while issues related to gender and race can arise during the career journey, a decrease in these types of experiences is often coupled with the attainment of a higher-level leadership position. For example, Serenity reflected on a time when she experienced gender and race issues, but once she became a campus president, those issues decreased tremendously. Grace also discussed her leadership abilities and the respect she has from her employees. As a vice president, Grace does not experience race and gender issues. She explains, "I hold the top-ranking position at my institution for a person of my ethnicity and gender, my salary is quite comparable, and I have the same opportunities to voice my opinion." This is significant to Grace because she is a significant part of the institution and she is valued. While Faith continues to overcome obstacles related to race and gender, she is aware that one day, she won't have to deal with such issues. She states, "I can't get mad every time that happens or I'd be mad all the time. There are just some things I have to put up with until I'm in a position where I don't have to put up with it anymore."

Destiny and Faith both explained that while Black women working in executive leadership positions at community college often encounter racial and gender barriers, it is important not to allow these issues to defeat you. Destiny believes that you must always stay focused because it is easy to become overwhelmed with all of the obstacles Black women face. Faith explains that you have to always remember why you do what you do.

> It's the coolest thing in the world to drive by a building and say, "I helped bring them here and I helped make sure that there are people and that their workers are all trained." It's a really cool thing. There are other days when you go to an event and someone asks you to get them coffee or they

put their hand in your hair because they have never seen locks. You have to have a clear understanding of why you're doing this. Those microaggressions over time, they can make you really angry and bitter or really steal the joy from the heart of what this work is really about.

CONCLUSION

This qualitative, phenomenological study allowed five women who serve in executive leadership positions at community colleges to share their journeys, their experiences, and how they ultimately obtained positions as vice presidents and campus presidents. Through the utilization of portraiture, illustrations of these women's lives and experiences in their pursuit of community college leadership positions were presented. This study explored the experiences of these women community college administrators. Challenges faced during the career journeys of the participants and strategies used to advance professionally and balance multiple roles were also examined. Several themes emerged from the qualitative data gathered during this study including (1) maintaining a strong support system; (2) work-life balance; (3) spirituality; and (4) overcoming barriers related to race and gender.

Several study participants discussed the importance of maintaining a strong support system. They noted their support systems as being influential in their success as community college administrators. When asked who they can depend on, the participants agreed that family, friends, and mentors have all contributed to their success. A strong support system is critical to the success of Black women who are pursuing executive leadership positions at community colleges. Because Black women often experience obstacles as they attempt to navigate the pathway to the community college presidency, having a network of supportive individuals can be essential in helping them overcome these hurdles. All the women interviewed depended on a combination of family, friends, and mentors during their career journey. Their strong support systems have played huge roles in their overall success.

Work-life balance also emerged as a common theme among the women interviewed for the purpose of this study. As wives, mothers, and daughters, women often have to balance multiple responsibilities related to work and family and they generally carry a disproportionate amount of childcare and elderly care duties. Further, Black women experience work-life balance differently when compared to White women. For example, 55% of Black children live in single-parent homes with most of those homes headed by women (Hamidullah & Riccucci, 2017). As a result, Black women must often balance the roles of wife, mother, and daughter with career responsibilities by finding ways to be everything to everyone. It is also common among Black women to seek alternative methods to balance family and work responsibilities. For many women this means that they count on family and friends to assist with childcare. While balancing a career and the demands of family is a concern for both women and men, it is particularly important to women because they often carry a significant amount of the load when it comes to taking care of the family (Hamidullah & Riccucci, 2017). All five women who participated in this study noted that the ability to balance work, family, and life has been significant during their journeys to their current executive leadership positions. These women agree that one must be able to rely on others for support and always include the demands of both work and family in their daily schedules.

The ability to remain grounded materialized as a common theme among three of the women interviewed. Spirituality and the existence of a faith system in their lives help to keep Destiny, Faith, and Grace grounded. This is necessary as the career journeys of Black women community college administrators can be especially challenging. Through an analysis of leadership traits of future community college leaders, Fulton-Calkins and Milling (2005) reveal that a sense of spirituality is necessary for community college presidents in order for them to be able to embrace and enhance their inward journey. As these women continue on their leadership journeys, their spirituality will continue to be essential to their success. They hold it extremely close because they are aware that challenges will continue to arise and they must be able to move forward and continue to be exceptional community college leaders.

Several of the women interviewed discussed the importance of being strategic in how you ask questions that include race and/or gender as well as how you respond to such questions. While the women interviewed acknowledged that they have faced obstacles related to race and gender, they were adamant that one should not allow racial and gender discrimination to control you. One participant noted that maintaining focus is the key because it is easy to become overwhelmed with issues such as these. In addition, three participants explained how they have experienced fewer race- and gender-related obstacles as they have moved up the career ladder. As executive-level community college leaders, they have gained the respect of their peers and those they supervise, thus decreasing the amount of discrimination in comparison to what they faced earlier in their careers.

This study examined the experiences of Black women who serve in executive leadership positions at community colleges. While the women who participated in this study faced challenges during their career journeys, they were able to implement a number of strategies that contributed to their success as leaders at community colleges. This research revealed that certain experiences are unique to Black women who are serving in leadership roles at community colleges. This is because many of these women encounter situations that White men, women, and even men of color do not experience. Much can be learned from the stories presented in this research. The portraits of the women and the themes that were illuminated by their stories are critical as community college leaders and board of trustee members look to increase diversity within their leadership teams. Further, the experiences of these women serve as models for Black women who also seek executive leadership positions within the pipeline to the community college presidency.

QUESTIONS TO PONDER

When seeking executive-level leadership positions at the community college, Black women should ponder the following questions:

1. What challenges might I face when pursuing the presidency at the community college level?
2. What strategies can I identify to assist me in overcoming barriers related to race and gender while navigating the community college presidential pipeline?
3. What tools do I need to successfully achieve my goals as a community college administrator?

4. What are my personal needs as a leader? Who are the people in my support system (family, friends, mentors) and what kind of support can those persons provide as I seek a healthy work-life integration?

KEY TAKEAWAYS

- Black women continue to face unique barriers while on their journeys to the community college presidency.
- The number of Black women serving in executive leadership roles at the community college level is still not comparable to the number of White males and White females serving in similar positions.
- The experiences of Black women who have achieved executive leadership at the community college level can provide other Black women who aspire to do the same with strategies to overcome similar obstacles.

KEYWORDS

Black women community college administrators; executive leadership; senior-level administrative position; community college; presidential pathway; presidential pipeline

REFERENCES

Agosto, V., & Karanxha, Z. (2011–2012). Resistance meets spirituality in academia: "I prayed it!". *The Negro Education Review*, 62/63(1–4), 41–66.

Berry, T. R. (2010). Engaged pedagogy and critical race feminism. *Educational Foundations*, 24(3–4), 19–26.

Carbado, D. W., Crenshaw, K., Mays, V., & Tomlinson, B. (2013). Intersectionality: Mapping the movements of a theory. *Dubois Review: Social Science Research on Race*, 10(2), 303–312.

Childers-McKee, C., & Hytten, K. (2015). Critical race feminism and the complex challenges of educational reform. *The Urban Review*, 47(3), 393–412.

Cook, S. G. (2010). Shattered glass ceiling still leaves jagged edges. *Women in Higher Education*, 19(3), 19–20.

Cook, S. G. (2012). For black women administrators, merit is not enough. *Women in Higher Education*, 21(4), 17–18.

Crenshaw, K. (1989). Demarginalizing the intersection of race and sex: A black feminist critique of antidiscrimination doctrine, feminist theory and antiracist politics. *University of Chicago Legal Forum*, 1989(1), Article 8, 139–167.

Creswell, J. W. (2003). *Research design: Qualitative, quantitative, and mixed methods approaches* (2nd ed.). SAGE.

del Mar Alonso-Almeida, M. (2014). Women (and mothers) in the workforce: Worldwide factors. *Women's Studies International Forum*, 44, 164–171.

Eddy, P. L. (2008). Reflections of women leading community colleges. *Community College Enterprise*, 14(1), 49–66.

Eddy, P. L. (2018). Expanding the leadership pipeline in community colleges: Fostering racial equity. *Teachers College Record*, 120(14), 1–18.

Eddy, P. L., & Khwaja, T. (2019). What happened to re-visioning community college leadership? A 25-year retrospective. *Community College Review*, 47(1), 53–78.

Evans-Winters, V. E., & Esposito, J. (2010). Other people's daughters: Critical race feminism and black girls' education. *The Journal of Educational Foundations*, 24(1/2), 11–24.

Fulton-Calkins, P., & Milling, C. (2005). Community college leadership: An art to be practiced: 2010 and beyond. *Community College Journal of Research and Practice*, 29(3), 233–250.

Giannini, S. T. (2001). Future agendas for women community college leaders and change agents. *Community College Journal of Research and Practice*, 25(3), 201–211.

Grant, C. M., & Simmons, J. C. (2008). Narratives on experiences of African-American women in the academy: Conceptualizing effective mentoring relationships of doctoral student and faculty. *International Journal of Qualitative Studies in Education*, 21(5), 501–517.

Hamidullah, M. F., & Riccucci, N. M. (2017). Intersectionality and family-friendly policies in the federal government: Perceptions of women of color. *Administration & Society*, 49(1), 105–120.

Harris, A. P. (2011). What ever happened to feminist legal theory? *Legal Feminism Now*, 9(2), 1–7.

Harris, A. P., & Gonzalez, C. G. (2012). Introduction. In G. Gutierrez y Muhs, Y. F. Niemann, C. G. Gonzalez, & A. P. Harris (Eds.), *Presumed incompetent: The intersections of race and class for women in academia* (pp. 1–14). University Press of Colorado.

Harvey, W. B. (Ed.). (1999). *Grass roots and glass ceilings: African American administrators in predominantly white colleges and universities*. State University of New York Press.

Jackson, J. F. L., & Daniels, B. D. (2007). A national progress report of African Americans in the administrative workforce. In J. F. L. Jackson (Ed.), *Strengthening the African American educational pipeline: Informing research, policy, and practice* (pp. 115–135). State University of New York Press.

Junior, N. (2015). Patricia Arquette's remarks explain why some black women don't call themselves feminists. *The Washington Post*. https://www.washingtonpost.com/posteverything/wp/2015/02/24/patricia-arquettes-remarks-explain-why-some-black-women-dont-call-themselves-feminists/

Longman, K. A., & Lafreniere, S. L. (2012). Moving beyond the stained glass ceiling: Preparing women for leadership in faith-based higher education. *Advances in Developing Human Resources, 14*(1), 45–61.

Opp, R. D., & Gosetti, P. P. (2002). Equity for women administrators of color in 2-year colleges: Progress and prospects. *Community College Journal of Research and Practice, 26*(7–8), 591–608.

Parker, L. (1998). Race is race ain't: An exploration of the utility of critical race theory in qualitative research in education. *International Journal of Qualitative Studies in Education, 11*(1), 43–55.

Patton, L. D., & Haynes, C. (2018). Hidden in plain sight: The Black women's blueprint for institutional transformation in higher education. *Teachers College Record, 120*(14), 1–18.

Phillippe, K. A. (2016). Female campus administrators. *Data Points: American Association of Community Colleges, 4*(5).

Pratt-Clarke, M. (2010). *Critical race, feminism, and education: A social justice model* (1st ed.). Palgrave Macmillan.

Rolle, K., Davies, T., & Banning, J. (2000). African American administrators' experiences in predominantly white colleges and universities. *Community College Journal of Research and Practice, 24*(2), 79–94.

Smith, D. W. (2013). *Phenomenology*. Stanford Encyclopedia of Philosophy. http://plato.stanford.edu/entries/phenomenology/

St. Rose, A., & Hill, C. (2013). *Women in community colleges: Access to success.* American Association of University Women.

Stephenson, G. W. (2001). Women as community college leaders. *Community College Journal of Research and Practice, 25*(3), 193–200.

VanDerLinden, K. E. (2004). Gender differences in the preparation and promotion of community college administrators. *Community College Review, 31*(4), 1–24.

Wiggins, M. J. (2001). The future of intersectionality and critical race feminism. *Journal of Contemporary Legal Issues, 11*, 677–903.

Wing, A. K. (Ed.). (2003). *Critical race feminism: A reader* (2nd ed.). University Press.

CHAPTER 3

The Future of Black Women in Community College Executive Leadership Positions

ABSTRACT

This chapter discusses the future of Black women in community college executive leadership positions. As the most diverse institutions in higher education, the makeup of community college executive leadership still does not mirror that of the student body. This chapter takes a closer look at the pathway to executive leadership at community colleges through the results of a resume-mapping process. In addition, typical pathways as well as support for how a pipeline for Black women can be developed and shared. Recommendations for institutions, administrators, and Boards of Trustees regarding how to increase the number of Black women in community college leadership positions are provided.

INTRODUCTION

Community colleges are centers of educational opportunity, and as compared to other educational sectors, they have an intentional focus on the community connecting the institution to business and industry, dual enrollment for high-school students, and university transfer (Eddy & Khwaja, 2019). Their commitment to accessibility and affordability has contributed to the diverse population of students, serving individuals who are diverse in age, ethnic and cultural background, socioeconomic background, and academic preparation levels. According to the American Association of Community Colleges (AACC), 57% of women and 45% of minorities are enrolled in community colleges; 43% of Black and 52% of Latino/Latina undergraduates are community college students (American Association of Community Colleges [AACC], 2017). In addition, among students, men are outnumbered by women across all races and ethnicities at community colleges and 3 out of every 10 women enrolled as students at community colleges are either Latina or Black (St. Rose & Hill, 2013). While the gender gap within community colleges favors women overall, the gap is largest for Black community college students; 63% are women. On the staff side, 58% of those employed at community colleges are women and 11% of all employed staff are Black. Further, 53% of women working at community colleges hold executive/managerial positions, while only 10% of Blacks are employed in those positions (AACC, 2016, 2017).

White students continue to surpass Black students in academic performance. Further, Black college students tend to exhibit a greater academic risk than White students due the fact that many are first-generation college students, they are likely to begin college academically underprepared, many are often juggling a variety of responsibilities, and they are more likely to experience cultural and institutional barriers (Greene et al., 2008). For community colleges to increase their graduation rates, they must focus on ways to assist Black students in persisting and achieving academically. One way to assist Black students as they move through their courses of study at community colleges is to offer them support from Black faculty and staff. This is essential for the success of Black students due to challenges they encounter when trying to pursue higher education opportunities.

While it is evident that the community college has a diverse student body, the composition of the professional workforce is not congruent to that diversity. As community colleges are identified by political leaders as being critical to assisting the United States in becoming the world leader in higher education again, it is imperative that we understand and support the students who attend these institutions (St. Rose & Hill, 2013;

The White House, 2016). Further, community college administrators must be able to relate to and understand the challenges that community college students face, especially given the diverse nature of the students who are enrolled. Jackson (2001) explains that the existence or absence of Black administrators at colleges and universities provides a sense of whether or not Black students will or will not feel welcomed at the institution. When considering the disproportionate and increasing number of Blacks, particularly women, attending community colleges, it would be a good practice for community colleges to attend to their staff being just as diverse as their student body.

As community college leaders and boards of trustees assess the need to diversify their staff to mirror the makeup of their student bodies, intentional planning must take place to ensure that Black women are at the top of the list of those who should hold executive-level administrative positions including the presidency. Conscious planning that includes Black women will also allow those Black women who take these executive-level administrative positions to mentor and assist in the professional development of other Black women. This, in turn, contributes to and develops the pipeline of Black women who pursue the community college presidency.

COMMUNITY COLLEGE LEADERSHIP: PREPARING FOR GENERATION NEXT—THE "GRAYING" OF LEADERSHIP

Community colleges are beginning to experience the consequences of a considerable leadership turnover in administrative and instructional capacities (De Los Santos, 2013). According to Shults (2001), research associated with senior-level administrators working in the community college reveals that there is a "graying" of individuals currently holding these positions. The average age of senior-level administrators in 1984 was under 50 and in 2000 the average age was 52 (Shults, 2001). According to Gagliardi et al. (2017), the majority of community college presidents are 61 years of age or older. Moreover, the AACC revealed in 2001 that 79% of community college presidents intended to retire within the next decade

(Leubsdorf, 2006). By 2006, this number increased to 84% (Weisman & Vaughn, 2007). Senior-level administrators who report to these presidents were also aging at a significant rate. As a result, leaders who began their tenure in the community college during the 1960s are now departing in droves (Leubsdorf, 2006). Fulton-Calkins and Milling (2005) explained that nearly 50% of community college presidents planned to retire by 2012. Over the past few years, this exodus of leaders has opened the doors to approximately 700 new community college presidents and 1,800 new senior-level administrators (Fulton-Calkins & Milling, 2005).

In 2003, Cohen and Brawer suggested that the time when baby boomers began employment at community colleges was one of the largest periods in community college history that experienced growth (Fulton-Calkins & Milling, 2005). In contrast, the American community college system is facing a decrease in the number of leaders due to the fact that senior-level administrators are retiring at a rate that surpasses the pace in which they are being recruited (Shults, 2001). The fact that new leaders are not emerging as rapidly as necessary to fill vacancies is of great concern and college boards and leaders continue to struggle with the most effective methods to acquire the next generation of leaders (Strom et al., 2011). In addition, since the majority of community colleges emerged in the 1960s and 1970s, many of the individuals who played a major role in the institutions' early development are now community college leaders who are nearing retirement. The history and experience possessed by these leaders along with their understanding of the culture and mission of the community college contribute to the gap that will be present as they retire (Shults, 2001). These concerns are extremely valid because institutions are looking to fill vacant positions with the next generation of community college leaders who will be able to offer innovative ideas while also learning from the past (Fulton-Calkins & Milling, 2005). Thus, as De Los Santos (2013) explains, it is mission critical to also prepare the next generation of community college leaders in order to meet the needs of the diverse student body and community.

Value of Succession Planning

As college presidents and senior-level administrators begin to exit their positions simultaneously, community college officials find it more difficult to fill these vacancies (Riggs, 2009; Strom et al., 2011). Warning signs of this substantial turnover of community college leaders have been visible for some time; however, many colleges were underprepared when it was time to replace those administrators who will be retiring (Leubsdorf, 2006). The continuous development of the AACC competencies has illustrated the importance of leadership development throughout the community college at all levels (Eddy & Garza Mitchell, 2017). This commitment to leadership development at multiple levels creates a foundation that allows leaders to apply skills in various ways and develop knowledge that will allow them to ascend to the next level. This type of leadership development coupled with careful planning for future leadership is a key to ensure that positions are filled and leaders who are chosen are the best fit (Eddy & Garza Mitchell, 2017).

As community college leaders and boards ponder over the most effective methods to fill vacant leadership positions, they can consider employing the notion of succession planning as a preparation strategy. The concept of succession planning and its principles have been present in the fields of business and industry for decades (Eddy & Garza Mitchell, 2017). A common theme that exists when defining succession planning is the execution of systematic methods for long-term leadership as it relates to succession, recruitment, and retention to meet the goals and adheres to the mission of an institution. Moreover, succession planning is utilized to address the planning of institutional employment with tactics that emphasize both internal and external candidates (Eddy & Garza Mitchell, 2017; Luna, 2010). It can ultimately ensure that organizations have the appropriate leadership for the future through a talent channel that is capable of nourishing the long-term goals of the institution (Wallin et al., 2005). After all, it is essential to "have the right people in the right place at the right time" (Wallin et al., 2005, p. 26).

While it can be a key instrument for colleges as they prepare for retirements and turnover in order to create a seamless transition for new leaders, according to Jones-Kavalier and Flannigan (2008), less than 12% of community colleges had created a succession plan (Riggs, 2009). Leubsdorf (2006) supports this statistic by noting that higher education leaders do not do a good job of planning for changes in leadership.

The culture of academic administration does not require leaders to cultivate their own replacements; therefore, there is a lack of preparation when it comes to filling vacant leadership positions (Leubsdorf, 2006). Fulton-Calkins and Milling (2005) explain that the concept of succession planning is valued within the community college, but it is not always implemented. More recently, organizations that focus on leadership development are highlighting the importance of developing leaders in planning for the future. AACC's competencies is just one example of this (Eddy & Garza Mitchell, 2017).

According to Klein and Salk (2013), Henri Fayol explained that it is an organization's responsibility to create stability. If organizations do not adhere to this responsibility, individuals who do not possess the necessary skills and characteristics will be placed in critical positions (Klein & Salk, 2013). Therefore, if community colleges want to be prepared for the impending need to make leadership replacements, it is imperative that effective succession planning procedures are used (Fulton-Calkins & Milling, 2005). Most importantly, leaders of color and Black women must be included in succession planning (Eddy & Garza Mitchell, 2017).

Klein and Salk (2013) provide four key components that will contribute to the success of filling vital leadership positions within the community college. Cognizance of the issue, a clear understanding of the needs of an institution, the consideration of talent outside of the "normal" profile, and constant professional development opportunities for employees are key components that can guarantee success when filling senior leadership positions within community colleges (Klein & Salk, 2013). Eddy and Garza Mitchell (2017) also highlight McMaster's (2012) best practices for succession planning. They include succession planning as an integral part of strategic planning and performance reviews; leadership development and opportunities for leadership for potential leaders; mentorship of potential leaders; an increase in mid-level leadership positions; and shared decision-making across the institution (Eddy & Garza Mitchell, 2017). While all these components are necessary, it is imperative that the concept of talent outside of the "normal" profile be highlighted. Wallin et al. (2005) explains that succession planning is not an extension of the "good ole' boy" system. It is a mechanism to pursue diverse candidates and provide opportunities for a larger category of talented individuals (Wallin et al., 2005).

Fulton-Calkins and Milling (2005) stress the importance of the hiring racially minoritized leadership. Succession planning can provide an opportunity not only to plan for the replacement of individuals when they retire, transfer, or find new opportunities, but it can also assist community colleges with adding to the diversity of their institutions (Klein & Salk, 2013). According to Gilliland (1991), stability is a product of diversity, which is the ability of a system to tolerate stress and to recognize and respond to opportunities. So, the utilization of succession planning to assist in leadership turnover and to enhance diversity can be extremely beneficial to community colleges.

THE COMMUNITY COLLEGE AND REFLECTIVE LEADERSHIP

As community colleges work to replace retiring leaders, it is necessary to discuss the origin and purpose of the community college, along with recent statistics related to the demographic makeup of the student body and staff. This provides significant support to the concept of reflective leadership and its relationship to the makeup of the community college administration. Further, it is critical to recognize the history of diversity within the administration of community colleges and how it compares to the present.

Efforts to increase diversity in higher education have resulted in an increase in the diversity of the community college student body. Community colleges are vital pathways for Blacks who go on to pursue associate and bachelor's degrees. Since 2000, enrollment rates of Black women at community colleges have increased significantly (Strayhorn & Johnson, 2014). This background information serves as a foundation and supports the notion of increasing diversity in the administrative makeup. Additionally, this evidence supports the concept of reflective leadership and its applicability to the community college.

The community college's open-door policy provides higher education access to those who may not otherwise qualify for admittance into four-year institutions (Jurgens, 2010). According to the AACC (2016), millions of individuals would not have the opportunity to pursue higher education if the community college did not exist. This is because it provides citizens with access to higher education and training in their communities that will ultimately prepare them for their next educational and/or career endeavor.

According to Brint and Karabel (1989), the community college was established in the early 1900s. Some decades earlier, the preparation of proposals to create junior colleges began to evolve. At that time, it was believed that junior colleges could minimize the burden experienced by universities by offering general education courses to high-school graduates. In turn, universities would be able to focus on research and higher levels of education (Jurgens, 2010). The community college soon evolved out of the junior college as the demand for access to higher education increased at a rapid pace. Unlike the original concept of the junior college, the community college would provide a more comprehensive education and have the ability to award associate of art and associate of science degrees. In addition, vocational and training programs would be offered to provide occupational training to students (Cohen & Brawer, 2003). The creation of the community college and its purpose of providing education and training have allowed the community college to become the entryway to higher education for working-class individuals and minorities (Dougherty, 1991). An example of this is illustrated by the fact that the majority of Black and Hispanic undergraduates have attended community colleges. Community college enrollment includes almost 2.7 million full-time students and 4.5 million part-time students across the United States. Of those students, 56% are females and 52% are minorities (AACC, 2017). The students served at community colleges across the United States are quite diverse in their academic levels as well as in issues related to their personal lives. Student populations can vary from those who are academically and personally prepared for the university experience, to those who are not strong academically and require some support to move forward in their educational quest (Husain, 2012). The beauty of this contrast is that community colleges have the ability to meet students where they are and assist them in succeeding in postsecondary education.

While it is evident that the community college has a diverse student body, the composition of the professional workforce is not congruent to that diversity. Gagliardi et al. (2017) revealed that 80% of community college presidents are White. According to the American Council on Education, only 5.4% of college presidents are Black women (Melidona et al., 2023). While the number of presidents from racially minoritized populations has increased at a slow rate over the past 30 years, women of color continue to be the most underrepresented group in the college presidency (Soares et al., 2018). This further proves that there is a mismatch between the number of racially minoritized individuals and women serving in administrative roles and the increasing number of racially minoritized and female students who are attending community colleges.

DETERMINING THE PATHWAY— RESUME-MAPPING PROCESS

To better understand the pathway to executive-level community college positions, it is important to take a closer look at the backgrounds of those who are in those positions. To accomplish this, a resume-mapping process was identified. In this process, resumes and curricula vitae were collected and analyzed to determine specific pathways to executive leadership positions. NVivo was utilized to compare the educational backgrounds and career trajectory of individuals employed in such positions.

A total of 25 resumes and curricula vitae were collected from participants who are members of the National Council on Black American Affairs (NCBAA) and National Council of Instructional Administrators (NCIA). The NCBAA consists of four regions that cover 50 states and the U.S. Virgin Islands. The regions include the north central region, northeast region, southern region, and western region. The NCBAA was established over 30 years ago and it is a council of the AACC. It is the principal professional development and networking organization for Black faculty, staff, and administrators of community colleges (National Council on Black American Affairs [NCBAA], 2016). The NCIA is an organization that is committed to the leadership and professional development of instructional administrators. The organization collaborates with the community college leadership program. Both are housed on the campus of the University of Nebraska at Lincoln. Formed in 1977, the overall goal of the NCIA is to enhance the performance of community college instructional administrators.

Members of NCIA represent eight regions within the United States (National Council of Instructional Administrators [NCIA], 2016). The membership of these organizations was utilized to identify individuals to participate in this process. Their participation allowed for an in-depth analysis that highlighted the paths taken by individuals working in executive leadership positions at community colleges.

This collection of resumes and curricula vitae supports a resume-mapping component that allows for the comparison of the education and career paths of those in executive leadership positions at community colleges. The evaluation of these documents provided essential information on education and career history. This also provides further insight into the paths executive leaders take to reach senior-level administrative positions in community colleges.

PATHWAYS TO COMMUNITY COLLEGE
EXECUTIVE LEADERSHIP

Pursuant to this study, 25 resumes and curricula vitae were collected from members of the NCBAA and the NCIA, which are both affiliate councils of the AACC. The purpose of the analysis of resumes and curricula vitae is to take a closer look at the career pathways of individuals serving in executive leadership roles at community colleges. During this analysis, the following categories related to the career pathways of those serving in leadership roles that report directly to community college presidents were identified: professional title, highest degree earned, higher education experience, community college experience, and area of experience.

Current professional titles emerged as a category through the resume-mapping process. Eleven leaders serve as chief academic officers (CAOs) with titles such as vice president of academic affairs, vice president of instruction, and vice chancellor of academic affairs. Six leaders serve as vice president of student services, while three serve as president. Two leaders work in the area of continuing education as vice president of continuing education and vice president of workforce development. One leader serves as vice president of institutional research, one serves as provost, and one is a vice president of academic and student affairs. These pathways are digested in the table below.

A majority of leaders who participated in the resume-mapping component of this study hold terminal degrees. Thirteen participants have earned doctor of education (EdD) degree, while 10 hold doctor of philosophy (PhD) degree. In addition, one leader holds a juris doctor (JD) degree. Lastly, one leader holds a master of business administration (MBA) degree.

Seventeen participants have only worked at community colleges, making their higher education and community college work experience comparable. The remaining eight participants have a combination of experience from four-year institutions and community colleges. The total number of years of experience for those participating in this portion of the research ranges from six years to 31 years. Only two participants have less than 10 years of higher education or community college experience, while 11 leaders have 20 or more years of experience. Ten participants have between 15 and 20 years of experience and two participants have between 10 and 15 years of experience.

Area of experience involves the division in which an individual works within the community college. These divisions or areas include academic affairs, student services, administrative services, and institutional advancement. Eleven leaders who participated in this study have worked in the area of academic affairs throughout their community college career. Academic affairs encompasses all areas of instruction at institutions. These areas are responsible for degree, diploma, and certificate programs at community colleges. All academic areas as well as continuing education and adult education are included in this category. Six leaders have significant experience in the area of student services. Student services include areas that support student access and success such as admissions, financial aid, and other services. One leader has experience in the area of administrative services. This area oversees financial and business activities for the institution. Seven leaders have a combination of experience from two or more of the previously mentioned areas. Most of these leaders have a combination of academic affairs and student services experience, while one leader has experience in all three areas (Table 3.1).

Table 3.1 Pathways

Pathway	Number of Participants ($n = 25$)
Professional title	
Chief Academic Officer	11
Vice President of Student Services	6
Campus President	3
Vice President of Continuing Education	1
Vice President of Workforce Development	1
Vice President of Institutional Research	1
Provost	1
Vice President of Academic and Student Affairs	1
Highest degree earned	
Doctor of education (EdD)	13
Doctor of philosophy (PhD)	10
Juris Doctor (JD)	1
Master of business administration (MBA)	1
Experience	
Higher education experience	8
Community college experience	17
Area of experience	
Academic affairs	11
Student services	6
Combination of two or more areas	7
Other	1

The resume-mapping process provides a closer look into the career pathways and educational backgrounds of individuals serving in executive leadership roles at community colleges. An analysis of resumes and curricula vitae revealed five categories that offer a better understanding of the leadership pathways of these individuals. They included professional title, highest degree earned, higher education experience, community college experience, and area of experience. The data from each of these categories show the existence of particular career pathways within the pipeline to the community college presidency. The pathways taken by individuals working in positions within the pipeline to the community college presidency vary. However, a common pathway is one where an individual moves up the ranks within the community college in order to obtain the presidency. For example, a community college faculty member often moves from department chair to academic dean and finally to vice president of academic affairs or student services before pursuing the presidency. A study by the Belk Center for Community College Research (Loovis et al., 2020) confirms that historically, the pathway to the presidency begins with faculty membership. In addition to the positions held within the pathway to the presidency, involvement in leadership development programs, fellowships, board service, and professional association membership also serve as preparation for those in the pipeline (Loovis et al., 2020).

BUILDING A PIPELINE OF BLACK WOMEN COMMUNITY COLLEGE LEADERS

Defining and refining a path is the key when one is pursuing leadership positions along the pathway to executive-level community college positions and the community college presidency, especially for Black women. In other words, it is essential that Black women identify their own paths and set specific objectives that will help to successfully navigate that path. Leadership development and networking are essential in planning and creating a successful path. Jones and Dawkins (2012) explain that involvement in professional organizations, leadership development opportunities, and some online resources can be essential as women progress through their careers. Further, Black women can purposely broaden their networks by becoming members of professional organizations, holding leadership positions in organizations, and attending conferences and trainings (Jones & Dawkins, 2012). Mentoring and institutional support are also critical to the success of Black women as they seek positions within the pipeline to the community college presidency. Mentoring promotes job satisfaction and career advancement (Crawford & Smith, 2005).

While Black women continue to define and refine their paths, it is critical that institutions and decision-makers identify ways to develop a pipeline of Black women community college leaders. Eddy (2018) discusses broadening the leadership pipeline early on. For instance, the majority of community college presidents began their careers as faculty. Well, when the bulk of faculty are White, it makes it much more difficult for people of color to achieve the presidency through a traditional pathway. Further, most non-White community college leaders are men of color, meaning that women of color have the least amount of opportunity to pursue and obtain a position as president of a community college. As a result, increased diversity at the faculty level can create a foundation for racial equity in community college leadership at the executive level (Eddy, 2018).

According to Eddy (2018), the importance of constructing a base by diversifying faculty is just one way that the pipeline can be broadened. Additionally, expanding the middle and providing opportunity and support to mid-level administrators is key. At this level, leaders are learning and they have the opportunity to prepare for higher-level leadership positions. Lastly, there needs to be a restructuring of leadership development. The focus should be on creating leadership development opportunities for those who do not represent the majority (Eddy, 2018).

The fact that Black women still fall behind Whites and men of color in executive leadership positions confirms that there continues to be issues within the system. As Black women determine the next steps in their journeys to executive leadership at the community college level, those who are involved in the hiring process at community colleges must take a closer look at current structures that prevent Black women from achieving these positions. Doing so and making significant changes can ultimately result in racial and gender equity in community college leadership (Eddy, 2018).

RECOMMENDATIONS

Five categories were identified through the analysis of resumes and curricula vitae that were provided by the interview participants and other individuals who currently serve in executive leadership roles. These categories, which include professional title, highest degree earned, years of higher education experience, years of community college experience, and area of experience provide significant data regarding common career pathways and educational backgrounds of those serving in executive leadership roles within the pathway to the community college presidency. Majority of the participants who submitted resumes currently serve as CAOs. Appiah-Padi (2014) notes that historically, the position of CAO has been the stepping stone to the community college presidency; however, new studies suggest that many CAOs are choosing not to pursue the presidency. This may allow leadership positions in administrative services and student services to also become more typical paths to the presidency. Twenty-four out of the 25 leaders whose resumes and curricula vitae were analyzed have terminal degrees. This is supportive of the notion that individuals seeking executive leadership positions at community colleges should have a terminal degree. In addition, areas of experience varied among the participants. Most leaders had academic affairs experience throughout the time they have been employed at community colleges. Several leaders had student services experience and a number of leaders had experience in two or more areas.

Ebbers et al. (2000) note that while community colleges have more women and racially minoritized people in administrative positions when compared to other sectors of higher education, the number of women and minorities in community college executive leadership positions still does not reflect the diversity of the student body. Further, it is essential that women and minorities serve in such leadership roles because it can positively affect the educational experience of racially minoritized students (Slater, 2007). These positive experiences can ultimately lead to favorable student outcomes and influence overall student success. Patitu and Hinton (2003) also note that individuals of color in higher education leadership positions provide an illustration of success and career advancement for minoritized students. Because of the connection between student success and the existence of Black women in leadership roles on college campuses, it is important to understand the experiences of Black women who are pursuing leadership positions within the pipeline to the community college presidency. Awareness of their career experiences, challenges, and successes can help to create a culture that will support Black women in their pursuit of community college executive leadership positions.

Jones and Dawkins (2012) explain that institutional support in the form of release time and financial assistance to attend conferences and other professional development opportunities is essential. Community colleges must be deliberate in providing opportunities for Black women to obtain mentors. This can be accomplished by encouraging supervisors and those in executive leadership positions to serve as mentors to individuals seeking to advance. Formal mentoring programs can also be established on community college campuses. These programs can also be formed across community college systems to allow Black women who are in or seeking executive leadership positions to network with individuals on other campuses. Internal leadership development institutes as well as those offered in local communities, statewide, and nationally are also essential to the career development of Black women community college administrators.

Further, institutions should encourage Black women to explore and become members of professional organizations. This will provide opportunities for networking, mentoring, and developing leadership.

CONCLUSION

The number of Black women serving in executive leadership roles at community colleges has increased over the years, but the numbers are still not comparable to that of White men and women serving in similar roles. As community college leaders look to implement methods to enrich the educational experience of a diverse student body and improve student success, it is important that they look to Black women to serve in executive leadership roles. Additionally, as presidents and senior-level administrators plan to retire, it provides an opportunity for community colleges to engage in succession planning. Klein and Salk (2013) explain that succession planning not only provides an opportunity to make plans when individuals vacate positions, but it also allows institutions to increase diversity within their organizations. This supports the idea of hiring qualified Black women to fill positions that are vacated due to retirement and/or relocation.

Community college leaders and boards of trustees must intentionally include Black women as candidates for leadership positions during the succession planning process. Further, hiring Black women for such positions will increase diversity within the college's administration and provide a more diverse group of role models for minoritized students.

As Black women continue to pursue executive leadership positions at community colleges, they should ponder the following questions:

1. How can I define my path?
2. What education, experience, and skills do I need to navigate the pathway to executive leadership positions at community colleges?

Community College Boards of Trustee members, administrators, and decision-makers should ponder the following questions:

1. Is there a succession plan in place that allows for leadership transitions and specifically includes Black women?
2. Has our institution addressed the need to diversify faculty?
3. How can we better support mid-level administrators, especially those who are Black women?
4. How can we restructure leadership development at our institution with Black women and people of color at the forefront?

KEY TAKEAWAYS

- While there has been progress, Black women remain underrepresented in community college executive leadership positions.
- Black women must be strategic when identifying next steps in their leadership journey. They must also recognize the barriers that exist for Black women who pursue executive leadership positions within the community college and how to successfully navigate those barriers.
- Those who are involved in the hiring process must recognize the importance of Black women serving in executive leadership positions and how it can positively impact the experience and success of racially minoritized students.

KEYWORDS

Black women; community college; executive leadership; presidential pathway; presidential pipeline; succession planning

REFERENCES

American Association of Community Colleges. (2016). *Community college trends and statistics*. http://www.aacc.nche.edu/AboutCC/Trends/

American Association of Community Colleges. (2017). *Fast facts—AACC*. https://www.aacc.nche.edu/research-trends/fast-facts/

Appiah-Padi, R. (2014). Job desirability: Chief academic officers opting out of the college presidency. *Sage Open*, 4(3), 1.

Brint, S., & Karabel, J. (1989). *The diverted dream: Community colleges and the promises of educational opportunity in America 1900–1985*. Oxford University Press.

Cohen, A. M., & Brawer, F. B. (2003). *The American community college* (4th ed.). John Wiley & Sons.

Crawford, K., & Smith, D. (2005). The we and the us: Mentoring African American women. *Journal of Black Studies*, 36(1), 52–67.

De Los Santos, G. E. (2013). The call for new leaders. *Diverse Issues in Higher Education*, 30(15), 21.

Dougherty, K. J. (1991). The community college at the crossroads: The need for structural reform. *Harvard Educational Review*, 61, 311–336.

Ebbers, L. H., Gallisath, G., Rockel, V., & Coyan, M. N. (2000). The leadership institute for a new century: LINCing women and minorities into tomorrow's community college leadership roles. *Community College Journal of Research and Practice*, 24(5), 575–382.

Eddy, P. L. (2018). Expanding the leadership pipeline in community colleges: Fostering racial equity. *Teachers College Record*, 120(14), 1–18.

Eddy, P. L., & Khwaja, T. (2019). What happened to re-visioning community college leadership? A 25-year retrospective. *Community College Review*, 47(1), 53–78.

Eddy, P. L., & Garza Mitchell, R. L. (2017). Preparing community college leaders to meet tomorrow's challenges. *Journal for the Study of Postsecondary and Tertiary Education*, 2, 127–145.

Fulton-Calkins, P., & Milling, C. (2005). Community college leadership: An art to be practiced: 2010 and beyond. *Community College Journal of Research and Practice*, 29(3), 233–250.

Gagliardi, J. S., Espinosa, L. L., Turk, J. M., & Taylor, M. (2017). *American college president study 2017*. American Council on Education.

Gilliland, J. R. (1991). Diversifying leadership in community colleges. *New Directions for Community Colleges, 1991*(74), 93–101.

Greene, T., Marti, C. N., & McClenney, K. (2008). The effort-outcome gap: Differences for African American and Hispanic community college students in student engagement and academic achievement. *Journal of Higher Education, 79*(5), 513–539.

Husain, S. P. R. (2012). Student success at the community college level. *Diverse Issues in Higher Education, 29*(7), 40–41.

Jackson, J. F. L. (2001). A new test for diversity: Retaining African American administrators at predominately white institutions. In L. Jones (Ed.), *Retaining African Americans in higher education: Challenging paradigms for retaining students, faculty, and administrators* (pp. 93–109). Stylus Publishing.

Jones, T. B., & Dawkins, L. S. (2012). Connecting the paths: Guiding institutions and administrators into the future. In T. B. Jones, L. S. Dawkins, M. McClinton, & M. Hayden Glover (Eds.), *Pathways to higher education administration for African American women* (pp. 122–130). Stylus.

Jones-Kavalier, B., & Flannigan, S. L. (2008). *The hiring game: Reshaping community college practices*. Community College Press.

Jurgens, J. C. (2010). The evolution of community colleges. *College Student Affairs Journal, 28*(2), 251–261.

Klein, M. F., & Salk, R. J. (2013). Presidential succession planning: A qualitative study in private higher education. *Journal of Leadership and Organizational Studies, 20*(3), 335–345.

Leubsdorf, B. (2006). Boomers' retirement may create talent squeeze. *The Chronicle of Higher Education, 53*(2), A51–A53. https://www.chronicle.com/article/boomers-retirement-may-create-talent-squeeze/

Loovis, K., Berry, R., Haley, K., Sepich, K., Davis, J., & Eddy, P. (2020). *Executive leadership research: Presidential pathways*. NCSU Belk Center for Community College Leadership and Research.

Luna, G. (2010). Succession planning: A doctoral program partnership for emerging community college leaders. *Community College Journal of Research and Practice, 34*(12), 977–990.

McMaster, S. M. (2012). *Succession planning for community colleges: A study of best practices* [Dissertation, University of Maryland University College, College Park, MD].

Melidona, D., Cecil, B. G., Cassell, A., & Chessman, H. M. (2023). *The American college president: 2023 edition*. American Council on Education. https://www.acenet.edu/Documents/American-College-President-IX-2023.pdf

National Council on Black American Affairs. (2016). *About us*. National Council on Black American Affairs. http://ncbaa-national.org/about/

National Council of Instructional Administrators. (2016). *About us*. National Council of Instructional Administrators. https://cehs.unl.edu/ncia/about-us/

Patitu, C. L., & Hinton, K. G. (2003). The experiences of African American women faculty and administrators in higher education: Has anything changed? In M. F. Howard-Hamilton (Ed.), *Meeting the needs of African American women* (pp. 79–94). Jossey-Bass.

Riggs, J. (2009). Leadership for tomorrow's community colleges. *Community College Enterprise, 15*(2), 27–38.

Shults, C. (2001). *The critical impact of impending retirements on community college leadership* (Research Brief, Leadership Series, no. 1 No. AACC-RB-01-5). American Association of Community Colleges.

Slater, R. (2007). Black student college graduation rates remain low, but modest progress begins to show. *Journal of Blacks in Higher Education, 50*, 88–96.

Soares, L., Gagliardi, J. S., Wilkinson, P. J., & Hughes, S. L. (2018). *Innovative leadership: Insights from the American College president study 2017*. American Council on Education. https://www.acenet.edu/Documents/Innovative-Leadership-Insights-from-the-ACPS-2017.pdf

Strayhorn, T. L., & Johnson, R. M. (2014). Black female community college students' satisfaction: A national regression analysis. *Community College Journal of Research and Practice, 38*(6), 534–550.

Strom, S. L., Sanchez, A. A., & Downey-Schilling, J. (2011). Inside–outside: Finding future community college leaders. *The Community College Enterprise, 17*(1), 9–21.

St. Rose, A., & Hill, C. (2013). *Women in community colleges: Access to success*. American Association of University Women.

The White House. (2016). Education: Knowledge and skills for the jobs of the future—higher education. https://obamawhitehouse.archives.gov/issues/education/higher-education

Wallin, D., Cameron, D. W., & Sharples, K. (2005). Succession planning and targeted leadership development. *Community College Journal, 76*(1), 24–28.

Weisman, I. M., & Vaughn, G. B. (2007). *The community college presidency: 2006* (Research Brief No. AACC-RB07-1). American Association of Community Colleges.

PART II

The Historically White Institutional Context

By Dr. Tamika Williams

Dr. Tamika Wordlow Williams serves as the Vice President of Student Formation and Dean of Students at Belmont University, Nashville, TN. In this capacity, she serves as the senior student affairs officer and is responsible for 11 departments that comprise the division for student formation. Dr. Williams has worked in student affairs for approximately 14 years, with experiences centered in residence life, student conduct, and the dean of student's office. As a student affairs practitioner, she has presented at national conferences, facilitated workshops, and initiated student leadership institutes. She has served on the Directorate of the National American College Personnel Association Student Conduct and Legal Issues Commission. She was selected to participate in the 2018 National Association Student Personnel Administrators (NASPA) Alice Manicur Symposium for women aspiring to the role of Vice President Student Affairs. Most recently, she was selected as a 2022–2023 TICUA Executive Leadership Institute Pressnell Fellow. A native of Little Rock, AR, and a first-generation college student, Dr. Williams earned an EdD in educational leadership from East Carolina University, an MPA in public administration from the University of Arkansas, and a BA in political science from Fisk University.

"Birds sing not because
they have answers but
because they have songs."

—African proverb

CHAPTER 4
Breaking Through the Glass Ceiling While Staying Off the Glass Cliff

ABSTRACT

This chapter focuses on access for Black women to formal leadership roles in higher education by reviewing challenges posed by the glass ceiling and glass cliff. Information presented here will be centered on the experiences of three Black women senior executive academic officers, at historically White research universities and how they worked to secure leadership positions on their own terms.

INTRODUCTION

Women, and more specifically Black women, are significantly underrepresented in senior executive positions (BlackChen, 2015; Diehl, 2014; Famiglietti, 2015; Hoyt & Murphy, 2016; Ryan & Haslam, 2007). In many professions, women's advancement is at a strikingly slow pace, yet the representation of women in roles that fall outside of this tier is overwhelming. Within academia, women generally and Black women particularly are not well represented in roles that lead to and include the college presidency (BlackChen, 2015; Field & Cunningham-Williams, 2021; Jones et al., 2012). The share of women presidents barely rose from just 30% of U.S. college and university presidents in 2016 to 32.8%

in 2022. Only 17.2% identify with a race/ethnic group other than White (Johnson, 2017; Melidona, 2023). Yet, women have outpaced men in educational attainment, as women now account for over half of all bachelor's, master's, and doctoral degrees in the United States (Fry, 2019; Warner & Corley, 2017) and comprise half of the college-educated labor force (Fry, 2019). It is evident that women have the necessary educational credentials to advance to senior executive roles, so the question remains: Why haven't they?

The 2016 ACE survey highlights a pattern whereby women have served as the senior executive academic officer (SEAO) prior to advancing to the college and university president (Johnson, 2017). While similar analyses of the 2022 data are pending, there are data reported in the 2022 survey that women are more likely than men to pursue traditional presidential pathways (Melidona, 2023). Historically, however, when considering the role next in line to the president, the narrative of the historic underrepresentation of minoritized groups seems to continue. Women accounted for just 38% of SEAOs in 2016, often referred to as chief academic officers (CAOs) or provosts, and more than half of them serve at a two-year institution (Johnson, 2017). Then, only 4% of SEAOs identified as Black (Johnson, 2017). More recent data suggest that among provosts, 9.2% are women of color and 7% are men of color (Melidona et al., 2023). It has been argued that women continue to lag substantially behind men because, when considering the traditional pathway to the presidency, women advance more slowly to full professorship (K. Davis & Brown, 2017), are not as likely to be considered for promotion (K. Davis & Brown, 2017; D. R. Davis & Maldonado, 2015), and are therefore overrepresented in low- and middle-rank positions (Chisholm-Burns et al., 2017; A. T. Davis, 2009; Dobele et al., 2014; Hung, 2012; Seo et al., 2016). Black women's salaries also tend to be lower than their counterparts (D. R. Davis & Maldonado, 2015) and women of color generally are more likely to report postponing a job search or promotion (26%) or leaving a position (8%) to care for a minor (Melidona et al., 2023). This pathway, through faculty tenure and promotion to academic executive leadership, is critical for Black women to gain minimal qualifications for senior academic roles (Croom & Patton, 2011).

Different schools of thought exist regarding the interpretation of these statistics. A subset of individuals may view these numbers and not see a concern. For example, some suggest that by questioning these numbers there is a minimization of the actual presence of women leaders (Adams et al., 2009; Darouei & Pluut, 2018; Dolan, 2004). To state more plainly, recognition is not given to the progress that has been made or the positive changes that have resulted. Others challenge the existence of barriers that impede upon the advancement of women leaders and suggest instead a lack of desire for advancement opportunities (Adams et al., 2009; D. R. Davis & Maldonado, 2015). And then, some question the effectiveness of women leaders (Eagly, 2005; Sczesny, 2003). While the list of dissenting opinions goes on, the trepidation with these viewpoints is that it does not resolve the real concern. "The question of whether or not [women] can lead is now a moot point, as the obvious is, [they] are seen in a variety of leading positions" (Glazer-Raymo et al., 2000, p. 244). The steady rise of women obtaining terminal degrees and the increase of women within the U.S. workforce also illustrates that they aspire to lead (Warner & Corley, 2017). Taking these factors into consideration, it is then necessary to understand why more women, including those from minoritized groups, are not better represented within positions of leadership. For example, when referencing minoritized groups, data are usually presented in larger categories which masks inequities that may exist (K. Davis & Brown, 2017; Dolan, 2004; Jones et al., 2012; Sharpe, 2019). By lumping subgroups together, it may also ignore the experiences that are unique to specific populations. This is a concern because it assumes that leadership experiences are identical for all minoritized groups, thus excluding incidents that shape and inform their individual perspectives.

Given the traditional trajectory, the experiences of women obtaining and leading in roles that prepare the way for the presidency become even more important to understand (Johnson, 2017). As articulated by Walton and McDade (2001), to better "understand the dynamics of women moving into presidencies it is necessary to study women in the CAO position, because the ascent of women into top positions does not happen by accident" (p. 86). On the one hand, scholars have stated that access for women to senior leadership roles is impacted by barriers that have impeded their ability to advance (D. R. Davis & Maldonado, 2015; Ryan &

Haslam, 2007; Sabharwal, 2013). On the other hand, when women are given opportunities to lead, it is often under conditions where the organization is in dire straits, either doomed to fail or saved by a miracle. In the following sections, I discuss the glass ceiling and the glass cliff as frames for understanding the pauses and pushes in women's professional trajectories.

GLASS CEILING

An impediment that contributes to the experiences of women leaders can be categorized as the glass-ceiling effect. The glass-ceiling effect is best described as the invisible barriers that hinder or prevent women from advancing to more senior leadership positions (BlackChen, 2015; Chisholm-Burns et al., 2017; Davies-Netzley, 1998; A. T. Davis, 2009; Diehl, 2014; Dolan, 2004; Famiglietti, 2015; Northouse, 2013; Ryan & Haslam, 2007; Sabharwal, 2013).

Various researchers have utilized the glass-ceiling effect as a means to define the experiences and lack of advancement opportunities for women in the United States. Thus, the low representation of women leaders can be attributed to several factors that contribute to the glass ceiling:

• Bias and discriminatory practices
• Lack of access to internal and external networks
• Isolation
• Lack of mentors, role models, and sponsors

To expound on the factors mentioned above, women may be subjected to discriminatory practices, conscious and unconscious bias, fueled by stereotypes and assumptions as it pertains to race and gender in their leadership roles (Butler & Ferriers, 2000; Chisholm-Burns et al., 2017; K. Davis & Brown, 2017; D. R. Davis & Maldonado, 2015; Eagly & Karau, 2002; Rosser, 2003). Specific to gender and leadership roles, these experiences are further explained using role congruity theory which holds the notion that female leaders are stereotyped as a result of the assumed incongruity of gender and leadership roles (Eagly & Karau, 2002). Women report that perspectives are often approached from a masculine lens, placing them at a disadvantage because their voice is not considered (Terosky et al., 2014). For example, "male characteristics are commonly used as the default or standard expectation by which women leaders are hired, retained, or promoted, while typically female characteristics are devalued" (Chisholm-Burns et al., 2017, p. 314). As a result, women are challenged with the difficult task of navigating conflicting gender and leadership role expectations: Be feminine but not too soft and carry out leadership traits and styles that have been branded as masculine, while not being viewed as unfeminine (Chisholm-Burns et al., 2017; Eagly, 2007).

In a study conducted by Diehl (2014), a total of 26 women in senior leadership roles, within higher education, reported facing 21 distinct barriers. Women reported that these barriers hindered advancement opportunities and success. These barriers were categorized as either personal (relationships, family, health), gender (discrimination, workplace harassment), or professional (discrimination, advancement issues, lack of leadership support).

Personal barriers further highlight the lack of organizational policies that offer work-life balance. Without supportive organizational policies that accommodate family and health obligations, women continue to carry the burden of being on the "second shift," wherein after completing an actual work shift women transition home for responsibilities that require equal and sometimes competing attention (Chisholm-Burns et al., 2017). The COVID-19 pandemic has compounded the issues and concerns of women leaders, and in many cases that of single mothers, within the workforce. Scholars have and continue to examine the impact of the COVID-19 pandemic on women in the academic workforce. Malisch et al. (2020) share that the COVID-19 pandemic has intensified the barriers women face in career advancement opportunities. Lechuga-Peña (2022) argues that "disruptions in productivity due to the COVID-19 pandemic have overwhelmingly affected women researchers" (p. 14). In this context, personal commitments have limited one's ability to engage in teaching, research, and service opportunities more fully (Lechuga-Peña, 2022). This is important to consider, given the significance, these have in the tenure process. Collins et al. (2021) highlight that as schools transitioned away from in-person learning, in response to COVID-19, working mothers were faced with double loads that exceeded traditional expectations.

Although many have sought to balance competing priorities, many women are "leaning out" and choosing to temporarily delay their career to address personal responsibilities. While understandable, the decision to pause their career also has an adverse consequence of further "off-tracking" career aspirations (Chisholm-Burns et al., 2017).

Another component contributing to the glass ceiling centers on the lack of access and opportunities to informal and formal networks (Chisholm-Burns et al., 2017; D. R. Davis & Maldonado, 2015). Access to such networks positions women to be connected to resources and opportunities that are more equal to their male counterparts. Critics, however, argue that the lack of advancement opportunities for women is not the result of access concerns but that of the "pipeline problem" (Carli & Eagly, 2001). This concept acknowledges that women are qualified to serve in senior leadership positions but suggests that they are not hired because they are not available when these positions are open. This is challenged by scholars who state that women may instead forgo leadership opportunities because of a "lack of leadership engagement" (Chisholm-Burns et al., 2017; D. R. Davis & Maldonado, 2015). More specifically, when organizations fail to empower and provide opportunities that groom women and particularly Black women for leadership roles, they do not develop a leadership mentality to eventually aspire to such roles (Chisholm-Burns et al., 2017).

Lastly, and a consistent theme in much of the literature, the lack of mentorship, role models, and sponsorship contributes to the glass ceiling (Chisholm-Burns et al., 2017; Clayborne & Hamrick, 2007). Research has continuously highlighted the benefit of mentorship for women leaders. For example, mentorship supports socialization experiences that better connect individuals to institutional culture (Niehaus & O'Meara, 2015). Mentorship helps protégés to develop their talents, to better understand organizational politics, and to become more proficient in their roles, and, overall, mentorship is crucial in supporting the retention and advancement of Black women at historically White institutions (HWIs) (Jackson, 2004; Jones & Dufor, 2012). Just as important is sponsorship, as it plays a significant role in advancement because it allows for voices of influence to aid in the promotion and advocacy of women (Niehaus & O'Meara, 2015). However, despite the benefits of mentorship and role models, the low representation of women in senior leadership positions results in fewer individuals serving as mentors, role models, and sponsors (Jones & Dufor, 2012; Northouse, 2013; Tran, 2014). Thus, women may navigate professional spaces with limited guidance and support.

The experiences highlighted above reinforce that a breakthrough in the glass ceiling is the key for women to have true progress in advancing into more senior leadership positions. While this is stated, those who are successful in breaking through the glass ceiling may also need to prepare for another experience that has been branded as the glass cliff.

GLASS CLIFF

As women are celebrated for their successes in breaking through the glass ceiling, it is not uncommon to find that women may encounter the glass cliff. The glass cliff is a term used to describe the unique timing when women are elevated into senior leadership positions, often during times of organizational crisis or turbulence (Issac et al., 2012; Peterson, 2016; Ryan & Haslam, 2007; Ryan et al., 2016). Thus, as women reach the height of their leadership careers, they also risk a downward spiral or falling off the glass cliff (Peterson, 2016; Ryan et al., 2010; Sabharwal, 2013). While some believe the rise to such positions and the unique times at which they occur is not a coincidence, other scholars debate the accuracy of the glass cliff concept (Adams et al., 2009; Darouei & Pluut, 2018). Rather than viewing it as a setup for failure, there is a belief that women may be selected for these opportunities because of their approach and ability to effectively manage crises and other emergencies (Peterson, 2016; Ryan et al., 2010). Scholars have termed this experience the "think crisis–think female" phenomenon (Ryan et al., 2007). Feminization is another term used to describe the unique timing at which women enter positions at an accelerated rate (England & Boyer, 2009; Peterson, 2016). On the one hand, this can be seen as a method to numerically capture occupations that have increased gender equality and transitioned away from being male dominated (Peterson, 2014). On the other hand, demographic feminization can also refer to roles being redefined as "women's work" as it becomes more time consuming, carries less prestige, provides few opportunities to advance, and comes with more risk but less job security (England & Boyer, 2009; Peterson, 2014). When taken together, shifts to demographic feminization during turbulent times can serve as the precursor to the glass cliff (Peterson, 2014).

To expound further, a study conducted by Peterson (2014) utilized two theoretical concepts, "glass cliff" and "feminization" to examine the increase in women leaders serving in Swedish HEIs. Between 1990 and 2010 Swedish higher education was transformed to survive the changing market. In response, efforts were made to compete with the recruitment of national and international students and to strengthen the financial status of institutions by overhauling traditional understandings through the implementation of an educational restructure (Peterson, 2014). It was during this period Sweden HEI experienced a demographic shift, holding the highest percentage of female vice chancellors in Europe (Peterson, 2014). Peterson (2014) sought to examine factors that contributed to the increase of women leaders within Swedish HEI. In total 22 women, serving in senior executive positions from Swedish HEI participated in interviews. Participants reported that following the restructure, roles were updated and had become administrative in nature, whereas in years past, it was more ceremonial and collegial (Peterson, 2014). In addition, participants reported facing highly complex problems resulting in burnout and exhaustion due to the extended time invested to meet the growing demands. Lastly, it was reported that the position held less value after changes were applied to the position.

While the focus of this study centered on women leaders in Swedish HEI, there are common themes consistent within the literature that apply to women leaders more broadly. In considering the experiences that may contribute to the glass ceiling or glass cliff, it is fair to question what steps could be taken to assist in reducing or eliminating factors that may hinder one's ability to advance and remain in senior executive roles.

LEADING WHILE BEING A WOMAN, LEADING WHILE BEING BLACK

This section will expound on factors that contribute to the glass ceiling and glass cliff for Black women leaders, as well as present items for consideration to navigate forward. Intentional efforts have been made to capture the experiences of women leaders; however, the discussion is often centered more broadly. Occurrences such as the glass ceiling are common among all women; however, it tends to impact Black women leaders to a greater extent due to their dual identities (Parker & Ogilvie, 1996).

Black feminist scholars argue that race and gender cannot be separated (Beal, 1970; Collins, 1990; K. Davis & Brown, 2017; hooks, 1984). Kimberlé Crenshaw coined the term intersectionality in 1989 and used it to describe how race and gender intertwine and form the many complex layers that comprise the experiences of Black women within the work-force (D. R. Davis & Maldonado, 2015). Consequently, Black women are often faced with "double jeopardy" or "double bind," which is defined as disadvantages that result because of Black women's intersecting and mar-ginalized identities (Beal, 1970; K. Davis & Brown, 2017; D. R. Davis & Maldonado, 2015). For example, a study conducted by Lloyd-Jones (2009) examined the experiences of Black women administrators at HWIs and concluded that Black women are subjected to racism, sexism, loneliness, and isolation, and have occurrences that reinforce a lack of trust that all impede upon their ability to advance.

Given their intersecting identities, Black women are subjected to unique structural challenges and therefore they offer a unique perspective on how to navigate challenges that are linked to biased practices, on the basis of gender AND race in the academic workforce (K. Davis & Brown, 2017). While studies have offered a glimpse into the lived experiences of women leaders, there is a benefit in understanding the experiences of Black women leaders (Collins, 1990; D. R. Davis & Maldonado, 2015). Specific to academia, there is limited research that exists and there is an opportunity to give voice to Black women leaders within the field of higher education (D. R. Davis & Maldonado, 2015).

This chapter draws from the work of a qualitative study (Wordlow, 2018) that examined the factors that may hinder and/or support the career advancement of Black women, serving in the capacity of SEAO at four-year public, doctoral degree-granting HWIs.

THEORETICAL FRAMEWORK

The theoretical framework that guided this study was Jackson's (2004) engagement, retention, and advancement (ERA) model. The ERA model is particularly salient because it identifies and examines elements that seek to attract, hire, retain, and advance Black administrators within HEIs (Jackson, 2004). Prince and Siegel (2017), for example, used the ERA model as a theoretical framework to explore the experiences of African American administrators within the development profession to elevate the discussion and aid in promoting opportunities for diversification in this field. Thus, the ERA model is significant because it elevates the discussion to go beyond diversity initiatives. Institutional action becomes more focused on creating environments that promote inclusive communities and a sense of belonging.

This model comprises of four overarching categories: Pre-engagement, engagement, advancement, and outcome. Each category consists of sub-categories that illustrate the various components needed for the successful recruitment, retainment, and ultimately advancement of Black professionals at HWIs.

Pre-engagement centers on access and the initial experiences Black administrators face upon entry at HWIs. Within this category, emphasis is placed on recruitment, orientation programs, and incentive packages (Jackson, 2004). The next category, engagement, goes deeper into the experiences of Black administrators, specifically in the areas of empowerment, leadership opportunities, mentoring, and in-service professional development (Jackson, 2004). The third category, advancement, pertains to professional release time, professional development funds, and involvement in experiences that goes beyond diversity work (Jackson, 2004). The final category, outcomes, provides considerations for upward mobility (Jackson, 2004). These four overarching categories are grounded by two principles: institutions have authentic relationships with the surrounding Black community and institutions are committed to diversity and affirmative action principles (Jackson, 2004).

RESEARCH METHOD

The present study was carried out using a narrative inquiry research design, respecting the stories of participants as data that can stand on its own (Clandinin & Connelly, 2000; Creswell, 2014; Patton, 2002; Webster & Mertova, 2007). Participants were recruited using a snowball method. Snowball sampling is an effective method to secure participants from populations that are concealed and may remain hidden otherwise (Atkinson & Flint, 2001). Data were collected using a method defined by Corbin and Morse (2003) as the "unstructured interview technique" which creates space for participants to convey their experience, ordering events based on what is most important to them. Participants were asked to speak on experiences they felt have brought them to this point in their career. This is referred to as the "grand tour question" because it allows participants to "tell their story as they see it, feel it, and experience it" while allowing the researcher to probe and ask additional questions based on the initial response (Corbin & Morse, 2003). This method also works to honor the individual experiences of each participant. Three participants took part in this study. Interviews occurred via phone or videoconference and lasted 60 minutes. Approval was received by Institutional Review Board (IRB) and consent was given by each participant prior to the interviews. The interviews were recorded, transcribed, and returned to the participants for review. NVivo (Wainright & Russell, 2010) was used to analyze the data.

FINDINGS AND INTERPRETATION
OF RESULTS

In review, participants' experiences aligned with that of the ERA model. Six of the 12 subcategories were present for each participant despite whether the experiences were self-initiated or carried out by the institution. They were recruitment, incentive packages, empowerment, leadership opportunities, mentoring, retention, and advancement (see Table 4.1). Participants did not share experiences that relate directly to professional development funds or orientation programs and are thus, beyond the scope of the study. Although implications from this omission will be shared. Additional themes emerged that included tools for navigating and responding to challenges; self-reflection and internal motivations; faith, spirituality, and religion; and paying it forward. These will be discussed in greater detail in Chapter 5.

Participants were provided pseudonyms to respect the privacy of their personal information. Michelle, Elizabeth, and Diane each have terminal degrees and have worked in higher education for a minimum of 30 years, with experiences that range from serving in the professoriate, to department chair, to associate dean, to dean, and to the SEAO. At the time of the interview, participants had served in their position for five years or less. Each had numerous accolades obtained throughout the course of their careers that highlighted research, publications, awards, service, donations, and contributions both internal and external to the institution. Participants were married and self-disclosed, had children in the early to mid-stages of their careers. Participants also noted that they were the first or of the few in their families to ever attend and graduate from college.

Table 4.1   Themes: Engagement, Retention, Advancement (ERA) Model

Categories and subcategories	N
Pre-engagement	
Recruitment	3
Orientation programs	0
Incentive packages	3
Engagement	
Empower administrator	3
Leadership opportunities	3
Mentoring	3
In-service professional	1
Advancement	
Professional release time	1
Professional development funds	0
Beyond diversity experience	1
Outcome	
Retention	3
Career advancement	3
Emerged themes	
Self-reflection and internal motivation	3
Faith, spirituality, and religion	3
Family upbringing and support	3
Paying it forward	3

PRE-ENGAGEMENT

Recruiting Black Women to Lead

Participants began their interview by sharing the path they took to reach the SEAO position. The information provided highlights that participants were encouraged to apply by the incumbent SEAO or by mentors, who also served in senior executive positions within higher education. In addition to meeting the required qualifications, one participant felt that institutions were also being intentional to diversify the makeup of faculty and staff.

For example, Michelle shared that

> …I think I was really at the right place at the right time, for which I am grateful but makes me sad for people coming along behind me. I grew up right at the time when people were looking to make opportunities for people of color; there I was. You know everybody today says they care about diversity, but they don't really, so I feel like I've [gotten] some opportunities [and] doors were thrown open for me.

This experience aligns closely with Jackson's (2004) guiding concept, found in the ERA model which outlines institutional commitment to diversity and affirmative action principles. However, not all participants expressed having similar experiences. For example, Diane explained that most SEAO positions are appointed through a process that is carried out by a search firm, sharing,

> Usually, a provost is selected by a search firm and the president of that institution. [With a search firm] there is not a tough negotiation process to go through or rather there should not be one. This is because the search firm and the president have determined that you are wanted and when you get to that level there is a general understanding as it pertains to these areas. So, it's important to take advantage of the fact that you are wanted and aim high.

Taking this into consideration we transition, to discuss practices that aim to attract and recruit talented Black administrators within HWIs. Institutions may utilize various approaches to recruit and select candidates for senior executive positions. This may include a search team that is internal to the institution, a search firm, or a hybrid model of the two. Search firms' involvement in higher education is increasing (Manfredi et al., 2019). While there is literature that examines factors that promote or hinder advancement for women leaders, there is also a need for research that expounds on the influence that search firms can have in contributing to or shattering the glass ceiling (Manfredi et al., 2019). For example, some argue that executive search firms (ESFs) continue the practice of "the old boys' network" because potential candidates must be connected or referred to the firm to receive further consideration for an executive position (Faulconbridge et al., 2009; Manfredi et al., 2019). Others state that search firms shape and define attributes that make the ideal candidate for positions within higher education (Manfredi et al., 2019; Tienari et al., 2013). And then, some have the viewpoint that search firms support both institutions and potential candidates in finding suitable matches that benefit both parties (Manfredi et al., 2019).

On the one hand, this process could perpetuate a system of bias, negatively impacting women and minoritized groups looking to advance. On the other hand, with the appropriate checks and balances, ESFs could serve as an additional layer of support for both institutions and candidates. A recent study, conducted by Manfredi et al. (2019), sought to evaluate ESFs' involvement, from a gender equality lens, in HEIs in the United Kingdom. Their study revealed that ESFs add meaning to the search process and provide marginalized groups with the necessary support as they navigate through the process; more specifically, they can serve in an advocacy role (Manfredi et al., 2019). Although this study centered on HEIs in the United Kingdom, there is a benefit in considering how these recommendations would fare in the United States.

Negotiation

While Diane, Elizabeth, and Michelle felt supported overall, they were also clear about the need for colleges and universities to provide greater access, by establishing compensation packages for women that are equitable to their counterparts. Participants' perceptions aligned with the literature. A recent study conducted by the College and University Professional Association for Human Resources (McChesney, 2018) found that within higher education, Black women administrators, faculty, and staff are paid at a rate that is less than all their counterparts. This suggests that for women to obtain competitive incentive packages, they may need to negotiate (i.e., self-advocate) terms of employment and compensation (Bowles et al., 2019; Reif et al., 2019). As articulated by Wade (2001), "negotiation is a critical [but not sole] element in finalizing job offers and accepting promotions and thus in determining pay" (p. 65). However, when it comes to negotiations, the potential costs of self-advocacy may lead women to be more accepting of initial offers presented and be less likely to expect a successful negotiation process (Bowles et al., 2019; Reif et al., 2019; Wade, 2001). Thus, negotiating can be a double-edged sword.

For example, Elizabeth shared,

> Well, I'm going to let you down here because I didn't really negotiate. I negotiate for everybody else, but when it came to doing it for myself, I defaulted back to all of the literature that says women are not as strong negotiators. You think it's a stereotype until it's you, and I didn't do it.

As Diane noted above, search firms can have an impact on the negotiation process. In addition, she offered the following words of wisdom, to encourage women to utilize resources at their disposal for the negotiation phase. She shared,

> It is important that one is knowledgeable about the mean salary. These data are available by public record at most public institutions. However, the position itself is rather limited, for example, there is only one CAO at any institution thus there is not another position to compare it to. So, it may be beneficial to review the salary of the previous CAO. While not absolute, it provides a starting place and can be used as a reference for the negotiation process.

And lastly, while Michelle did not negotiate her salary, she offered her reflections on the process by sharing,

> It has been my experience that men negotiate as if it's going to affect how many days they live. And women just say gee thanks. It's amazing. It's really difficult for me as a leader, in that regard, to know how to respond

to that because I've always been sort of fair in life ... I say all that to say that I think women by and large are really bad at [negotiating]. And that's unfortunate because men end up getting more if they are asking for things that aren't all that difficult. For example, let's say you offer a man $25,000 and they respond with, could it be $25,000 and an extra week of vacation? You are inclined to accept this request. So, I think women need to know their worth. I also think it's complicated by the fact that it isn't always pleasant.

The experiences described by this participant are common for many women leaders. Scholars highlight women leaders are less likely to negotiate because they are concerned about the impact of professional relationships or social norms in which assertiveness does not align with presumed gender roles (Bowles et al., 2019; Hoyt & Murphy, 2016). While the potential risks of self-advocacy should be considered, women leaders must also evaluate the adverse consequences that can result when they do not advocate for themselves. Stated more directly, if Black women are paid at a rate less than all their counterparts (McChesney, 2018), this means that every pay increase thereafter will continue to lag and potentially cause the pay inequity gap to widen (Babcock & Laschever, 2003).

Despite the fact that women may be less inclined to initiate negotiation for themselves, literature does suggest that women tend to make requests on behalf of others (Wade, 2001). Participant experiences align with the literature, as each expressed that while they did not advocate for themselves they do work to encourage others or engage in third-party advocacy for professionals to negotiate better offers. This can serve as an effective tool to address concerns with self-advocacy. Another alternative to negotiating includes making offers that go beyond the salary (Wade, 2001). It is possible that requests unrelated to salary are mutually beneficial for both the employee and employer. This was the experience for Michelle as she shared that there were "only two things that I cared about. I didn't negotiate over salary, starting date, or title..." This raises the question, what are other items that should be considered?

There is no perfect strategy, and weighing the potential costs is very important to consider. However, it does not eliminate institutional responsibility to create an environment that promotes equitable practices.

Institutions can develop a practice of offering the best package to each candidate in order to avoid putting women at risk through negotiations. It is in the institution's interest as well to ensure they are getting the best candidate, not just the best candidate at a reasonable expense. McChesney (2018) recommends that institutions conduct an audit and review equity for representation and pay internally, evaluate institutional data with that of peer institutions to ensure fair market wages, and gather information that goes beyond pay and representation, such as reviewing turnover and experiences to address systemic issues. This is stated because pay inequity can be costly for an institution in long term, both financially as well as with staff and faculty relationships that can lead to retention concerns.

ENGAGEMENT AND ADVANCEMENT

Empowerment, Leadership Opportunities, and Professional Development

Participants highlighted that as they grew more confident in their role, and had a general understanding of responsibilities, they sought to go deeper by transitioning their focus to leadership opportunities that would help groom them for more advanced positions. Internally, these included involvement in formal leadership training and mentoring programs, serving on committees that are often geared to budgeting and fundraising, development, or academic planning. In addition, participants noted that serving as the SEAO required visibility on campus and just as important, within the community. For example, Michelle shared,

> In this role, you wear many hats, one of which is the ability to engage and connect with the community. It is a necessity to be present [in the community] to help people understand [the] universities role and contribution to the larger picture. This is how you find and create opportunities for students. If you are at a play you may watch it and begin to think, our students could benefit from this! Then you must find a way to make it happen. This is why participation on boards is so important. As a senior administrator, you must have some visibility. Boards allow you to take the name of your organization, your university, out into the community.

Such experiences contributed to participants becoming more empowered and leaning further into their roles. However, each emphasized that, in addition, to being empowered there was also a need to trust yourself. Michelle and Diane shared that at times you will make decisions that are not favored by others, but you must remain confident in the choices you make, and understand that this comes with experience, sometimes learning through mistakes, and of great importance, remaining ethical. Elizabeth stated directly,

> I am older. I am at a point where I do not really care what other people think of me. I am here to do the work that is important for our students. So, don't worry about being liked, worry about being respected and being able to sleep at night. I do not have any trouble sleeping because I'm exhausted. And I do not have integrity issues where I am saying, I wish I had not done that … I work with the information that I have and try to make the best decision. Do not be afraid to be who you are in this environment. If people don't like it, then it may be the wrong environment for you.

While the participants' experiences proved to aid in their development as well as career advancement, BlackChen (2015) notes that women are not always able to advance successfully into leadership roles, within higher education, largely due to a lack of empowerment. Thus, to empower women leaders, organizations should work to build environments and provide opportunities that prepare Black women to take on leadership roles (D. R. Davis & Maldonado, 2015). Institutional actions such as these validate and support a sense of belonging and place Black women in a position to become more engaged within the organization. However, Jackson (2004) highlights that these opportunities should be at a pace that aligns with the strengths of the individual to avoid the adverse impact, and feelings of being overwhelmed or unprepared which may result in others questioning the readiness for advancement opportunities.

Mentorship

Mentorship, both formal and informal, serves as another meaningful tool to support Black women leaders in navigating through such experiences.

In discussing participants' advancement to the role of SEAO each acknowledged the intentionality of mentors and sponsors that empowered them to pursue leadership and advancement opportunities. This is supported by literature, as mentorship provides a space for seasoned professionals to shed light on the official and unofficial rules of the organization as well as offers advice and guidance (Jackson, 2004). A theme within literature illustrates that mentorship is a powerful tool in combating the stereotypes and challenges that aspiring Black women leaders face (BlackChen, 2015; Jones et al., 2012).

Participants in this study spoke about the impact of positive mentorship. For example, Diane not only expressed that individuals should be intentional about seeking out a mentor, but she also added that there is benefit in being open to having a mentor of a different background. This was stated to reiterate that "at times, you can't wait [to have a mentor of the same background] because you may be the first of your kind." Elizabeth went further to highlight the benefits of having multiple mentors by stating,

> If you want to have a mentor who is at the top of the university, you generally get a male person. There's nothing wrong with that, but they don't give you insight into how women navigate this space. So then, you need another person who may not be at the top of the university but has had some experiences you haven't had that can help you with that. Then, if you're a woman of color it's really hard to find someone of color who can be a mentor. But if you can, it's not likely to get that all in one person, [so] now you have [multiple] people.

Elizabeth's statements reinforce the intersecting identities present in Black women leaders. It also supports the recommendation provided by another participant. Michelle highlighted the significance of Black women leaders serving as mentors to expand resources and networking opportunities for the up-and-coming Black women leaders.

In addition to growing through mentorship, participants did highlight the benefits of other engagement opportunities to provide professional development. Participants provided recommendations that Black women leaders should have intention to gain exposure and a diversity of experiences.

For example, participants reported that any professional seeking to advance within higher education should focus intently on budgeting and fundraising opportunities because this is how many agendas can move forward. Elizabeth mentioned that she participated in a Harvard institute for educational management and gained insight into institutional budget operations. Additionally, through practice, she has learned how to be creative when there are competing priorities. Another item to consider, as it pertains to professional development, centers on service within the community. For example, Michelle shared, "It seems to me not a duty but a responsibility, and the right thing to do, to engage with members of the community."

Black women leaders carry out responsibilities for which they are hired and may also find themselves involved in work that exceeds the description of the work they are appointed to do. A study conducted by Reynolds-Dobbs et al. (2008) examined images of Black women leaders and whether or not these other duties as assigned hindered career advancement. From their study five themes emerged, one being that of superwoman. In this context, the definition of "superwoman" pertains to someone with a strong work ethic and talent and who is able to do many things well (Reynolds-Dobbs et al., 2008). This illustration comes with a false narrative that Black women leaders can, want to, and will do it all. On the surface, this appears to be a very positive attribute applied to Black women leaders. However, individuals with authority should consider the motivation behind ancillary assignments or tasks. In addition, work to eliminate or compensate for initiatives that take additional time outside of the traditional work schedule, as well as consider how assignments may be equally distributed among employees to balance out the load (Reynolds-Dobbs et al., 2008). This is important to consider to avoid extreme burnout.

To help avoid experiences of burnout, participants provided advice that centered on setting boundaries. Specifically, participants shared that there is no such thing as "work-life balance" but rather that of "maintenance." Each acknowledged that at their level there are many competing priorities, and it is not possible to do all things. For this reason, participants shared that for items outside of their scope of responsibility, they say yes to what they can do and say no to those things they cannot do. However, participants acknowledged they can have this mindset because they have family support as well as talented professionals on their team to whom they can delegate responsibilities.

While setting boundaries is important, it is also beneficial to be intentional about the things that Black women leaders decide to take on or not. For example, saying yes to too many ancillary assignments may have the same impact as taking on additional responsibilities that fall within a certain category. Each has the opportunity to generate burnout to some degree while failure to diversify the professional portfolio may result in Black women leaders being considered only for assignments of a specific nature. For example, involvement in diversity, equity, and inclusion work is significant in removing barriers and challenges faced by people from marginalized groups. However, Black women leaders seeking advancement may find it beneficial to include additional experiences in their portfolio. This may entail work related to fundraising, service in community or advisory boards, and participation in committees or task forces that connect to larger institutional objectives.

BREAKING THROUGH THE GLASS CEILING WHILE STAYING OFF THE GLASS CLIFF

Taken together these experiences illustrate measures that offer meaningful support to Black women's retention and professional advancement. While it is significant to have institutional influences, initiated by a top–down approach, it is also important not to discount the personal strategies and perspectives implemented by women leaders (Amon, 2017).

Participants in this study were able to use their personal tenacity and institutional support to break through the glass ceiling. They were actively recruited and had advocates who spoke highly of them in settings in which they were not present. They were provided competitive salaries for which they did not feel necessary to enter into negotiations, for purposes of their salary. They were empowered and engaged in leadership opportunities to further develop and serve others in their roles.

They sought mentorship from professionals who were able to provide guidance and understanding. They have built relationships that benefit internal and external stakeholders. While participants were successful in breaking through the glass ceiling, there is no evidence to suggest that participants had experiences with the glass cliff. However, this could be due to the participants' years of expertise. Given the length of service, it is possible that participants are politically savvy and understand how to navigate and avoid pain points, thereby reducing these occurrences. No matter the reasoning, it is evident that the participants have a passion for this work. In the following chapter, I examine several themes that emerged as part of this study. These include tools for navigating and responding to challenges; self-reflection and internal motivations; faith, spirituality, and religion; and paying it forward.

REFLECTION QUESTIONS TO PONDER

1. What am I looking for in a mentor? What will I contribute as a mentee?
2. In a review of my portfolio, what experiences are missing? How will I diversify my experiences?
3. How will I show up and lead as my authentic self?
4. What is my wellness plan? How will I pour back into myself?
5. How do I define and articulate my worth to prospective employers?
6. What items are important to present as part of the negotiation process?

KEY TAKEAWAYS

- Know your worth and remember your WHY. This will serve as your inner compass.
- Trust yourself and practice ethical leadership.
- Be intentional to seek mentorship from individuals who are interested in your success.

KEYWORDS

Black women; women in leadership; glass ceiling; glass cliff; intersectionality; mentorship

REFERENCES

Adams, S. M., Gupta, A., & Leeth, J. D. (2009). Are female executives over-represented in precarious leadership positions? *British Journal of Management, 20*, 1–12. https://doi.org/10.1111/j.1467-8551.2007.00549.x

Amon, M. J. (2017). Looking through the glass ceiling: A qualitative study of STEM women's career narratives. *Frontiers in Psychology, 8*, 236–246.

Atkinson, R., & Flint, J. (2001). Accessing hidden and hard to reach populations: Snowball research strategies. *Social Research Update, 33*, 1–3.

Babcock, L., & Laschever, S. (2003). *Women don't ask: Negotiation and the gender divide*. Princeton University Press.

Beal, F. M. (1970). Double jeopardy: To be black and female. In T. Cade (Ed.), *The Black woman: An anthology* (pp. 90–100). New York: Signet.

BlackChen, M. (2015). To lead or not to lead: Women achieving leadership status in higher education. *Advancing Women in Leadership, 35*, 153–159.

Bowles, H. R., Thomason, B., & Bear, J. B. (2019). Reconceptualizing what and how women negotiate for career advancement. *Academy of Management Journal, 62*(6), 1645–1671. https://doi.org/10.5465/amj.2017.1497

Butler, E., & Ferriers, F. (2000). *'Don't be too polite, girls!': Women, work, and vocational education and training: A critical review of the literature*. National Centre for Vocational Educational Research.

Carli, L. L., & Eagly, A. H. (2001). Gender, hierarchy, and leadership: An introduction. *Journal of Social Sciences, 57*(4), 629–636. https://doi.org/10.1111/0022-4537.00232

Chisholm-Burns, M. A., Spivey, C. A., Hagemann, T., & Josephson, M. A. (2017). Women in leadership and the bewildering glass ceiling. *American Journal of Health-System Pharmacy, 74*(5), 312–324. https://doi.org/10.2146/ajhp106930

Clandinin, D. J., & Connelly, F. M. (2000). *Narrative inquiry: Experience and story in qualitative research*. Jossey-Bass.

Clayborne, H. L., & Hamrick, F. (2007). Rearticulating the leadership experiences of African American women in midlevel student affairs administrations. *Journal of Student Affairs Research and Practice, 44*(1), 123–146. https://doi.org/10.2202/1949-6605.1758

Collins, C., Ruppanner, L., Landivar, L. C., & Scarborough, W. J. (2021). The gendered consequences of a weak infrastructure of care: School reopening plans and parents employment during the COVID-19 pandemic. *Gender & Society, 35*(2), 180–193. https://doi.org/10.117/08912432211001300

Collins, P. H. (1990). *Black feminist thought*. Routledge.

Corbin, J., & Morse, J. (2003). The unstructured interactive interview: Issues of reciprocity and risk when dealing with sensitive topics. *Qualitative Inquiry*, *9*(3), 335–354. https://doi.org/10.1177/1077800403251757

Creswell, J. W. (2014). *Research design: Qualitative, quantitative and mixed methods approaches* (4th ed.). Thousand Oaks, CA: Sage.

Croom, N., & Patton, L. (2011). The miner's canary: A critical race perspective on the representation of Black women full professors. *Negro Educational Review*, *62–63*(1–4), 13–39.

Darouei, M., & Pluut, H. (2018). The paradox of being on the glass cliff: Why do women accept risky leadership positions? *Career Development International*, *23*(4), 397–426. https://doi.org.10.1108/CDI-01-2018-0024

Davies-Netzley, S. A. (1998). Women above the glass ceiling: Perceptions on corporate mobility and strategies for success. *Gender and Society*, *12*(3), 339–355. https://doi.org/10.1177/0891243298012003006

Davis, A. T. (2009). Empowering African American women in higher education through mentoring. *Journal of the National Society of Allied Health*, *6*(7), 53–58.

Davis, D. R., & Maldonado, C. (2015). Shattering the glass ceiling: The leadership development of African American women in higher education. *Advancing Women in Leadership*, *35*, 48–64.

Davis, K., & Brown, K. (2017). Automatically discounted: Using Black feminist theory to critically analyze the experiences of Black female faculty. *NCPEA International Journal of Educational Leadership Preparation*, *12*(1), 1–10 https://files.eric.ed.gov/fulltext/EJ1145466.pdf

Diehl, A. B. (2014). Making meaning of barriers and adversity: Experiences of women leaders in higher education. *Advancing Women in Leadership*, *34*, 54–56. http://www.advancingwomen.com/awl/Vol34_2014/Makingmeaning.pdf

Dobele, A. R., Rundle-Thiele, S., & Kopanidis, F. (2014). The cracked glass ceiling: Equal work but unequal status. *Higher Education Research & Development*, *33*(3), 456–468. https://doi.org/10.1080/07294360.2013.841654

Dolan, J. (2004). Gender equity: Illusion or reality for women in the federal executive service? *Public Administration Review*, *64*(3), 299–308.

Eagly, A. H. (2005). Achieving relational authenticity in leadership: Does gender matter? *The Leadership Quarterly*, *16*(3), 459–474. https://doi.org/10.1016/j.leaqua.2005.03.007

Eagly, A. H. (2007). Female leadership advantage and disadvantage: Resolving the contradictions. *Psychology of Women Quarterly*, *31*(1), 1–12. https://doi.org/10.1111/j.14716402.2007.00326.x

Eagly, A. H., & Karau, S. J. (2002) Role congruity theory of prejudice toward female leaders. *Psychological Review*, 109(3), 573–598. https://doi.org/10.1037/0033-295x.109.3.573

England, K., & Boyer, K. (2009). Women's work: The feminization and shifting meanings of clerical work. *Journal of Social History, 43*(2), 307–340.

Famiglietti, R. R. (2015). *Discerning the glass ceiling: A phenomenological study of the glass ceiling, social role theory, role models, mentors, sponsors, and champions* [Doctoral dissertation, Drexel University, Philadelphia, PA].

Faulconbridge, J. R., Beaverstock, J. V., Hall, S., & Hewitson, A. (2009). The war of talent: The gatekeeper role of executive search firms in elite labour markets. *Geoforum, 40*(5), 800–808. https://doi.org/10.1016/j.geoforum.2009.02.001

Fields, L. N., & Cunningham-Williams, R. M. (2021). Experience with imposter syndrome and authenticity at research-intensive schools of social work: A case study on Black female faculty. *Advances in Social Work, 21*(2/3), 354–373. https://doi.org/10.18060/24151

Fry, R. (2019). *U.W. women near milestone in the college-educated labor force* (Research report). Pew Research Center. https://www.pewresearch.org/fact-tank/2019/06/20/u-s-women-near-milestone-in-the-college-educated-labor-force/

Glazer-Raymo, J., Bensimon, E. M., & Townsend, B. K. (Eds.). (2000). *Women in higher education: A feminist perspective*. Pearson Learning Solutions.

hooks, b. (1984). *Feminist theory: From margin to center:* S o u t h   E n d   P r e s s.

Hoyt, C. L., & Murphy, S. E. (2016). Managing to clear the air: Stereotype threat, women, and leadership. *The Leadership Quarterly*, 27, 387–399. https://doi.org/10.1016/j.leaqua. 2015.11.002

Hung, J. L. (2012). *Navigating power and politics: Women of color senior leaders in the academe* [Doctoral Dissertation, University of Maryland, College Park, MD].

Issac, C. A., Kaatz, A., & Carnes, C. (2012). Deconstructing the glass ceiling. *Sociology Mind, 2*(1), 80–86. https://doi.org/10.4236/sm.2012.21011

Jackson, J. F. L. (2004). An emerging engagement, retention, and advancement model for African American administrators at predominantly White institutions: The results of two Delphi studies. In D. Cleveland (Ed.), *A long way to go: Conversations about race by African American faculty and graduate students in higher education* (pp. 221–222). Peter Lang.

Johnson, H. L. (2017). *Pipelines, pathways, and institutional leadership: An update on the status of women in higher education*. American Council on Education.

Jones, T. B., Dawkins, L. S., McClinton, M. M., & Glover, M. H. (2012). *Pathways to higher education administration for African American women.* Stylus Publishing.

Jones, T. B., & Dufor, W. (2012). Direction along the path: Mentoring and Black female administrators. In T. B. Jones, L. S. Dawkins, M. M. McClinton, & M. H. Glover (Eds.), *Pathways to higher education administration for African American women* (pp. 27–36). Stylus Publishing.

Lechuga-Peña, S. (2022). Navigating pre-tenure and COVID-19: A testimonio of a BIPOC junior faculty mother. *Feminist Inquiry in Social Work, 37*(1), 13–19. https://doi.org/10.1177/08861099211048432

Lloyd-Jones, B. (2009). Implications of race and gender in higher education administration: An African American woman's perspective. *Journal of Advances in Developing Human Resources, 11*(5), 606–618. https://doi.org/10.1177/1523422309351820

Malisch, J. L., Harris, B. N., Sherrer, S. M., Lewis, K. A., Shepard, S. L., McCarthy, P. C., Spott, J. L., Karam, E. P., Moustaid-Moussa, N., Calarco, J. M., Ramalingam, L., Talley, A. E., Cañas-Carrell, J. E., Ardon-Dryer, K., Weiser, D. A., Bernal, X. E., & Deitloff, J. (2020). In the wake of COVID19, academic needs new solutions to ensure gender equity. *Proceedings of the National Academy of Sciences of the United States of America, 117*(27), 15378–15381. https://doi.org/10.1073/pnas.2010636117

Manfredi, S., Clayton-Hathway, K., & Cousens, E. (2019). Increasing gender diversity in higher education leadership: The role of executive search firms. *Social Sciences, 8*, 1–17. https://doi.org/10.3390/socsci8060168

McChesney, J. (2018). *Representation and pay of women of color in the higher education workforce* (Research report). CUPA-HR. https://www.cupahr.org/surveys/research-briefs/2018-representation-pay-women-of-color-higher-ed-workforce/

Melidona, D., Cecil, B. G., Cassell, A., & Chessman, H. M. (2023). *The American college president: 2023 edition.* American Council on Education. https://www.acenet.edu/Documents/American-College-President-IX-2023.pdf

Niehaus, E., & O'Meara, K. (2015). Invisible but essential: The role of professional networks in promoting faculty agency in career advancement. *Innovative Higher Education, 40*, 159–171. https://doi.org/10.1007/s10755-014-9302-7

Northouse, P. G. (2013). *Leadership: Theory and practice.* SAGE.

Parker, P. S., & Ogilvie, D. T. (1996). Gender, culture, and leadership: Toward a culturally distinct model of African-American women executives' leadership strategies. *The Leadership Quarterly, 7*(2), 189–214. https://doi.org/10.1016/S1048-9843(96)90040-5

Patton, M. Q. (2002) *Qualitative research and evaluation methods* (3rd ed.). SAGE.

Peterson, H. (2014). An academic glass cliff? Exploring the increase of women in Swedish higher education management. *Athens Journal of Education*, *1*(1), 33–44. https://doi.org/10.30958/aje.1-1-3

Peterson, H. (2016). Is managing academics "women's work"? Exploring the glass cliff in higher education management. *Educational Management Administration & Leadership*, *44*(1), 112–117. https://doi.org/10.1177/1741143214563897

Prince, T. G., & Siegel, D. J. (2017). The lived experiences of African American development administrators at public universities. *Philanthropy & Education*, *1*(1), 29–47. https://doi.org/10.2979/phileduc.1.1.03

Reif, J. A. M., Kugler, K. G., & Brodbeck, F. C. (2019). Why are women less likely to negotiate? The influence of expectancy considerations and contextual framing on gender differences in the initiation of negotiation. *Negotiation and Conflict Management Research*, *13*(4), 287–303. https://doi.org/10.1111/ncmr.12169

Reynolds-Dobbs, W., Thomas, K. M., & Harrison, M. S. (2008). From mammy to superwoman: Images that hinder black women's career development. *Journal of Career Development*, *35*(2), 129–150. https://doi.org/10.1177/0894845308325645

Rosser, V. J. (2003). Faculty and staff members' perceptions of effective leadership: Are there differences between women and men leaders? *Equity & Excellence in Education*, *36*(1), 71–81. https://doi.org/10.108/10665680303501

Ryan, M. K., & Haslam, S. A. (2007). The glass cliff: Exploring the dynamics surrounding the appointment of women to precarious leadership positions. *The Academy of Management Review*, *32*(2), 549–572.

Ryan, M. K., Haslam, S. A., Hersby, M. D., & Bongiorno, R. (2007). Think crisis-think female: The glass cliff and contextual variation in the think manager-think male stereotype. *Journal of Applied Psychology*, *96*(3), 470–484. https://doi.org/10.1037/a0022133

Ryan, M. K., Haslam, S. A. & Kulich, C. (2010). Politics and the glass cliff: Evidence that women are preferentially selected to contest hard-to-win seats. *Psychology of Women Quarterly*, *34*(1), 56–64. https://doi.org/10.1111/j.1471-6402.2009.01541.x

Ryan, M. K., Haslam, S. A., Morgenroth, T., Rink, F., Stoker, J., & Peters, K. (2016). Getting on top of the glass cliff: Reviewing a decade of evidence, explanations, and impact. *The Leadership Quarterly*, *27*(3), 446–455. https://doi.org/10.1016/j.leaqua.2015.10.008

Sabharwal, M. (2013). From glass ceiling to glass cliff: Women in senior executive service. *Journal of Public Administration Research and Theory, 25,* 399–426. https://doi.org/10.1093/jopart/mut030

Sczesny, S. (2003). A closer look beneath the surface: Various facets of think-manager-think-male stereotype. *Sex Roles, 49,* 353–363. https://doi.org/10.1023/A:1025112204526

Seo, G., Mehdiabadi, A. H., & Huang, W. (2016). Notes from identifying core competencies to advance female professors careers: An exploratory study in US academia. *Journal of Further and Higher Education, 41*(7), 741–759. https://doi.org/10.1080/0309877x.2016.1177167

Sharpe, R. V. (2019). Disaggregating data by race allows for more accurate research. *Nature Human Behaviour, 3*(12), 1240–1240. https://doi.org/10.1038/s41562-019-0696-1

Terosky, A. L., O'Meara, K., & Campbell, C. M. (2014). Enabling possibility: Women associate professor's sense of agency in career advancement. *Journal of Diversity in Education, 7*(1), 58–76. https://doi.org/10.1037/a0035775

Tienari, J., Meriläinen, S., Holgersson, C., & Bendl, R. (2013). And then are none: On the exclusion of women in processes of executive search. *Gender in Management, 28*(1), 43–62. https://doi.org/10.1108/17542411311301565

Tran, N. A. (2014). The role of mentoring in the success of women leaders of color in higher education. *Mentoring & Tutoring: Partnership in Learning, 22*(4), 302–315. https://doi.org/10.1080/13611267.2014.945740

Wade, M. E. (2001). Women and salary negotiation: The costs of self-advocacy. *Psychology of Women Quarterly, 25,* 65–76.

Wainright, M., & Russell, A. (2010). Using NVivo audio-coding: Practical, sensorial, and epistemological considerations. *Social Research, 60,* 1–4.

Walton, K. D., & McDade, S. A. (2001). At the top of the faculty: Women as chief academic officers. In J. Nidiffer & C. T. Bashaw (Eds.), *Women administrators in higher education: Historical and contemporary perspectives* (pp. 85–100). State University of New York Press.

Warner, J., & Corley, D. (2017). *The women's leadership gap: Women's leadership by the numbers.* Center for American Progress. https://www.americanprogress.org/issues/women/reports/2017/05/21/432758/womens-leadership-gap/

Webster, L., & Mertova, P. (2007). *Using narrative inquiry as a research method: An introduction to using critical event narrative analysis in research on learning and teaching.* Routledge.

Wordlow, T. (2018). *Second in command: Examining the factors that impact the career advancement of black women chief academic officers* [Doctoral Dissertation, East Carolina University, Greenville, NC]. http:hdl.handle.net/10342/7052

CHAPTER 5

When Perception Meets Reality: Reflections on Leading Oneself and the Institution

ABSTRACT

This chapter will take a closer look at the experiences of three Black women senior executive academic officers, at historically White research universities. Information will be presented on the strategies used by Black women leaders to maintain a sense of self as they navigate through challenging situations.

INTRODUCTION

Women have steadily gained a presence in the college-educated labor force and they continue to excel in the obtainment of advanced degrees (Fields & Cunningham-Williams, 2021; Fry, 2019); yet, they remain underrepresented in senior leadership roles (BlackChen, 2015; Croom & Patton, 2011; Famiglietti, 2015; Fields & Cunningham-Williams, 2021; Hoyt & Murphy, 2016; Jones et al., 2012; Ryan & Haslam, 2007). Taking into consideration what is known through existing literature, women are more than capable of serving in senior executive leadership roles, so the question remains: why haven't they?

The previous chapter highlighted two factors that contribute to the makeup of women in executive leadership positions, the glass ceiling and the glass cliff. While the glass ceiling is defined as a barrier that impedes upon women transitioning into advanced senior leadership positions (BlackChen, 2015; Chisholm-Burns et al., 2017; Davies-Netzley, 1998; Davis, 2009; Diehl, 2014; Dolan, 2004; Famiglietti, 2015; Northouse, 2013; Ryan & Haslam, 2007; Sabharwal, 2013), the glass cliff is characterized by the timing in which women enter into senior executive roles, often at times when an organization is faced with a crisis or is going through turbulent times (Issac et al., 2012; Peterson, 2016; Ryan & Haslam, 2007; Ryan et al., 2016).

To better understand the challenges faced by women leaders in top executive positions, a review was done of women serving in leadership capacities within academia. It was found that within higher education, women are overrepresented in positions that have low and middle ranking status; yet, their presence decreases significantly when moving up the higher education ladder to full professor, department chair, assistant/associate dean, dean, or senior executive academic officer (SEAO) (Chisholm-Burns et al., 2017; Croom & Patton, 2011; Fields & Cunningham-Williams, 2021; Seo et al., 2016). The makeup of women leaders within U.S. higher education reveals that women represent 30% of college or university presidents and account for just 38% of all SEAO positions (Johnson, 2017). Specific to race/ethnicity, only 4% of SEAOs identify as Black/African American (Johnson, 2017), suggesting that the makeup of Black women SEAOs is less than 4% overall. This pattern continues when reviewing the professorship, as Black women account for only 18% of college professors within the United States (National Center for Education Statistics [NCES], 2019). And when disaggregated for institutional type, the composition is significantly less, with only 4.1% Black-tenured faculty at research intensive (R-1), doctoral granting institutions (Vasquez Heilig et al., 2019; Fields & Cunningham-Williams, 2021).

Why is this significant? This is important because the trajectory of women leaders moving into more senior positions, such as the college and university presidency, is often a progression through the aforementioned roles (Johnson, 2017). Hill and Wheat (2017) assert that "the projected vacancy in presidential positions will present greater opportunities for qualified and talented women to advance to presidencies" (p. 2091). Thus, the experiences of women serving in roles that precede the presidency become important to understand, specifically the factors that contribute to or hinder advancement opportunities.

Given the limited research and small percentage of Black women SEAOs (Fields & Cunningham-Williams, 2021), greater awareness regarding personal experiences is needed for Black women who have advanced to such positions. This chapter presents themes that emerged from the work of a qualitative study (Wordlow, 2018) that examined the career advancement of Black women, serving in the capacity of SEAO at four-year public, doctoral degree-granting, historically White institutions. The next section will present a review of relevant literature and will be followed by a discussion on emerging themes from this study which include self-reflection and internal motivations; faith, religion, and spirituality; and paying it forward.

THE IMPOSTER SYNDROME AT WORK

The term "imposter syndrome," coined by Clance and Imes (1978), is used to define individuals who are overall high performers but may feel uncertain about their success (Fields & Cunningham-Williams, 2021; Hutchins, 2015) or who consistently doubt their own ability and intelligence (Hutchins & Rainbolt, 2017). Individuals suffering from imposter syndrome may view their success as luck or based on external factors that they do not control (Clance & Imes, 1978).

There is a growing interest to explore imposter syndrome among faculty, as many studies look at graduate and medical residents (Hutchins & Rainbolt, 2017). For example, a study conducted by Fields and Cunningham-Williams (2021) examined how Black women faculty interpreted themselves as it pertained to imposter syndrome and authenticity. In total, nine Black women faculty, specializing in the area of social work from research intensive (R1) doctoral granting institutions, took part in this study and reported experiences of imposter syndrome that at times impacted their professional performance (i.e., decline or over-perform), led to concerns that colleagues had negative perceptions or assumptions of them and that these feelings had, in some ways, hindered them from being their authentic self (Fields & Cunningham-Williams, 2021). In a separate study, conducted by Hutchins and Rainbolt (2017), it was found that as it relates to imposter syndrome "faculty who persistently question their professional legitimacy are at a higher risk for experiencing adverse psychological outcomes with implications to career retention, advancement, and job performance" (p. 96). This raises the question if Black women reported that they were unable to be their authentic self in the workplace, how then did they show up to work and what are the potential implications? Respondents from this study reported that they engaged in practices that included self-management (i.e., managing the discomfort of others through their speech, research), code-switching (i.e., altering tone or vernacular to address diverse constituencies), or monitoring one's appearance and demeanor while at work (Fields & Cunningham-Williams, 2021).

Experiences of imposter syndrome are not isolated to a particular group or profession; thus, various approaches may be used in response. In many ways, the techniques used by respondents can be likened to strategies used to respond to stereotype threat. Stereotype threat theory "holds the perspective that one will be judged based on social identity group membership rather than actual performance or potential" (Block et al., 2011, p. 571). In response, one may fend off the stereotype through dis-identification or de-emphasis of the characteristic under scrutiny (Hippel et al., 2011). For example, one may feel a need to over-perform in a role to justify that they are worthy of the position. While this does serve as a strategy to deploy, it is important to consider the adverse consequences. The efforts made to prove the stereotype wrong can result in burnout, exhaustion, or physical/mental health concerns (Davis, 2009; Hutchins, 2015). Another response may result in one becoming discouraged by the stereotype (Block et al., 2011) leading to disengagement or decreased sense of belonging or connection to the job (Hippel et al., 2011) which may impact performance, retention, or advancement opportunities (Hutchins, 2015). Lastly, one may illustrate that they are resilient to the stereotype by challenging assumptions that are incongruent with the individual's actual performance or potential (Block et al., 2011).

Specific to academia, scholars have captured techniques used by faculty to respond to experiences of the imposter phenomenon (Hutchins, 2015). Based on findings from their research, Hutchins and Rainbolt (2017) identified three supportive approaches faculty have used to cope with imposter syndrome: (a) seeking social support; (b) correcting negative thoughts through exercises that challenge perceptions with facts that validate successes; and (c) engaging in positive affirmatives and self-talk. Similar to social support, other studies recommend securing a mentor who can aid in challenging feelings of self-doubt through positive reinforcement (Hutchins, 2015). Another method for combating imposter syndrome centers on the role of faith, spirituality, and religion. These will be discussed further in the next section.

THE POWER OF EFFECTIVE MENTORSHIP

Mentorship has been known to contribute to the development of women leaders. Brown (2005) defines a mentor as an "experienced individual who provides guidance, assistance, and support to help pave the path for mentees in achieving their career goals" (p. 659). Scholars have researched the benefits that mentors have in the advancement of aspiring leaders (Jones et al., 2012). Mentors help up-and-coming leaders learn formal and informal rules as well as socially constructed norms (BlackChen, 2015; Hill & Wheat, 2017). Mentors can positively support women leaders in combating experiences of imposter syndrome, stereotypes, and challenges (BlackChen, 2015; Jones et al., 2012; Wordlow, 2018). Mentors offer guidance, support, and career advice that support job advancement opportunities (Madesen, 2012; Smith & Crawford, 2007). Mentors also play an integral role to help aspiring leaders avoid as well as navigate barriers that are often associated with bias or discriminatory practices (Kurtz-Costes et al., 2006; Pfafman & McEwan, 2014; Schipani et al., 2009).

Given the underrepresentation of women leaders, there is a need to consider that the availability of women mentors in senior executive positions may be scarce. To this end, those seeking mentorship can consider it advantageous to secure multiple mentors as well as mentors who may identify differently (Brown, 2005; Hill & Wheat, 2017; Madesen, 2012; Tran, 2014; Wordlow, 2018). For women leaders, diversifying mentorship can assist in preparing for advanced leadership positions, to gain insight into different perspectives and approaches that exist (Hill & Wheat, 2017). Securing mentors of different ages, races/ethnicities, genders, faiths, and other identities may also assist women leaders in better understanding and leading diverse populations. However, these experiences should not take away from the added value of having mentorship that can help inform how one navigates the leadership space as a woman.

Hill and Wheat (2017) examined how women leaders make meaning of and experience mentorship. As part of their study, they interviewed 4 women presidents and 12 additional women who served (retired) or were serving in senior executive roles. From their study, a majority of participants considered mentorship as a secondary role in their career path. One possible explanation provided by researchers highlighted that participants in that study did not initially have aspirations to serve in senior executive positions and entered into these roles toward the latter stages of their careers. This presents for consideration that a possible connection exists between the scarcity of women leaders to serve as role models and the level of interest in up-and-coming women leaders to explore advancement opportunities (Hill & Wheat, 2017).

THE ROLE OF FAITH, SPIRITUALITY, AND RELIGION

Just as mentorship has a strong role in the development of up-and-coming women leaders, there is literature (Aponte, 2002; Bacchus & Holley, 2005; Everett et al., 2010) that speaks about the role that faith, spirituality, and religion play in supporting women, particularly Black women, when faced with adversity.

While spirituality and religion are closely connected, they are not the same. Bacchus and Holley (2005) define religion as the "outward expression of one's faith, marked by worship practices, personal beliefs, and ethical codes of behavior" (p. 67). Spirituality is defined as "a universal dimension of life that lends meaning to our existence, sets a moral standard for living, and assumes some sense of moral connection among people at the very heart of our humanity. Spirituality may be based in the supernatural realm of deity or based on ethics and philosophy" (Aponte, 2002, p. 16).

Several studies speak about the impact spirituality has made on Black women coping with adversity. A 2010 study explored how Black women coped with everyday conflict and daily stressors. A total of 41 women, between the ages of 18 and 55, took part in the study (Everett et al., 2010). Through six focus groups, it was learned that Black women experience multiple stressors, with the primary being competing priorities of work and family life as well as financial stress (Everett et al., 2010). In addition to learning the stressors that Black women faced, researchers also sought to understand how Black women coped with stress. Coping is defined as, "constantly changing cognitive and behavioral efforts to manage specific external and internal demands that are appraised as taxing or exceeding the resources of a person" (Lazarus & Folkman, 1984, p. 141). Participants' coping strategies included prayer, church attendance, and participation, as well as meditation (Everett et al., 2010). This aligns with scholars Bacchus and Holley (2005), whose exploratory study on professional Black women highlighted that spirituality serves as a coping mechanism that offers an "inner peace" and "strategies shaped by biblical example." As a coping strategy, spirituality supported Black women in dealing with work-related stress in five ways (Bacchus & Holley, 2005):

1. as a protective factor,
2. source of personal strength,
3. resource for general guidance,
4. resource for guidance in decision-making, and
5. resource for reappraising stressors, including considering whether to accept negative situations

This is further supported by the work of Mattis (2002) who examined Black women's experiences coping through spirituality and through religious practice. Their study revealed that Black women used religion and spirituality to cope in defined ways. Black women saw religion and spirituality as a way to let go of things they could not control by turning their problems over to a higher power and to be at peace with circumstances as they are. Not overly ruminating over how they would wish things to be (Mattis, 2002).

The literature review serves as an overview for the following section that presents themes that emerged from the work of a qualitative study (Wordlow, 2018). This study examined the career advancement of Black women, serving in the capacity of SEAO at four-year public, doctoral degree-granting, historically White institutions.

RESEARCH DESIGN

The purpose of the study undergirding this chapter was to explore the lived experiences of Black women who served in SEAO positions. The engagement, retention, and advancement (ERA) model served as the theoretical framework that guided this study (Jackson, 2004). A fuller discussion of this framework is available in Chapter 4.

The study was carried out using a narrative inquiry research design (Clandinin & Connelly, 2000; Patton, 2002; Webster & Mertova, 2007). Participants were recruited using a snowball method (Atkinson & Flint, 2001). Data were collected using a method defined by Corbin and Morse (2003) as the "unstructured interview technique." Three participants took part in this study. Interviews occurred via phone or videoconference and lasted 60 minutes. Approval was received by IRB and consent was given by each participant prior to interviews. The interviews were recorded, transcribed, and returned to the participants for review. NVivo (Wainright & Russell, 2010) was used to analyze the data.

Limitations

Participants were very positive toward their institution and appeared reluctant to speak in ways that would alter this image. More often, participants would describe or explain the experience as part of the process. Similarly, when participants did expound on personal experiences that hindered their abilities, responses shifted from personal accounts to general observations. On the one hand, it is possible that given the participants' role they may view themselves as part of the institution and choose not to share information that would negatively portray the university. On the other hand, it is also possible that participants may have had negative encounters during the earlier parts of their careers. Thus, as they advanced into senior leadership roles these became less prevalent or participants learned to view them differently (i.e., interpreting them as part of the experience). This presents opportunities for future considerations that may involve interviewing Black women leaders within higher education who are retired, as the distance from the position may offer more ability to freely share their experiences. Lastly, there is a limitation as it pertains to the criteria for participation, Black women SEAOs/CAOs (chief academic officers) from four-year public, doctoral degree-granting institutions that are not classified as historically Black colleges and universities (HBCUs). Thus, future considerations may involve interviewing Black women leaders using expanded criteria.

FINDINGS AND INTERPRETATION OF RESULTS

Participants were provided pseudonyms to respect the privacy of their personal information. In review, participants' experiences aligned with that of the ERA model. Six of the 12 subcategories were present for each participant. They were recruitment, incentive packages, empower administrator, leadership opportunities, mentoring, retention, and advancement (see Chapter 4). In addition, themes emerged that included tools for navigating and responding to challenges; self-reflection and internal motivations; faith, spirituality, and religion; and paying it forward. These are discussed in greater detail in the following section.

I can't leave! Because that work is not done…

Participants reported that the SEAO role is not an easy path, there will be trying times due to the nature of the job, and other times the experiences may be compounded because of the intersecting identities of Black women leaders. Participants shared that increasing access for Black women leaders as well as students serves as one of many motivators to continue in the role. For example, Elizabeth shared,

I might have left if the work had gotten done, but as I move forward in my career, I see we're still dealing with recruiting students of color. We're still dealing with recruiting faculty of color. I can't leave! Because that work is not done, and it's clearly never going to get done, so I'm committed to the end. But every year—we had all these movements, and all these task forces and all these initiatives to change higher education. I would dare say that some of them have been effective but there is still a need. I'm still out here trying to make sure our students are getting represented. There's too much work for me to walk away.

And another participant shared, "I'm a ferocious fighter for our students, all of our students, and especially for our students of color. If we are going to have them here we're going to treat them right." To further add to these experiences, Michelle, Diane, and Elizabeth expressed that it is important to remember "your why." Elizabeth expounded to share that, no matter the field, "there will be people who don't want you in any high-level environment."

RESPONDING TO CHALLENGES

Participants were asked to speak on approaches they utilized to navigate and respond to challenges. The techniques shared by participants align with a study conducted by Diehl (2014) that sought to evaluate how women leaders in higher education form meaning to the barriers or challenges faced. From Diehl's (2014) study, five themes emerged: (a) out of adversity comes opportunity or growth if you survive it; (b) perspective matters; (c) privacy in adversity is important; (d) finding a meaning for adversity connects to self-esteem; and (e) you are a survivor.

In review, the approaches utilized by Diane, Elizabeth, and Michelle closely align with ways in which other women leaders think through and respond to challenges faced. For example, participants reported that to be successful in this role one must understand that perspective frames the experience. Elizabeth shared that whenever she is faced with a challenging experience, she leans on a reference that was often made by her mom, "well, what are you doing there if you're not going to make a difference?" To this end, she understood that her work served more than

just herself or understanding that her work serves a greater purpose. This
is true of all participants, as they spoke on the limited visibility of Black
women leaders in higher education and factors they believe hinder retention and advancement.

Special Challenges: Visibility

Diane stated, "One of the things I think of, except for HBCUs, we don't
have a lot of African American women college presidents who any of us
regularly see." Elizabeth shared, "I think part of what contributes to
being so low in representation is that it's just a path you don't see. So,
you don't know how to best position yourself." And Michelle shared, "If
you haven't seen those opportunities, it's hard to move in that direction."
Through their work, individually and collectively, participants in this
study understand that a path for aspiring Black women leaders within
higher education is being created.

Special Challenges: Discretion and Discernment

Participants also shared that during challenging times they lean on the
motto that privacy is the key. Michelle highlighted that maintaining
privacy is part of the reason for her success. The discretion with which
she operates has "supported her in moving agendas forward, involving
the right partners at the right time, to do what was in the best interest of
the students, without unnecessary push back from others." This is similar to
Diane who expressed the need to use discretion and to also be "selective
with your battles [because] sometimes peace is better than proving to
others that you are right." All participants highlighted the importance of
knowing the formal rules of engagement; highlighting that experience
has taught them when they needed to exercise discretion versus when
they needed to be present at the table and use their voice.

The Challenge of Negativity

Although participants sought to be positive, they recognized that Black
women leaders may face experiences that result in them questioning their
place or readiness to advance. For example, Elizabeth shared "people still

hold stereotypes about women of color; [from] how we act, to what we bring [to the table], or what we study ... I usually blow right through those stereotypes." While this participant has been able to combat assumptions, in reference to her position or readiness to advance, it is not the case for all Black women leaders and can lead many to doubt themselves.

Self-doubt is a common experience for Black women leaders. And if left untreated can fester into experiences of imposter syndrome. However, one method for combating stereotypes and imposter syndrome involves active mentorship with professionals who will challenge negative thoughts and assumptions.

THE RESOURCES OF FAITH AND SPIRITUALITY

While not listed as a subcategory within the ERA model, participants conveyed the impact that faith, spirituality, and religion have had on their professional careers. As highlighted by Michelle,

> I feel professionally I was set on a course. I believe that God has shaped the path that I travel, by many people over the years who have encouraged me to explore things I had not even contemplated. It [my faith] has been a huge part of my life; it has given me an anchor. It has let me stay calm. I think it has helped me remember what is important and what is not. I think that is associated with the characteristics I possess. I have the ability to let things roll off my back and not take them personally. People often say, "How can you do that knowing that person just did a really crappy thing to you?" But it did not end up hurting me. I think that comes from faith ... I think the reason I can see past that is a calm that informs my life that I just think is rooted in my faith.

Participants' experiences are supported by literature that suggests spirituality helps to manage stress (Jones et al., 2012). The emphasis on faith serving as "an anchor," helping her to "stay calm," and "remember[ing] what is important and what is not" confirms the work of Bacchus and Holley (2005), who share that spirituality is a great method to address environmental stressors, build strength to address responsibilities as it pertains to work, and provide reassurance during decision-making.

PAYING IT FORWARD

The final theme that emerged relates to participants paying it forward. Participants reflected on their advancement, acknowledging the impact of others through their care and support, and expressed that with their power comes the obligation to pay it forward. For example, Elizabeth shared, "I am not a person who gets to a position and says, 'Well, I'm here now everybody else figure it out.' I didn't have to figure it out by myself." Diane shares, "One thing I have tried to do as a professional is to work with people coming in behind me and have them open their minds to all ideas and different kinds of jobs that their family upbringing may not have exposed them to." Participants stressed that one impactful way to pay it forward is to serve as a mentor for aspiring leaders. They shared that mentorship is mutually beneficial and vital, therefore they work to serve as a mentor when asked.

CONCLUSION

This chapter sought to present themes that emerged from this study. The items shared by participants centered on experiences that can better serve Black women leaders and expand opportunities for this population. In addition, participants sought to provide strategies to navigate the glass ceiling and glass cliff, as these may play a role in the advancement of Black women leaders. While participants' experiences were largely positive, they acknowledged challenges faced by Black women leaders and reinforced that a breakthrough in the glass ceiling is the key for women and Black women to have true progress in advancing into more senior leadership positions.

IMPLICATIONS FOR FUTURE RESEARCH

Reflecting on this study retroactively, while participants provided experiences that relate to their intersecting identities, the ERA model focuses on Black administrators and does not evaluate the intersections of race and gender. Thus, there is an opportunity to further evaluate the ERA model in relation to Black women in leadership. In addition, participants shared information that presents opportunities for further exploration as it pertains to the use of search firms in the recruitment and selection process of Black women leaders in senior positions. Finally, there is a need for future research that explores self-care strategies implemented by single mothers serving in senior leadership roles, that aid in supporting their overall health and well-being as they continue to lead through and navigate the challenges of the COVID-19 pandemic.

REFLECTION QUESTIONS TO PONDER

1. As I advance, what will my contribution be to this field?
2. Do I experience imposter syndrome? If so, how does imposter syndrome manifest itself in work life? How should I work to combat experiences of imposter syndrome?
3. How do I cope with stressors? What mechanisms do I use to stay grounded?

KEY TAKEAWAYS

- Be selective with your battles, sometimes peace is more important than proving to others that you are right.

KEYWORDS

Black women; women in leadership; imposter syndrome; mentorship; spirituality

REFERENCES

Aponte, H. J. (2002). Spirituality: The heart of therapy. *Journal of Family Therapy, 13*, 13–27.

Atkinson, R., & Flint, J. (2001). Accessing hidden and hard to reach populations: Snowball research strategies. *Social Research Update, 33*, 1–3.

Bacchus, D. N. A., & Holley, L. C. (2005). Spirituality as a coping resource: The experiences of professional Black women. *Journal of Ethnic & Cultural Diversity in Social Work, 13*(4), 65–84. https://doi.org/10.1300/J051v13n04_04

BlackChen, M. (2015). To lead or not to lead: Women achieving leadership status in higher education. *Advancing Women in Leadership*, *35*, 153–159.

Block, C. J., Koch, S. M., Liberman, B. E., Merriweather, T. J., & Roberson, L. (2011). Contending with stereotype threat at work: A model of long-term responses. *The Counseling Psychologist*, *39*(4), 570–600. https://doi.org/10.1177/0011000010382459

Brown, T. M. (2005). Mentorship and the female college president. *Sex Roles*, *52*(9), 659–666.

Chisholm-Burns, M. A., Spivey, C. A., Hagemann, T., & Josephson, M. A. (2017). Women in leadership and the bewildering glass ceiling. *American Journal of Health-System Pharmacy*, *74*(5), 312–324. https://doi.org/10.2146/ajhp106930

Clance, P. R., & Imes, S. A. (1978). The imposter phenomenon in high achieving women: Dynamics and therapeutic intervention. *Psychotherapy: Theory, Research, and Practice*, *15*(3), 241–247. https://doi.org/10.1037/h0086006

Clandinin, D. J., & Connelly, F. M. (2000). *Narrative inquiry: Experience and story in qualitative research*. Jossey-Bass.

Corbin, J., & Morse, J. (2003). The unstructured interactive interview: Issues of reciprocity and risk when dealing with sensitive topics. *Qualitative Inquiry*, *9*(3), 335–354. https://doi.org/10.1177/1077800403251757

Croom, N., & Patton, L. (2011). The miner's canary: A critical race perspective on the representation of Black women full professors. *Negro Educational Review*, *62–63*(1–4), 13–39.

Davies-Netzley, S. A. (1998). Women above the glass ceiling: Perceptions on corporate mobility and strategies for success. *Gender and Society*, *12*(3), 339–355. https://doi.org/10.1177/0891243298012003006

Davis, A. T. (2009). Empowering African American women in higher education through mentoring. *Journal of the National Society of Allied Health*, *6*(7), 53–58.

Diehl, A. B. (2014). Making meaning of barriers and adversity: Experiences of women leaders in higher education. *Advancing Women in Leadership*, *34*, 54–56. http://www.advancingwomen.com/awl/Vol34_2014/Makingmeaning.pdf

Dolan, J. (2004). Gender equity: Illusion or reality for women in the federal executive service? *Public Administration Review*, *64*(3), 299–308.

Everett, J. E., Camille Hall, J., & Hamilton-Mason, J. (2010). Everyday conflict and daily stressors: Coping responses of Black women. *Journal of Women and Social Work*, *25*(1), 30–42. https://doi.org/10.1177/0886109909354983

Famiglietti, R. R. (2015). *Discerning the glass ceiling: A phenomenological study of the glass ceiling, social role theory, role models, mentors, sponsors, and champions* [Doctoral dissertation, Drexel University, Philadelphia, PA].

Fields, L. N., & Cunningham-Williams, R. M. (2021). Experiences with imposter syndrome and authenticity at research-intensive schools of social work: A case student on Black women faculty. *Advances in Social Work*, *21*, 354–373. https://doi.org/10.18060/24151

Fry, R. (2019). *U.W. women near milestone in the college-educated labor force* (Research report). Pew Research Center. https://www.pewresearch.org/fact-tank/2019/06/20/u-s-women-near-milestone-in-the-college-educated-labor-force/

Hill, L. H., & Wheat, C. A. (2017). The influence of mentorship and role models on university women leaders' career paths to university presidency. *The Qualitative Report*, *22*(8), 2090–2111. https://doi.org/10.46743/2160-3715/2017.2437

Hippel, C., Walsh, A., & Zouroudis, A. (2011). Identity separation in response to stereotype threat. *Journal of Social Psychological and Personality Science*, *2*(3), 317–324. https://doi.org/10.1177/1984550610390391

Hoyt, C. L., & Murphy, S. E. (2016). Managing to clear the air: Stereotype threat, women, and leadership. *The Leadership Quarterly*, *27*, 387–399. https://doi.org/10.1016/j.leaqua.2015.11.002

Hutchins, H. M. (2015). Outing the imposter: A study exploring imposter phenomenon among higher education faculty. *New Horizons in Adult Education & Human Resource Development*, *27*(2), 3–12. https://doi.org/10.1002/nha3.20098

Hutchins, H. M., & Rainbolt, H. (2017). What triggers imposter phenomenon among academic faculty? A critical incident study exploring antecedents, coping, and development opportunities. *Human Resource Development International*, *20*(3), 194–214. https://doi.org/10.1080/13678868.2016.1248205

Issac, C. A., Kaatz, A., & Carnes, C. (2012). Deconstructing the glass ceiling. *Sociology Mind*, *2*(1), 80–86. https://doi.org/10.4236/sm.2012.21011

Jackson, J. F. L. (2004). An emerging engagement, retention, and advancement model for African American administrators at predominantly White institutions: The results of two Delphi studies. In D. Cleveland (Ed.), *A long way to go: Conversations about race by African American faculty and graduate students in higher education* (pp. 221–222). Peter Lang.

Johnson, H. L. (2017). *Pipelines, pathways, and institutional leadership: An update on the status of women in higher education.* American Council on Education.

Jones, T. B., Dawkins, L. S., McClinton, M. M., & Glover, M. H. (2012). *Pathways to higher education administration for African American women.* Stylus.

Kurtz-Costes, B., Helmke, L. A., & Ulku-Steiner, B. (2006). Gender and doctoral studies: Perceptions of Ph.D. students in an American university. *Gender and Education, 18*(2), 137–155.

Lazarus, R., & Folkman, S. (1984). *Stress, appraisal and coping.* Springer.

Madesen, S. R. (2012). Women and leadership in higher education: Learning and advancement in leadership programs. *Advances in Human Resource Development, 14*(1), 3–10.

Mattis, J .S. (2002). Religion and spirituality in the meaning-making and coping experiences of African American women: A qualitative analysis. *Psychology of Women Quarterly, 26,* 309–321.

National Center for Education Statistics (NCES). (2019). *Degrees and other formal awards conferred.* U.S. Department of Education. https://nces.ed.gov/programs/digest/d19/tables/dt19_324.20.asp

Northouse, P. G. (2013). *Leadership: Theory and practice.* SAGE.

Patton, M. Q. (2002) *Qualitative research and evaluation methods* (3rd ed.). SAGE.

Peterson, H. (2016). Is managing academics "women's work"? Exploring the glass cliff in higher education management. *Educational Management Administration & Leadership, 44*(1), 112–117. https://doi.org/10.1177/1741143214563897

Pfafman, T. M., & McEwan, B. (2014). Polite women at work: Negotiating professional identity through strategic assertiveness. *Women's Studies in Communication, 37,* 202–219.

Ryan, M. K., & Haslam, S. A. (2007). The glass cliff: Exploring the dynamics surrounding the appointment of women to precarious leadership positions. *The Academy of Management Review, 32*(2), 549–572.

Ryan, M. K., Haslam, S. A., Morgenroth, T., Rink, F., Stoker, J., & Peters, K. (2016). Getting on top of the glass cliff: Reviewing a decade of evidence, explanations, and impact. *The Leadership Quarterly, 27*(3), 446–455. https://doi.org/10.1016/j.leaqua.2015.10.008

Sabharwal, M. (2013). From glass ceiling to glass cliff: Women in senior executive service. *Journal of Public Administration Research and Theory, 25,* 399–426. https://doi.org/10.1093/jopart/mut030

Schipani, C. A., Sworkin, T. M., Kwolek-Folland, A., & Maurer, V. G. (2009). Pathways for women to obtain positions of organizational leadership: The significance of mentoring and networking. *Duke Journal of Gender Law and Policy, 16*(8), 89–136.

Seo, G., Mehdiabadi, A. H., & Huang, W. (2016). Notes from identifying core competencies to advance female professors careers: An exploratory study in

US academia. *Journal of Further and Higher Education*, 41(7), 741–759. https://doi.org/10.1080/0309877x.2016.1177167

Smith, D. T., & Crawford, K. (2007). Climbing the ivory tower: Recommendations for mentoring African American women in higher education. *Race, Gender, & Class*, 14(1), 253–265.

Tran, N. A. (2014). The role of mentoring in the success of women leaders of color in higher education. *Mentoring & Tutoring: Partnership in Learning*, 22(4), 302–315. https://doi.org/10.1080/13611267.2014.945740

Vasquez Heilig, J., Flores, I., Souza, A., Barry, J., & Barcelo Monroy, S. (2019). Considering the ethnoracial and gender diversity of faculty in the US College and university intellectual communities. *Hispanic Journal of Law and Policy*, 2(1), 1–31. http://stcl.edu/Journals/HispanicLaw/2019/2019Heilig1-31.pdf

Wainright, M., & Russell, A. (2010). Using NVivo audio-coding: Practical, sensorial, and epistemological considerations. *Social Research*, 60, 1–4.

Webster, L., & Mertova, P. (2007). *Using narrative inquiry as a research method: An introduction to using critical event narrative analysis in research on learning and teaching*. Routledge.

Wordlow, T. (2018). *Second in command: Examining the factors that impact the career advancement of black women chief academic officers* [Doctoral Dissertation, East Carolina University, Greenville, NC]. http://hdl.handle.net/10342/7052

PART III

The Historically Black Institutional Context

By Dr. Nichole R. Lewis

Dr. Nichole R. Lewis is the Assistant Vice Chancellor of Student Affairs/ Dean of Students at Elizabeth City State University. She joined the executive team of student affairs in October 2020. Dr. Lewis progressed through the ranks for higher education in various roles in career and professional development, having last served as the Director of the Women's Center at North Carolina Central University where she is credited for rebranding of the Center, to expand offerings aimed at building cultural capital, leadership development skills, and career readiness. She also served as the Executive Director of Professional and Leadership Development at a private historically Black college and university (HBCU) in North Carolina. Dr. Lewis had a robust career in human resource management and consulting, and she has worked in health care, association management, and retail. Dr. Lewis spent a great deal of her professional career rising through the ranks of one of the nation's leading pediatric healthcare systems, in the Greater Philadelphia area.

Dr. Lewis is the author of *Just Write*, a collection of poetry and short stories. Samples of her early work were featured in Yolanda Coleman's 2008 novel *Sugar Rush: Love's Liberation*. She has been a featured guest on the Anchor podcast, Black Girl Mentor, and served as the keynote speaker for multiple mentoring organizations. She holds a doctorate in higher education leadership from East Carolina University. Her dissertation is entitled *Herstory: The exploration of the lived experiences of first female HBCU presidents.*

Dr. Lewis earned an undergraduate degree in mass media arts from Hampton University, and an MBA from the Fox School of Business at Temple University. She has maintained a certificate as a professional in human resources since 2004.

Lewis is a fourth-generation member of Delta Sigma Theta Sorority, Inc., a member of The Links, Incorporated, and is the mother of one daughter, Taylor.

"Ears that do not listen to advice, accompany the head when it is chopped off."

—African proverb

CHAPTER 6

The Culture and Climate Surrounding Black Women in HBCU Presidencies

ABSTRACT

In this chapter, I examine the experiences and interactions of three women who served as the first woman president at a historically Black college and university. Herein will be the exploration of hidden organizational challenges that women faced in leading a school in crisis. The women will describe their outsider perspective and what adjustments were made to fulfill job duties at a private and public university. Also, there will be an exploration of the local media and its influence or hindrance to a woman leader's success.

INTRODUCTION

Though no two college presidencies are the same, there are points of comparison, similarities, and themes heard within the telling of the stories of Black women presidents. In the 1990s with the shift in college attendance, particularly the relative increase in Black women's enrollments as compared to Black men, governing boards were beginning to select women to lead historically Black colleges and universities (HBCUs).

Those women seemed to be selected to lead schools that were in crisis or major transitions (Allen & Jewel, 2002; Bower & Woverton, 2009). In the present chapter, I explore the unique experiences of being the first woman to lead a historically Black institution at a time when the mere category of the institution places it in crisis. While the intention is not to singularly focus on institutions in North Carolina, there were striking similarities in the experiences of women who primarily led HBCUs operating in the state of North Carolina. I begin with a discussion of the participants, the narrative approach utilized in this study, and the theoretical framework of the glass ceiling which undergirds this study. I then discuss the significance of HBCUs in the education of underserved students, the legacy of leadership HBCUs proudly enjoy, and how women in HBCU presidencies challenge traditional leadership conceptions. I then turn to a discussion of my findings. The hope is that through the exploration of these experiences, boards of trustees will be able to draw meaning and counsel from their role in the periods of transition for new presidents. In addition, this study may assist women who are currently in senior leadership roles, who may be better equipped to plan for their own transition into, and possibly out of the role as the chief campus-level executive at an institution with not only a history of challenges, but also a history of impact.

THE PARTICIPANTS

Of the 38 Black women who were leading colleges and universities in 1998, the majority were leading community colleges or HBCUs. Participants in this study are among the Black women hired to lead HBCUs from 1994 to 2014. They are identified by pseudonyms to protect confidentiality: Dr. M.D. Browning at Conversion State University (CSU); Dr. Blue Golden at Made it Better University (MIBU); and Dr. Dana B. Smith at Saint Monica's University (SMU). Dr. Browning pursued a traditional faculty career. After rising to the rank of full professor, she served as a senior executive leader for two university systems. She was then tapped for leadership at CSU where she grew enrollments by 21%, increased distance-education offerings, as well as articulation agreements with the state community college system. The number and percentage of faculty with terminal degrees grew under her administration and several programs, including the MBA and nursing programs, received national attention during her tenure. Dr. Golden rose from the position of an instructor to become the first full professor at a state institution before assuming the presidency at MIBU. While at MIBU, she became a fundraising champion and led in the restoration of the historic campus infrastructure. She significantly increased the technological infrastructure of the institution as well as became nationally renowned for her work in intercollege athletics. Dr. Smith's pathway was comparatively less traditional, beginning her career in the K–12 sector. She was selected as the president of St. Monica's after holding a senior executive academic position at another private liberal arts historically Black institution. Her accomplishments included growing enrollments and athletics, overseeing the institution's transition from a college to a university, and the developing high-demand professional academic degree programs.

There are few studies that explore specific experiences of Black women who have served in the role of historically Black college president or chancellor. Through the narratives of these women, those who aspire to the presidency of an HBCU will be able to gain insight into what that experience may bring. These stories stand to shed light not just on how to get there but to provide insight on staying and "staying too long" (Smith, personal communication, April 2014).

RESEARCH APPROACH

This study was conducted using narrative inquiry method. Narrative inquiries are most effective when a researcher is looking to explore what occurred in a period of time and if there was significance within the occurrence. In her paper, designed to make the argument for narrative inquiry as a central and not complementary research method, Thomas (2012) simply defined the research method as a method best used to "investigate what happened, the significance or meaning of that, and how it is told or shared" (para. 15). In this current study, the narratives of the participants' individualized experience as the first Black female president/chancellor will consider three distinct time frames of their presidency: ascendance to the presidency, the first 100 days in office, and the end of their presidency. This approach is modeled after Suber (1995) and is discussed in detail below.

Given the scrutiny under which HBCUs and the leadership therein often operate, it is unlikely that a survey, focus groups, or extensive reviews of secondary data, would reveal or give evidence regarding the challenging events in a college or university presidency.

Ryan et al. (2006) introduced the conceptual theory of glass cliff, the idea that women and racially/ethnically minoritized persons are selected to lead organizations amid crises. As such, if the institution fails, the individuals can be scapegoated for their leadership, but if the institution succeeds, the board can claim credit for making an innovative hire. It was conjectured that the existence of a potential glass cliff in the lived experiences of these presidents would be revealed accurately as an interpretation through their narratives by a trusted member of the HBCU community. This study uses the glass cliff as an interpretive framework as a consideration of the selection and shared experiences of these women at HBCUs.

HISTORICALLY BLACK COLLEGES AND UNIVERSITIES

Considering the status of HBCUs historically and in more recent history, one cannot discount the experiences of its leaders set against the greater context of the impact and influence of HBCUs in the United States. HBCUs comprise a small fraction of the total postsecondary education market, 101 out of over 4,000 institutions in the United States. In 2021, there were 99 HBCUs in 19 states, the District of Columbia, and the U.S. Virgin Islands. Of the 99 HBCUs, 50 were public institutions and 49 were private nonprofit institutions (NCES, 2021). HBCUs represent only 3% of all higher education institutions but educate 14% of Black undergraduates, and award roughly 24% of bachelor, graduate, and professional degrees each year to Black Americans (Esters & Strayhorn, 2013). In addition, HBCUs are foundational to the successful completion of PhDs for Blacks, particularly in the science and engineering fields. Seventy-three percent (73%) of Black women and 57% of Black men holding

PhDs in the sciences completed their undergraduate degrees at an HBCU (Gasman & Commodore, 2014; Strayhorn et al., 2013), among other accolades (Covington et al., 2022).

Largely situated in the southeast, HBCUs stretch as far west as Texas and as far north as Pennsylvania. Given this geography, HBCUs are the preservers and curators of the Black experience in the United States, a bastion of knowledge, and a safe place for students to learn. Since 2016 there has been a significant increase in the number of students attending HBCUs. They provide students a robust education, connect them to a rich history, and help promote a culture of diversity and inclusion nationally (Covington et al., 2022).

A LEGACY OF LEADERSHIP AT HBCUS

> I found a special, intangible something at Morehouse in 1921 which sent men out into life with a sense of mission, believing they could accomplish whatever they set out to do. (Mays, 1971/2003, p. 257)

Benjamin E. Mays is but one of the iconic leaders of historically Black colleges. Among other things, as the President of Morehouse College, he led the institution to financial stability and greater institutional prestige. Black leaders coming-of-age under the Mays dynasty include Howard Thurman, Thomas Kilgore, and Martin Luther King, Jr. Over Mays' tenure, Morehouse graduated 4,000 students; but of Black people with doctorates, one out of 18 was a Morehouse graduate. His legacy is nothing less than legendary.

Mays came to the office of the president during a time when the expected commitment to a campus presidency was for life. In addition, the expectancy for leadership even among Black women's colleges was that the leader is a man. As such, the continued viability of HBCUs is largely attributed to the leadership of men, leading to leadership succession practices that favor men over women in presidential roles. Schools such as Tuskegee, Hampton Xavier, and Morehouse, all had leadership that made significant shifts to remain viable and relevant during the late 1990s and 2000s (Allen & Jewel, 2002). Hampton University, under the

44-year leadership of Dr. William Harvey, Morehouse College and Xavier University, under the 40-year and 46-year leadership of Dr. Benjamin Mays and Dr. Norman Francis, respectively, all have stories involving the dynamic leadership of its presidents. Each president in his way provided a level of continuity and stability that comes with leading an institution through multiple decades against an ever-changing landscape of industry and politics. What is missing from the narrative, are the accomplishments of several women who also led, providing growth and stability to HBCUs over the past three decades.

For certain institutions, there are iconic Black women HBCU presidents such as Johnetta B. Cole (Spelman/Bennett), Beverly Tatum (Spelman), and Julianne Malveaux (Bennett), each of whom served at an HBCU for women. Well-known Black women presidents who served/are serving at coeducational institutions include Mary Sias (Kentucky State), Trudie Kibbie Reed (Bethune-Cookman), Rosalyn Artis (Benedict), and Karrie G. Dixon (Elizabeth City State). Yet, only nine of the United Negro College Fund's 2022 37-member HBCUs are headed by Black women. That fraction is greatly diminished among the 47-member public institutions of the Thurgood Marshall College Fund.

A review of existing literature allows for the establishment of a foundation and framework to interpret and better understand the narratives of the Black women HBCU presidents. Herein, I attempt to not only make connections between previous studies but also highlight missed opportunities to explore the unique experiences of women who served as the first Black women to lead historically Black colleges.

The Dilemma of Being a Black Woman and a Leader

Success is often defined based on one's perception of their trajectory from a relative starting point to one's current status. Merriam-Webster defines success as "the fact of getting wealth, respect or fame; alternately achieving the correct or desired result of an attempt" (2016). Therefore, to make a comparison or to attempt to describe the nuances, differences, or the varying success of Black men in America against that of Black women maybe to consider what is deemed as the "correct" result of an attempt. One must also consider if success is the result of an attempt or an amalgamation of attempts. Does this paradox of success look different based on gender and society's expectations? Is success mitigated by the starting point of a person's attempt? How is wealth, respect, and fame actualized among an ethnic group that has similarly situated marginalized beginnings?

Bond (2011) considers Dr. Julianne Malveaux's concept of the paradox of success for Black women in HBCUs. The article and the associated study look specifically at the experience of Black women students at an HBCU; however, there is some transference that can be considered in the way in which the concept is described. In Malveaux's (2009) book, she describes a third burden borne by Black women. Bond, quoting Malveaux (2009), posits "that the intersection of race and gender, additionally create a third burden for African-American women in that, part of our status, is a function of the way that majority society marginalizes and demonizes African American men" (*quoted in* Bond, 2011, p. 133). Thus, Black women can be similarly targeted by Black men. Such an approach creates an adversarial, zero-sum game, in which Black women are seen as winning only at the loss of a Black man. In her review of existing literature, Bond considers data that suggest Black women's success in the boardroom and classroom has come at the expense of Black men. Given this type of argument, that as Black women continue to appear to outperform Black men it "renders [Black women] less visible as administrators," it demonstrates the degree to which Black women campus leaders operate on college campuses in a system grounded in patriarchy (Bond, p. 137).

Emblematic of this zero-sum game approach, Kaba (2005) makes the argument that there has been a gradual shift in power and economic influence trending upward for Black women. The article sets as a base for comparing the status of Black men and women in politics, economics (business), and education. Of note, Kaba (2005) acknowledges several observations related to the imbalance between Black men and women:

> An important development ... in the United States is that although Black males as of 2003 are still in more leadership positions within the Black population, Black females are on the verge of overtaking black males in leadership positions in a variety of important sectors. (p. 33)

Regarding Black college presidents, Kaba observes this:

> ...in the September 2001 issue of *Ebony*, the names and pictures of 79
> Black college presidents were listed, entitled "Black College Presidents:
> Pioneering on the Frontiers of Education." Of the 79 Black college presi-
> dents, only 20% were females. Many of the men whose pictures were
> shown on this list were older Black males, most of whom would retire
> soon. Their replacements will most likely be Black females because com-
> pared to Black males they will be more likely to have the academic
> credentials required to become future Black college presidents. (p. 35)

Guy-Sheftall in Cole and Guy-Sheftall (2003) recounts a letter to an
editor from a Black man in which the author suggests that Black men
and women can certainly come to resolution on a discourse of race and
gender "behind closed doors," without the validation of White people.
The authors posit that very statement as a reality of the challenges Black
women face when they are in positions to be vocal and lead or push
against social norms in the community. The authors offer that Black
women often must contend with the persona of being an angry Black
woman when they are addressing issues within a certain community, especially if to do so, would lead to the possibility of criticism of a Black man.

In Cole and Guy-Sheftall (2003), the authors facilitated a multilogue
between Black men and women of note in the American political, educational, and literary scene. Their text covers a myriad of topics under the
auspices of the title *The Struggle for Women's Equality in African
American Communities*, but of note, for this study, are a few realizations
that may aid in the understanding of the role of gender in the slow rise
of women in university leadership in the HBCU setting.

Cole (1993)—the first Black woman to serve as president of Spelman
College—writes about sexism, racism, and oppression in her book
Conversations. In the chapter on being Black and female she says this:

> Not every woman's "adventure" with sexism has been the same. There
> have always been enlightened men and oppression-tolerant women ...
> economics has [also] played a role in the tone and timbre of the oppres-
> sions a woman experiences ... When sexism is then superimposed not
> only on poverty but on racism ... if African Americans are less than

Whites and women are less than men, then African American women are least of all—least of all even among their sisters of color ... [So when Black women] find themselves confronted by racism ... and sexism, they [in fact] find themselves between a rock and a hard place. (pp. 85–86)

Cole (1993) discusses how society would attempt to make sexism and racism parallel challenges and calls into question or rather points out that often times the most devastating battles a Black women experiences come through her involvement with Black men. She goes on to describe that the nature of sexism is that men and women are equal as human beings but that patriarchal systems are designed to preserve men hierarchically. This is no less true in Black communities than other cultures in the United States.

Jones (2013) explores Black women's career paths, challenges, and barriers to the presidency, using Black feminist theory as a conceptual framework. As part of the delimitations and universality of Jones' (2013) study is a distinction between the experiences of Black women presidents at historically Black colleges and those at predominantly White institutions. Given the breadth of her study, Jones is unable to capture the in-depth experience of Black women leading at Black colleges and universities specifically.

Confrontations: Black Men and Black Women in Leadership

In May 2022, a city council meeting held in Portsmouth, VA, went viral. The council meeting held on May 24, 2022, involved a vote to terminate city manager, April Jones, a Black woman. The video went viral because of the reaction and statements made by the only woman on the council (Hall, 2022). Subsequently, the council woman was asked to issue an apology for the language used in her outrage (Web Staff, 2022). Of relevance to this chapter is the deeper consideration of what led to the decision to end the Black female city manager's tenure, after just one year in the position. Following the spread of the story, journalists, CNN contributor, and TV One commentator interviewed the councilwoman. In that interview and the discussion that ensued with the guest panelists on Roland Martin's *Unfiltered*, the matter was raised that the people who had initially supported, and verbally touted praise for the city manager's performance, were the same four Black men on the council who "conspired" to vote Jones out of the role (2022).

Roland Martin: So these four Black men, voted against this sister, to get her up outta there?

Councilwoman: Yes!

While unfortunate, this situation in which Black women are undermined by Black men in the community is not unique. Cole (1993) reflected on the experiences where she said that the most damaging encounters for Black women occurred through their engagement with Black men.

Land Mines: HBCU Culture, Climate, and the Media

The significance of prevailing climate is not as evident in the literature as other factors of success for Black HBCU presidents but it serves as a constant backdrop in these women's narratives. The existing culture of a university can present a challenge for any incoming president. In a panel discussion in March 2016, Dr. Blue Golden spoke candidly about her belief that culture cannot be changed, particularly within the first few years of a presidency. What another sitting president on that same panel provided as a counter, was the fact that the existing nature of the way in which entities on a campus participate in decision-making processes from can impact how a new president is able to maneuver in the beginning of her tenure. Together, these presidents suggest that beyond the immediate campus culture, new presidents must contend with the perception of attentive publics off campus in addition to boards of trustees. As such, media portrayal, positive or negative, can frame a presidency.

Given the negative portrayals of Black women in the media, the challenge of perceptions and positive imagery is significant for Black women presidents (Gasman, 2007a). Gasman (2007b) examined the media influence and coverage of one specific HBCU. The women in this study found parity between their experiences with local media and those denoted in Gasman's findings, which highlighted the influence of media on the perception of the success or impact of HBCU leadership. Particularly insightful were the analyses regarding the differences in media attention by gender, with women's work portrayed in a more negative light.

Professors Shauntae Brown-White and Kandace Harris compiled *Representations of Black Womanhood on Television: Being Mara Brock*

Akil, an edited book that introduced the significance of images and stories told in the media about Black women into academic literature. Detailed herein were similar descriptions of how local media influenced perceptions of leadership efficacy. Imani Cheers, in the foreword of Brown-White and Harris' (2019), *Representations of Black Womanhood on Television* had this to say about the influence of media on the institutions we hold sacred in this country:

> For the first time in close to three decades Black women are starring in leading roles and not only in films, sitcoms, and dramas but as showrunners, directors ... Along with the increase in media visual in media ownership. A surge in visual representation and ownership is directly related to the political, social, educational, and economic progress made by Black women in the United States in the last half century. (p. ix)

Contemporary media provide a venue to promote an anti-Black women agenda that constantly assaults African American humanity through stereotypical portrayals of Black women in current popular representation and perceptions of Black womanhood. Therefore, "Black women must play a key role in defining authentic Black womanhood" (Gammage *quoted in* Brown-White & Harris, 2019, p. 2).

There is a level of preparedness every Black woman leader believes that she possesses when she competes for and is then selected for, a leadership position in academia. There are tenets of the business of higher education that leaders learn to consider as one rises through the ranks of any university system. Academic leaders know they must not only be familiar with the context of finances and fundraising, enrollment management, and accreditation, but also the politics of agenda setting. Moreover, leaders who chose HBCUs also know to review and become familiar (quickly) with those areas that tend to be the areas that can jeopardize the standing of their institution: operating budgets, financial and technological infrastructure, alumni giving, enrollment history and threats, campus master plan, state of facilities and the actual physical plant, and strategic plan, and status/schedule for accreditation. While one can prepare oneself through education and professional development to lead through these nuts and bolts, navigating institutional culture as fed by the media often means driving around, over and through potholes, and in some cases land mines.

Birnbaum (1988) describes two specific prevailing campus culture—that of the *locals* and that of the *cosmopolitan*. In a letter sent to a former HBCU president, which accompanied copies of the positive articles that had been written about her successes, from the renowned publisher Rolfe Neill, of the *Charlotte Observer*, Neill wrote:

> ...[Well] You done done it! What a joy to watch you raise the academic achievements and [of that school's] aspirations over nearly two decades. And you don't need to apologize for not being "Miss Charlotte Civic." That was the problem with some of your predecessors who confused being well known with the job they were hired to do, which went unfulfilled! ... (Neill, personal communication, July 2, 2008)

The sentiment in Neill's letter reflects the idea of a culture that prioritizes local perspectives over cosmopolitan gains. Here the example of Gwendolyn Boyd at Alabama State is apropos. While over her less than two-year tenure, she was successfully able to steer the university off an accreditation watch list, her rocky relationship with the board and their parochial expectations of a Black woman as a leaders interrupted institutional progress in the making (Web Staff, 2016).

Black Women: Leading from the Margins

In her pinnacle work, hooks (1984/2000) shifts feminist conversations from a space in which race, class, and sexuality were on the margin to centralizing those who were traditionally marginalized in feminist work. Similarly, Black women breaking into spaces traditionally occupied by men encounter resistance. Boards comprised of local leaders from churches and industry, who are often tied to traditions of leading that tend to be gendered in favor of men. Thus, women seeking to be included as leaders not just in title but in cultural respect, make decisions between leadership styles and tactics that are traditionally associated with men (e.g., charismatic, inspirational leader), or become authentic leaders with their own voices, and draw from experiences grounded in academic or nontraditional leadership. Thus, culturally and in terms of leadership traits, Black women tend to be at a competitive disadvantage for senior leadership. In order to ascend, they often find themselves adapting as perennial outsiders.

Howard-Hamilton and Patitu (2012) in their chapter "Decisions to Make (or not) Along the Career Path" present a case study on career transitions and decisions. In the study, the Black woman at the center of the case was said to have learned to compartmentalize her experiences of being overlooked, hitting the "glass ceiling," and even her invisibility. Howard-Hamilton and Patitu found that 86% of the 201 Black women administrators they interviewed stated that knowledge of organizational culture was very important in the fulfillment of their responsibilities. Their study also drew meaning from various responses connecting the concept of being respected, and the ability to think outside the box and beyond the organizational culture. Therefore, it seems likely that the foundation for implementation of innovative initiatives hinges on one's ability to be respected, and one's ability to implement a strategy for success hinged on the ability to build relationships.

Institutional or organizational culture negates the addition and blending of the campus culture and that of the area, district, or location of the college campus. As Black women presidents of HBCUs, their accountability and need, to be able to build a rapport and set an agenda, goes beyond the gates of the university. That need is impacted by the prevailing climate that is inclusive of the campus community.

CONCEPTUAL FRAMEWORK

I am intentionally challenging the normative language of the literature to make a distinction between a generalized institutional culture and the idea of the prevailing climate. The prevailing climate is inclusive of existing relationships and how the president was introduced to the environment, and even how the predecessor and his exit was perceived and managed.

To analyze the key factor of consideration for the importance of the assumption of a role of senior leader in a bound academic system, I use Suber's (1995) dissertation on the initiation and transition periods for new public-school superintendents as a guide. While not exactly a one-to-one match for the university presidency, superintendents certainly have similar challenges as those experienced by university presidents. Suber loosely compares the initiation and transition to the new superintendency to the periods of time experienced by U.S. presidents from the time they win the election to the time they first take office, through their first 100 days on the job. What Suber uncovers in her interviews is a consistent theme around some of the challenges in play with the prevailing climate. Of note, in her interviews with the two women superintendents, both indicate coming into a system behind an outgoing superintendent and/or a recent history of short-term superintendents who were just not good fits with the system. In both cases, the women followed men who no longer were able to match the vision the board of supervisors had for those particular counties or school systems. In addition to depicting the influence of the prevailing climate that may pose a challenge to a new leader in an educational system, Suber's (1995) findings are telling and shed light on the phenomenological concept of establishing a climate for the transition, and on the need to use the interview process to establish potential allies. The women interviewed in the study also talk about personal sacrifices of time and commitment to ready themselves for their role of superintendent, far before the opportunity actually was presented.

Suber (1995) found that a significant influence for first-year superintendents was that of the prevailing climate in the district where they were expected to push an agenda and make improvements. Institutional culture negates the addition and blending of the campus culture and that of the area, district, or location of the college campus. Similarly, as Black women presidents of HBCUs, their need to be able to build a rapport, set an agenda, and be accountable to the community and accreditors goes beyond the gates of the university.

RESEARCH METHOD

The strategy of narrative inquiry is to illustrate a phenomenon or event(s) from the perspective of individuals who lived through the experience. With "re-storying" there is a limitation of chronological sequencing, in which memories are recalled out of sequence. Another element of narrative inquiry is that participants' retelling of life events is shaped by the storyteller's memory, and the perception of those events. In an effort to account for those elements, I used secondary data, including real-time newspaper articles and articles in established educational leadership journals to support the stories told by each participant. Direct citations are omitted to preserve confidentiality. I also reviewed official documents shared with me directly by each participant. I consulted the universities' annual report where it was available. I also considered the tone or slant of news articles to verify the participants' recollection of the role the local media played in telling stories about their contributions or shortfalls during their tenure.

I gathered the stories of three women who served as the first woman president at an HBCU, which were all located in North Carolina. One president I will refer to as Dr. Blue Golden, who assumed the presidency in 1994, of a private HBCU (Make It Better University) in a major metropolitan city in North Carolina. She had served as faculty for a large, Research 1 institution in another state. She served for 15 years at MIBU, and subsequently led another private HBCU as its first women in an interim role—twice. My second participant will be referred to as Dr. M. D. Browning; she served at a public HBCU (CSU), in a broader system, in a metropolitan city in North Carolina as well. She had previous leadership experience in HBCUs, in major cities, and an experience in a university system in another state. She was in the role for four years. The third participant was Dr. Dana B. Smith who was appointed to serve the then-Saint Monica's College which under her leadership developed to Saint Monica's University (SMU). It is a private HBCU. She had served in multiple leadership roles at a private HBCU in Virginia, as a second career. Her first career was in leadership in K–12, also in Virginia. Each woman was no longer serving in any presidential roles at the time of the study, and all were over the age of 50 when appointed; and when we interviewed, they were over 60. While Dr. Browning was married, the other participants were divorced or widowed at the time of their appointments.

I had each participant review a transcript of the interview, make edits to clarify meaning, and consulted with each woman at least once in follow-up as I recorded my findings. Two women supplied additional written comments, with permission for me to use those as well to draw meaning from their experiences. I do not suggest that three narratives were enough for generalizability but do posit that it was a starting point for further research. Each woman's story was not the same and an argument could be made that not all stories seemed congruent for interpretation through the glass cliff concept (see Chapter 4). What these narratives provided had enough similarity to suggest that their experiences have multiple points of intersectionality that could be considered by those interested in pursuing this career path.

This study aroused my own thoughts and feelings about the experiences of these women, particularly during their last 100 days. I was present for the final days of Dr. Smith's tenure, therefore I intentionally referred solely to her accounts, those of the newspaper, and heavily relied on what I was able to extract from over 12 documents related to communication between her and her board. I even referenced the preparatory documents that she willingly provided of the gender-discrimination case she lodged against the university. Finally, during this process, as I stated above, the Chancellor of North Carolina Central University where I was employed at the time of the study—Dr. Debra Saunders White passed away. As a way of unsolicited professional coaching, Dr. Golden called me to tell me of my obligation to the university, as a Black woman administrator on that campus, and *told* (italics for emphasis) me that I *would not fly* to Atlanta to interview her in the same week of Saunders White's passing, that I *would* be present on campus and then in Virginia for the final services. This experience added to the meaning I was able to make for myself as I traverse through leadership as a Black woman at an HBCU, considering the multiplicity of the role of an administrator.

FINDINGS

Perennial Outsiders

All the women leaders interviewed for this chapter came from campus cultures that would have most closely resembled Birnbaum's description of a cosmopolitan culture. They quickly learned that that cosmopolitan persona followed them, and added to the perception of these women as "outsiders." Each woman at some point used this phrase. One of the women specifically used the terminology to describe her realization of people's perception of her. She had this realization while she was fund-raising to meet the goal of the capital campaign which was underway when she began in the role:

> What I discovered was that I was an outsider, even though I had gradu-ated from [the school], I had never been there and the faculty and staff all saw me as an outsider ... I was [a daughter of the university kind of] person in the eyes of the alumni. I had to explain to the business commu-nity that I was a product of [the institution]. They didn't see me as being there either. You had these different constituents that had different views of where you had come from because you had been somewhere else. I had not spent my life there and I had never worked there ... I was considered to be an outsider; I had come from [a large PWI in another state].

The same experiences are detailed for folks who work for HBCUs in more remote parts of a state, or on campuses with lower attrition rates at the frontline and mid-manager ranks due to geography and family sys-tems. It is also a realization of Black women who transition into higher education from outside higher education. There are in fact "little things" in terms of campus culture that were an unexpected adjustment and add to the feeling of being an outsider. In addition to the vast difference in the level of technological infrastructure, at schools considered to be in crisis, Black women must consider the impact of the prevailing culture in every-day operational decision-making. One president shared this quip:

> My first surprise was when the Xerox machine didn't staple because they bought one that didn't staple, and it was brand new. Little things were the things that would bother me. I was accustomed, and I still did it, to typing my own letters, doing my own exams, making my own reservations, mak-ing my own phone calls, so there was very little for a secretary to do [for me]. I was out there making copies of something. The copy machine was right there where the secretary was sitting. I said, "Who bought this? Who would buy a machine that won't staple?" [The lady who bought it was standing there—the vice president]. I learned that I had to watch what I said because they already decided I thought I was better than they were because I'd been [at a whole different kind of organization for] 20 some-thing years. I had to travel a lot and they used the travel agency. I learned that our benches were so shallow; that you can't let people make your

travel plans who never left the city limits. There's no sense in getting mad with them. Just go on and do it.

Another president who served at another HBCU noted the following:

> What I found was an institution that was very much different from the institution that I had left on a number of levels ... what I did not plan for in the first 100 days but that you need to plan for is the differences in cultural environments. What I discovered ... is that The City traditionally is a very white male bastion, and so they ... the culture was unaccustomed to women being in charge. Unaccustomed to African Americans being in charge and certainly not used to a what-comes-up-comes-out personality which is pretty much what I am.

Of her exploratory visit to the campus prior to even applying for the position, this president made statements about ways in which she could have better prepared during her transition:

> We went and looked at [the college] but what we didn't look at was the culture of the community. It was the culture of the community [people in these roles need to consider.] If I had looked at the magazines from business leadership, if I had looked at the rosters of boards of the United Way and all of that, what I would have realized is that that white male dominance, that Southern white male dominance, was a factor I was going to have to deal with.

In terms of being an outsider, one thing to think through are the unspoken facts about the culture of the city or town in which the school is located. Prevailing climate encompasses connectivity to the area or the region. One of the stories pointed out basic considerations that one may only think of as a bonus to have, but not a necessity for long-term success.

> What I had to deal with was the push back from African Americans who were not used to that kind of African American person in that community remembering that this is a community that has 1 African American councilman, 1 African American county commissioner, 1 African American legislator, and *those* (italics for emphasis) all rotate ... [When we first were looking for money to help build the football stadium], which was during the period when the conference basketball tournament was still in

our city as the host city, we were the first Black organization to ever ask
for money out of the inter-local tax fund in all those years because the
Blacks in that community don't see themselves as viable players in that
city. [When I] pushed the chairman of the Chamber of Commerce on why
the economic development conversation did not include leaders from the
Black community, he says to me "Well, we don't know who the African
American leadership is in The City."

This is not to suggest that any of these areas are also not in play at other
institution types, or in cities where the Black or African American population may have a greater presence in the political and business community.
It is to bring to light the reality of an organizational culture and a prevailing climate that are interconnected but should be part of one's overall
analysis—equally.

As the first female president of MIBU in Charlotte, NC, Dr. Blue Cowser
Golden had direct and deliberate access to the departing president, who
left completely on his own, and she jumped into the role as an interim,
with no real expectation of staying or even applying for the position. This
transition period provided the greatest foundation for her.

Browning and Smith's transition periods were shorter than Golden's,
with Browning's (30 days) being the shortest of all the three women
interviewed. Perhaps that limited transition period, behind a Black man
as predecessor, who resigned under duress, could be seen as a predictor
of a short tenure.

Dr. Smith states that one of the areas she had to deal with immediately
was academic affairs as it was related to accreditation preparation. More
specifically, she had to deal with practices that had been put in place by
the provost who was there when she arrived. What she did not learn during the interview process, nor during her transition, was that he had
submitted an application during the early stages of the presidential
search, but did not advance as a finalist; however, the board had made
him an interim president (Lee, 1999). During the period he served as an
interim, before that the board appointed trustee member Dale Dennis to
serve as an Interim, the provost had developed policies that gave "the
provost" ultimate authority. "When I got to St. Monica what I found was
that almost all the policies, whether they were student affairs' policies, or …

business policies or whatever, started and stopped with him as the last word or the decision maker" (D. Smith, personal communication, October 16, 2016). The information shared about the provost's actions was significant. Smith says "his undermining and second guessing consumed a great deal of energy and effort. The strategy to limit his authority in the middle of transition was difficult to develop without creating media coverage" (personal communication, December 29, 2016). Smith shared an example that ultimately resulted in the provost's separation from the institution; the referenced separation occurring just outside of her first 100 days.

> Eventually we ran into a situation where he made an arbitrary decision to fail about 16 or 17 seniors that were in a class which would've kept those kids from graduating. It was a math class, and his decision was that ... they would fail and that this was from the [fall 1999] semester. When we looked at ... exactly what had occurred.... There were prerequisites for the course that they failed, that the students had not taken, had not been required to take. We were able to make a decision that, because the institution had failed to meet its obligation to ensure that the students were prepared, we would pull those seniors, and set up a separate section for just those seniors, where they could pass with a minimal grade. It would get them out of the system rather than fail 16 seniors when [their lack of preparedness] it could be argued, was really our fault. It was a line that was drawn in the sand, and the provost indicated that if I went through with it, he would quit. I gave him a directive to follow, and on Monday, he did quit. (Personal communication, October 16, 2016)

Relationship With the Board

Boards of trustees continue to be an ever-present distraction in the accomplishments of, and sustainability of, HBCUs. Schools spend resources to select board members who will add to the success and provide a level of support and visibility for these institutions, but it seems the board composition has demonstrated an added burden for Black women HBCU presidents. The board's agenda seems to be often in conflict with the prescribed goals and objectives set out by the selection committee, and often there are internal factions that were unmanaged that hinder the forward movement and stability of these institutions. Who is the puppeteer and who are the marionettes? Who is really in charge? What are the goals of those who make the selection, boast of being forward thinking in moving women through the ceiling, all the while knowing they have set these women up to fall off the cliff? HBCUs have a distinct place in American higher education, yet those who are making decisions about its leadership, seem to be doing so ignoring the ramifications, of alienating the exact women—Black women—who have proven successful in solidifying that place in recent history. There are women who have managed to stabilize, build, and grow these institutions. For each of these women, the relationship with her board of trustees was the turning point, whether in her first 100 days or her last.

Dr. Blue Golden also, had previously been an active member of the MIBU board of trustees prior to her appointment to the interim role. There was a very specific task Dr. Blue Golden began to consider and address during her period of transition, permanently into the role. Reflecting on her first 100 days, one journalist posited "…while thorough investigation and excavation of [fiscal and technological infrastructure] was partly accomplished while serving as a member of the Board of Trustees' Strategic Planning … Golden's first statement to the then vice president of finance was, 'Show me the books'" (*citation omitted to preserve confidentiality*, p. 20). According to Golden what she found during the transition period was "there was no money for July and August. You had to figure out how to live for July and August." As aforementioned, the school had very limited unrestricted funds, and modest cash on hand upon her arrival. Golden's efforts through what has been described as "fierce tenacity and persistence" resulted in her first formal President's fiscal report to the board of trustees be recorded as "end[ing] the fiscal year June 30, 1994, with a balanced budget and monies to place into the Fund Balance" (*citation omitted to preserve confidentiality*, p. 20). As she entered her last 100 days, she had made undeniable strides.

About her second capital campaign she said:

> I started this one. The goal was $75 million. I could never get my board to come up with a leadership group for the campaign. I was in the middle of it, and someone said "Blue, you know what you should do if they don't lead it? You should finish [it] and announce victory." That made me say "… that's a good idea."

She said that the Southern Association of Colleges and Schools Commission on Colleges (SACSCOC, a.k.a. SACS) review is ongoing, but of the SACSCOC reaffirmation during the latter part of her tenure she recalls:

> I had two campaigns and two SACS official review cycles. I told myself, "I can't leave until I finish [the campaign]; can't leave until I finish SACS. We got the social work program and education reaffirmed.

In each of the explored experiences, the women presidents noted pivotal moments during their tenure as the first. Golden noted multiple pivotal moments related to her board of trustees. First was the exit of her first board chair:

> The board chair was also up for the interim presidency position [but he was not selected]. He tortured me for three years. I was ready to leave. Mrs. Blande was on my board. She helped me move him off the board.

There was also the election of new (her third and last) board chair:

> He should have never been on the board … he always wanted to go in a different direction…. he wanted me gone, as much as I wanted to be gone. I told him and the vice president of the board I was going to leave and told them when I planned on doing it … but they did not know the day I'd make the actual announcement.

As a board-related act she discussed the provost appointment and resignation:

> The board insisted I hire a number two. He was working against me [especially in the preparation for accreditation] … I had to take SACS back from him … and call SACS to tell them I was having difficulties with him … He wanted to run the whole school … I figured out I couldn't trust him, but I could not let him go in middle for SACS … so I isolated him … the day we finished SACS, he resigned.

Different than the other participants who's last 100 days coincided with the announcement of their departure, Dr. Golden's announcement occurred one year prior to her actual departure ergo, her last 100 days. Her pivotal moments reveal greater insight into decision and timing of the announcement of her exiting the university. Golden says her goal was to get a perfect score on SACS, and to complete the $75 million capital campaign.

> When I got my money right, for my campaign, I announced my departure all in the same day. I said, "I might as well announce a victory and departure at the same time." That's what I did. I went and got me a new suit and put it on. I did. I went to New York and bought a new St. John's. I had it that day. I had a little meeting with my various people. I told them what I was doing. They were all surprised, but I wasn't. I had been thinking about that for some time. You look good when you arrive, and you look good when you leave.

Dr. Browning's tenure was a four-year tenure, marked with several accomplishments that seem to have raised the profile of CSU. She had "quadrupled enrollment in distance-education courses, catapulting CSU into the 3rd place in distance-education across the 16-member UNC system" (*citation omitted to protect confidentiality*). She had established dual-enrollment agreements with 14 community colleges spread throughout North Carolina. The university had become an international institution with partnership campuses in Shanghai and Mongolia. Faculty positions were filled with 93% of faculty holding doctoral or first-professional degrees. She had significantly increased fundraising from $952,364 to $1,725,4004, and grants from $4,729,213 to $11,335,271 during the four years of her tenure (2003–2004 Annual report; 2005–2006 Annual report; personal documents presented on November 12, 2016).

CSU fundraising efforts had seen the highest level of success under Browning's leadership inclusive of the successful completion of a capital campaign to raise $1.5 million in 3 months. That campaign concluded during what would be Browning's last 100 days "not only [meeting] the goal, [but] exceeding it by 15 percent" (*citation omitted to preserve confidentiality*).

Browning has also raised the number of non-African Americans in the state attending CSU, making it a true intercity competitor of Jesuit University. It also competed for Black students with UNC Nash, the university with which the initial nursing relationship was formed and had proven successful.

For Browning, it may have been the not knowing about the significance of culture and the level of crisis of the institution that would have been a predictor—not as much about the length of tenure—but internal and external support. Browning's relationship with the CSU board was not part of her narrative but rather with the UNC System Board of Governors, which for a public university in North Carolina, has a great, if not greater impact, on one's ability to succeed and grow an institution. Findings for Browning and her time at CSU, were made within the larger context of the UNC system's politics in mind. Throughout this inquiry, influence of the board of governors and board of trustees was evident.

In order to properly document the information gathered about what Dr. Browning notes as the beginning of the end of her tenure as CSU's first woman president, I have included her statements related to her expectation of the success for the program. The nursing program's approval was considered complete as of the 2003–2004 annual report. Students in fall 2004 were able to declare nursing as a major with accounts. The program began in 2005, and had perfunctory success in that there was an existing template for the program already in place at CSU soon after her arrival.

> The RN to BSN program just requires students to complete the general education courses and other courses they need because they already have their licenses … That's what Conversion State had been doing with Nash. They took a couple other courses that were nursing related … [but they] already had their licenses and … the measure of success of a nursing program is the licensure … Blooming [State University, where I was on faculty and in administration for 20 years] had a four-year nursing program. It was very successful. Grayfield State College [*pseudonym*] had a successful nursing program. I made an assumption that if these HBCUs could have high quality nursing programs, Conversion State could do the same thing. I was wrong.

Dr. Browning confirms that her push for the program resulted in it being approved and accredited, and the completion of hiring of staff including a program director.

Dr. Smith noted as something she had to contend with during the beginning of her tenure was a "big battle with certain Board members who challenged whether I really 'understood how things were done.'" The first board of trustee chairperson under whom she served was part of a historically prestigious family legacy, a strong point of pride for the college. Personally, other than the familial connection, that chair had very little affinity for HBCUs, having grown up in New York, attending private primary schools and Ivy League colleges (according to Smith, and a Bloomberg.com corporate profile). According to Dr. Smith, "he was an avid supporter of former president Richardson, whose retirement was forced by the Board after 28 years of service."

Her interview exposed that while there was a president between Smith and Richardson, she inherited not only faculty, and an alumni base who were still loyal to him, but also a board that "for the most part" remained loyal to him. Smith says in her first 100 days, he was "perfunctorily respectful." He advised her that "[she couldn't] fix it with the people who broke it." However, soon after she notes even that level of respect waned.

The first milestone for Smith involving her relationship with her board, represented a solid level of support and a show of confidence in her ability to set and implement a vision for the institution—it was the resignation of her first board chair. He [who was himself African American] demonstrated open disdain for women, African Americans, and southerners:

> Eight months after I assumed the presidency … his efforts to demonstrate how I had not "fixed things" failed. He resigned at the end of 2000.

As part of Smith's discovery, one of the things she quickly realized at the beginning of her tenure was the school's lack of readiness for the pending SACSCOC review. Her next noted milestone was the successful completion of the accreditation process:

> First time the team came we went on warning for finances, which was fine for me because they identified issues that needed to be addressed … it gave me leverage to make some necessary changes. The following year, we were accredited, fully with no compliance issues. As is often the case, true impact takes time to be realized. Changes to curriculum, and the development of student affairs initiatives designed to build cultural capital were not as evident in the first year.

Smith talked about her fourth commencement ceremony as evidence of the impact of her leadership in that regard. She says of the graduation of the first full class in May 2004:

Those students who were freshmen in Fall 2000 … at their graduation we were able to see the things we'd put in place like student leadership organizations, the honor society, all things that were not there, that class acknowledged it had been a great experience.

Though she acknowledges the success of St. Monica's student athletes during her first couple of years, Smith does not attribute their "wins" as a direct result of her leadership. She did however, consider their success as a milestone. Smith reflected on her ability to build rapport with them in a real way, a way that demonstrated how committed she was to holistic student success, during one of their most memorable experiences early on in her tenure. Smith considers her attending the 2000 Olympics in Australia as a milestone for another unexpected reason.

The first year I was there I had seven students compete in Australia and 4 gold medalists. I did go to Australia. I took my own money and went to Australia … that was a milestone because I was there when they competed and afterwards, the publicity that that got … opportunity to meet with the mayor … and governor … gave me opportunity to be introduced to that part of [of the city] and North Carolina.

Perhaps one of the most notable milestones for Smith was the reintroduction of football:

When people write about me, [it's always] "Smith, who brought back football after 37 years" … [I consider it a milestone because] it gave alums a reason to come back to campus. It generated a level of pride and … excitement in the alumni base … I was also the person who convince the CIAA to start giving award for high academic achievement for teams … then for 8 of the 9 years of football, the football program at St. Monica's always had the highest academic achieving athletes.

Lastly, in the narrative, Smith discussed one of the most lasting impacts of her presidency which was the elevation in the status of the institution. It was under her leadership that Saint Monica's College became SMU. The change from college to university. Simply stated she says of that major change:

It was a very unifying act that raised the profile of the institution.

Smith considered the aforementioned experiences milestone as the noted events signaled significant points of success or achievements for her in her role as president. Below are those experiences she considered as pivotal moments—those experiences that demonstrated a shift in direction either for the university or for her within the context of her role as its leader. These experiences, in combination with the accomplishments previously discussed, brighten the light on the theme of these women's relationships with their boards.

Needing little description, and therefore giving none, Smith's first recollection of pivotal moments in her 14-year tenure were the two cycles of successful SACSCOC reaccreditation. She then touts the new construction on campus. She reflects fondly of one board member, who facilitated the building of a new residence hall on campus with 320 beds. That was significant. She found him as one of the more supportive board of trustee members. His support resulted in yet another pivotal moment—the reacquisition of a local golf country club.

> He purchased it and then four years later gifted it to the University. We were able to restore, renovate and upgrade the greens. It became a focal place for the community, and the remaining original owners who were African American.

Smith also considered offering of new academic majors that specifically set SMU apart from its peer institutions, for example, property management, biophysics, and communications with a film and interactive media option.

> Development of these kinds of majors that would ensure we were not just a good HBCU to attend, but a desirable, full, comprehensive institution that happens to be an HBCU.

Her final two pivotal moments, we discussed, were directly related to the composition and influence of her board of trustees. One was specific to the cycles of board chairs:

> I had 2 cycles of board chairs who actually were visionary in their thinking, and who were supportive ... for that period of about 4–5 years we experienced unprecedented growth ... in enrollment ... visibility.

In Smith's experience, results indicate the greatest conflict with the board of trustees, most notably as she considered them the pivotal moments of her tenure. In the moments as recorded, she recalled those key periods when her attempts to grow the institution and expand its profile proved to be the alternative to the plan of certain members of her board (primarily the three White males who were staples of the local community). She also noted a pivotal moment during her first 100 days when the board of trustees' chair, a Black man, commenced to discredit her efforts and abilities. However, in that instance, other board members were able to combat the chairman's efforts, which resulted in his resignation from the board. Smith shared details regarding the gender composition of her board, but what seemed to have had a greater impact was the prevailing climate of presiding at a school in the state's capital city region, even when the composition of the board became more balanced.

There are striking parallels in Smith's experiences at St. Monica's University, with the board's interference in Williamson's (2004) research on now-nonexistent Campbell College, and the way in which the freedom of private HBCUs not only made them a gift to the civil rights movement but also made those private college's leadership a target for groups that did not want to see growth or systematic change. Is it possible, given the recent history of the SMU presidency that Smith was brought in because of her successes, because she was uniquely qualified for the challenge, without the selection committee considering and therefore preparing her for the greater influence of prevailing climate? In her retelling of her story, it appeared that when the governing body itself was not successful in containing the school's unexpected growth under her leadership, the external entities found a way to contain it, from the inside and alleviate her from her seat at the table.

Across literature on higher education and leadership, the interaction with the board of trustees is noted as one of the challenges of the presidency. Throughout this volume, the literature helps to frame the challenge; however, in discussions with multiple Black women presidents, governing board interference and interaction were discovered to be major contributors to the success or perceived failure of a college president. At face value, the board of trustees' involvement is considered as one of the external entities for which a president is held accountable, but the board's involvement has the propensity to add unrealistic pressure on the day-to-day work of the university president.

By means of the accounts of three of the first Black women to head an HBCU, the interaction with the board of trustees took many forms, but those interactions were strongly emphasized in the experience of each woman. In considering her last 100 days and the correlated pivotal moments, Smith reflected on those (multiple) cycles the governance and administration relationship being "as it was supposed to be." The other was about her realization of a misalignment of the plan for SMU:

> I guess the most significantly pivotal piece was when I realized that there
> was an element on the board that had a vision and a plan for St. Monica's
> that was different than the direction in which we had been growing.

It is that final pivotal moment, Smith says was what ultimately resulted in her leaving the university.

The Media

When the U.S. higher education system was seeing a surge in the appointment of Black women to the role of president at HBCUs and community colleges, there was also an insurgence of articles and literature about the role the media, in particular print and television, played on the perception of the effectiveness or relevance of historically Black institutions. From 2012 to 2014 there was a definitive peak in the appointment of Black women as first-time presidents, and at the same time, there was a notable increase in the presence of Black women in the media itself—both on and off screen—in leadership roles. Each woman considered for this chapter discussed a phenomenon of the influence or the role of the media, but in particular that of the local newspaper.

While Gasman (2007b) examined the media coverage of one specific HBCU, this phenomenon seems more significant in the retelling of these three women's experiences over a collective 20-year time span. It was eye-opening to know how the local media influenced the perception of their leadership, and their ability, creating challenges with building rapport and making shifts on campus, and repositioning the school. Browning and Smith had more stories related to media challenges than

Golden. There were inferences in the news that set out to discount Golden's accomplishments because she worked unapologetically in a way that would "build a school," and not necessarily in a way that would endear her to locals (*citation omitted to protect confidentiality*).

In her first 100 days, Dr. Smith encountered a phenomenon of the media's coverage of the college and the points of her transition as the new president.

> I found that for the first time, I was garnering headlines that were nega-
> tive. I had also never been in a situation where the media outlets took
> anonymous letters and people complaining and printed it. There were a
> series of [articles based on] anonymous letters that [questioned who I was
> and challenged whomever as to] "who have they have brought to The City
> to run this school." (Personal communication, October 16, 2016)

An additional fact that posits support of the media contribution to the perception of others during Smith's early tenure is the action taken by the provost when he quit:

> What he did was he sent a letter to the newspaper indicating that I had
> arbitrarily changed grades so that these students could pass, and so the
> paper printed it without any verification. They apparently were not used
> to consulting with women about situations. I had that debacle to deal with
> as well.

Thus, just as in the case of Browning, media involvement was an emergent theme.

Just as her narrative revealed succinct milestones of noted accomplishments, Browning was clear about her pivotal moments as well. Those were her commitment to honor the Aramark contract:

> I was under a lot of pressure, as soon as I arrived, to open [the dining
> services] contract up for [bid] as soon as it was legally possible ... I think
> people thought I would be malleable and that they could persuade me ...
> once it was determined I wasn't ... people who had been my supporters
> the first 100 days were not my supporters any longer ... Senator Smith
> sent negative letters to The System President about me; she told me about
> them. She spoke throughout the interview about the support of UNC
> system president, and as discussed during her transition period the role

that board member advocacy had on her initial wins. Therefore, a pivotal moment that occurred early in her short tenure—the departure of board member W.T. Brown, who had pushed for her to have a contract, left during her first year in the position. He said things when he was leaving about me … I don't think the intention was to harm me … but it was interpreted as him not supporting me … it gave the Conversion Times permission to write negative things about me.

Of the things Dr. Browning encountered and could have anticipated having to manage and learn in her first 100 days, given her 20 plus years of education at an HBCU, the influence and relationship with the local news media was not one. However, much that she learned about the anticipated matters in her first few months, she learned from the media—not directly from her team. By making comparisons to her experience at one of the two HBCUs in the other major cities, she had not had experiences where an HBCU garnered as much interest for a newspaper to print articles pointing out issues, when there were several other competing matters in the city.

> Of course, newspapers will print stories that sell papers. Unfortunately, in Conversion what I found is there was no greater consumer of bad news about CSU than the Black people who lived in Conversion.

Emphasizing the point, earlier in the data results, Dr. Browning disclosed that she was unaware of the year-end audit results until she had officially begun and was at a seminar at Harvard; however, she makes this point about the local paper:

> One of the newspapers, right after I was announced, printed a cartoon of me coming into an office at CSU and encountering all these audit findings.

One prompt for her listening tours was her receipt of anonymous letters from people who had issues with things at the university. Browning remembers going to campus and spending whole days there, only to return to the hotel, and hotel staff handing her envelopes for her with "unsigned" letters. She learned the local newspaper would also print articles based on accounts that may or may not have been verified, based on unsigned letters or anonymous calls to the paper—by faculty and staff.

In 2019, 25 women were presidents of the nation's 100 HBCUs, according to Thurgood Marshall College Fund and the United Negro College Fund (Eversley, 2019). Each Black woman President in this study accomplished goals that had not been reached in the school's recent history. Yet, at their respective institutions, a scan of the milestones for each is but a mere mention, or a footnote. Images featuring these women, wall wraps denoting their legacy and contribution to the university as part of library archives have been removed. Many of the first women presidents were required to sign nondisclosure agreements so that they are unable to discuss the facts and experiences of their contributions or the closing out of their tenure. This work preserves for posterity the contributions of these women to HBCU leadership. There were more Black women hired between 1994 and 2014 who met initial criteria for inclusion in this study, but who were excluded because they had not at the time of study experienced their last 100 days. Additionally and unfortunately, there are now several other possible participants for studies conducted by researchers looking to draw meaning from the experiences of a Black woman who was the first to lead an HBCU.

Transitions

The largest portion of those experiences missing in the literature is the recorded and lived experiences of those women's last 100 days. At the beginning of my research, I selected five women. One woman went on to another presidency, so her willingness to be candid diminished greatly. The other woman, upon learning that the scope of my research would include the last 100 days of her tenure, had to decline participation because of the confidentiality terms of her separation.

In retrospect, Browning shared that the most telling memory about the culture, came as a reflection during her first few days in the role as CSU's first woman chancellor. Closing out a comment about her last 100 days and the financial management staff still not having proper training,

> History kept repeating itself, and it was a campus culture. I remember when I was new, the chief of police said to me, when he picked me up on my first day of work, "Ma'am" he said, "You have gotten yourself in a mess and you don't even know it." I said, "What do you mean?" He said,

"You're going to do things, and you're going to have an impact on people who are connected to other people in ways that you'll never know. You may do something, and you think it's the right thing to do, and you're going to make all these enemies, and you won't know that you've made them because you don't understand the connections" …That was my first day, and he was right, and I didn't know it … I was told [by broad] I had to make changes, and make them fast … I had not anticipated that some of those changes were going to rock the boat in such a way. [My lesson is this], know the culture of the place because, again, I've been in an HBCU before but those people at Grayfield, even though they might have hated everything about Grayfield, would have died before they would have told the press about what was going on.

Dr. Golden's revelation about the difference in culture was not as pointed as the experiences recalled by Browning and Smith. Different from the other two women, Dr. Golden did have a connection. She was not only an alumna of the school she was chosen to lead but had also accepted the interim president role as a current member of the MIBU board of trustees. Yet, she specifically used the same terminology to describe her realization of people's perception of her:

Although having graduated from university, I found that I was an outsider. … the faculty and staff all saw me as an outsider … [Yet,] I was a Made It Better person in the eyes of the alumni. [Nevertheless,] I had to explain to the business community that I was a product of Made It Better. They didn't see me as being there either. You had these different constituents that had different views of where … [I] had come from because … [I] had been somewhere else. I had not spent my life there and I had never worked there … I was considered to be an outsider; I had come from Georgia….

Dr. Golden recognized this perception of herself as an outsider. She talked about the "little things" in terms of campus culture that was an unexpected adjustment, and part of her discovery. Those little things, however, over time can add up.

DISCUSSION

What has been learned from the lived experiences of three women who were the first to lead HBCUs is the greatest, and unexpected impact of prevailing climate on how women led schools that were considered to be in crisis. The Black women at these institutions share, in informal settings, and during periods of reflection among each other those ways in which they considered the differences and nuances between organizational culture and prevailing climate. A few stories include significant references to the "not knowing, and discovery" and the significance of researching the more-than-just-the-campus community. This condition of prevailing climate goes beyond just researching the campus and its programs. It's crucial during one's transition period (the time between accepting a position and officially assuming the role) one adds to or expect that discovery will include researching social norms and historical relationships of the institution with the geographic location that is critical as well.

The literature considered race and gender "institutionally" in a broader context, but it was evident in each of the lived experiences of my study participants, that challenges raised regarding perception of these women's skills and abilities were raised by Black men within the governance structure. The challenge to the women's authority that was initiated by men was more apparent, and in two of these instances, specifically by Black men. In some scenarios, possible derailment of Black women in the president's seat came at the expense or detriment of the school. To provide balance to that narrative, each woman also talked about Black men who were critical to points of success for them as well. The women did not see themselves as being in competition with men, as they were mostly driven by the calling to improve, stabilize, and raise the profile of the institution, far beyond the gratification of raising themselves.

As the industry experiences what has come to be known as the great resignation, rising leaders believe that organizational culture can be defined or easily determined by what is printed, reported, or viewed in limited campus visits. Corporations and foundations are capitalizing on the brand of HBCUs' universal "organizational culture" as they offer financial support during an upsurge of attention on these institutions. This increased visibility of HBCUs, and their unique organizational cultures have even begun to make them attractive to those external to the academia, entering pools for the role of president. What if the normative idea of institutional culture was to be challenged and we posited that there is a difference, and limitation of that terminology? How might the distinction play into the level of success for new leaders, particularly Black women?

Studying the tenures of the Black women who were the first to lead HBCUs in North Carolina—boasting the largest number of historically Black colleges as compared to any other state in the union, increases the richness and draws meaning from the narratives in a way that will add to the literature in the field. The focus allows this research to serve as a resource to aspiring HBCU college presidents. However, in their experiences of being the first woman president or chancellor at the respective HBCUs in a provincial environment, the findings confirm that all three women had a realization that they must contend with the duality of their identity as a Black person and a woman. In each instance, gender was not something present in their responses to the initial questions, which had a slant toward the three-time frames of focus for this study—their transition period, their first 100 days, and their final 100 days. Rather, each woman's narrative revealed their awareness of their womanhood in response to the question reserved for the end of the interview. Each woman, in her way, acknowledged how their womanness or gender was not something they had ever considered, at least not the same way in which their Blackness had been an element of their identity. Their gender had not been made a focal point or posed a dilemma in their career before they assumed their role as college president of an HBCU.

The significance of the prevailing climate was not as evident in the reviewed literature as other factors of success for Black college presidents but served as a constant backdrop in two of the three narratives. However, each woman used or described their initial experiences as that of being "an outsider." How quickly one adjusts to the prevailing climate seemed to make the difference in the speed with which the first woman president was able to make strides, build relationships, and get things moving in a stronger direction, or how quickly she stalled out.

QUESTIONS TO PONDER

1. What is the prevailing climate at my institution? With this understanding, what is an appropriate leadership style and what are the types of

goals the organization can attain in the short-term and long-term? (Cox, 2001).
2. Who can I rely on for navigational support for culture, organization, finance, and so on?
3. How do I build a positive relationship with the local media, local civic, and religious leaders?
4. How do I cultivate trust within my cabinet?

KEY TAKEAWAYS

- Perception matters. Proactively building a positive relationship with the media may temper the desire for negative sensationalism in the future.
- Boards of trustees need to be oriented toward supporting the academic and organizational mission. This includes financial support. Board members can be cultivated over time but in the meantime, they connect and build trust.
- Know when to say when. Preserve your dignity and sanity.

KEYWORDS

Prevailing climate; women presidents; HBCU; organizational culture; leadership

REFERENCES

Allen, W. R., & Jewel, J. O. (2002). A backward glance forward: Past, present and future perspectives on historically Black colleges and universities. *Review of Higher Education, 25*(3), 241–261.

Bond, H. (2011). Black females in higher education at HBCUs: The paradox of success. In Chambers, C. & Sharpe, R. *Support systems and services for diverse populations: Considering the intersection of race, gender, and the needs of Black female undergraduates* (Vol. 8, pp. 131–144). Emerald Group Publishing Limited.

Bower, B. L., & Wolverton, M. (2009). *Answering the call: African American women in higher education leadership*. Stylus Publishing, LLC.

Birnbaum, R. (1988). *How colleges work: The cybernetics of academic organization and leadership.* San Francisco: Jossey-Bass.

Brown-White, S., & Harris, K. (2019). *Representations of Black womanhood on television being Mara Brock Akil.* Lexington Books.

Cole, J. B. (1993). *Conversations: Straight talk with America's sister president.* Doubleday.

Cole, J. B., & Guy-Sheftall, B. (2003). *Gender Talk.* Penguin Random House.

Covington, M., McClendon, Njoku, N., & Priddie, C. (2022). *The HBCU effect: An exploration of HBCU Alumni's peer networks and workforce outcomes.* The United Negro College Fund. https://cdn.uncf.org/wp-content/uploads/The-HBCU-Effect_FINAL.pdf?_ga=2.98384735.1356466227.1678719317-1946911967.1678719317

Cox Jr, T. (2001). *Creating the multicultural organization: A strategy for capturing the power of diversity* (Vol. 6). John Wiley & Sons.

Eversley, M. (2019, March–April). *Changing herstory* (pp. 17–23). Currents – Council for Advancement and Support of Education. https://www.case.org/resources/issues/march-april-2019/changing-herstory

Esters, L. L., & Strayhorn, T. L. (2013). Demystifying the contributions of public land-grant historically black colleges and universities: Voices of HBCU presidents. *Negro Educational Review, 64*(1), 119–135.

Gasman, M. (2007a). Swept under the rug? A historiography of gender and black colleges. *American Educational Research Journal, 44*(4), 760–805.

Gasman, M. (2007b). Truth, generalizations, and stigmas: An analysis of the media's coverage of Morris Brown College and Black colleges overall. *The Review of Black Political Economy, 34* (1–2). https://doi.org/10.1007/s12114-007-9001-z

Gasman, M., & Commodore, F. (2014). The state of research on historically Black colleges and universities. *Journal for Multicultural Education, 8*(2), 89–111.

Hall, B. (2022, May 24) *Council fires Portsmouth city manager in tense meeting.* https://www.wavy.com/news/local-news/portsmouth/portsmouth-city-manager-angel-jones-fired/

hooks, b. (1984/2000). *Feminist theory: From margin to center.* Pluto Press.

Howard-Hamilton, M., & Patitu, C. (2012) Decisions to make (or not) along the career path. In T. B. Jones, L. S. Dawkins, M. M. McClinton, & M. H. Glover. *Pathways to higher education administration for African American women* (pp. 85–102). Stylus.

Jones, T. A. (2013). A phenomenological study of African American women college and university presidents: Their career paths, challenges and barriers.

Proquest Dissertation and Thesis Global. http//search.proquest.com.jproxy. lib.ecu.edu/docview/131853689?accountid=10639

Kaba, A. (2005). The gradual shift of wealth and power from African American males to African American females. *Journal of African American Studies*, *9*(3), 33–44.

Malveaux, J. (2009). The status of African-American women: Shouldering the third burden. *State of black America: In a black woman's voice.* http://www. juliannemalveaux.com/downloads/THE_STATUS_OF_AFRICAN_ AMERICAN_WOMEN.pdf.

Mays, B. E. (1971/2003). *Born to rebel: An autobiography.* University of Georgia Press.

National Center for Education Statistics (NCES). (2021). *HBCU fast facts.* https://nces.ed.gov/fastfacts/display.asp?id=667

Ryan, M. K., Haslam, S. A., Hersby, M., & Bongiorno, R. (2006), *Think crisis—think female: Glass cliffs and contextual variation in the think manager—think male stereotype.* University of Exeter.

Strayhorn, T. L., Williams, M. S., Tillman-Kelly, D., & Suddeth, T. (2013). Sex differences in graduate school choice for Black HBCU bachelor's degree recipients: A national analysis. *Journal of African American Studies, 17,* 174–188.

Suber, D. B. (1995). A descriptive study of the factors identified in the initiation and transition of individuals into a new superintendency [Dissertation, Virginia Tech University, Blacksburg, VA].

Thomas, S. (2012). Narrative inquiry: Embracing the possibilities. *Qualitative Research Journal, 12*(2), 206–221.

Web Staff. (2022, May). 'I apologize for not saying it sooner': Portsmouth Councilwoman Lisa Lucas-Burke responds to criticism after heated city council meeting. *WKTR.* https://www.wtkr.com/news/portsmouth-councilwoman-lisa-lucas-burke-apologizes-for-language-used-during-heated-city-council-meeting

Williamson, J. A. (2004). "Quacks, quirks, agitators and communists" private black colleges and limits of institutional autonomy. *History of Higher Education Annual, 23,* 49–81.

CHAPTER 7

The Calling to Lead: A Black Woman's Commitment to Run HBCUs

ABSTRACT

In this chapter, I focus on the personal commitments the woman made and the responsibility of leading while also being an African American and a woman. This chapter dives into the challenges the women faced and the strategies taken to maintain and preserve the mission of historically Black colleges and universities, even when it put the presidency, and their careers, in jeopardy.

INTRODUCTION

Retired Dillard University president, Walter Kimbrough, shared his perspectives on opportunities for Black leadership in academe. His response to *The Boston Globe's* conjecture that "With a large number of college presidents stepping down, vacancies may open the door for more diverse leaders" simply was "Nope. Door still largely closed." Although the article is not about historically Black colleges and universities (HBCUs), and does not include elite colleges in the South, Selig (2022) recounts data that matched with what were discovered through the narratives of my study participants and reviewed in other literature. However, there are some leaders who are beating the odds.

The December 2021 edition of *Diverse Issues in Higher Education* high-lighted the extraordinary strides of three HBCU presidents in the area of major gifts. The donations were made by billionaire philanthropist and novelist MacKenzie Scott, who is the ex-wife of Amazon CEO Jeff Bezos. All told, Scott selected 384 organizations to donate, with an unexpected number of those institutions being HBCUs. The *Diverse* article focused on three of those schools. These institutions announced the receipt of a multimillion-dollar gift; no strings attached. "For many schools, that was the largest one-time gift that they had ever" (Kelliher, 2021, para. 1). The university administrator for advancement at Norfolk State University (NSU) explains the significance of the gift of $40 million for his/her insti-tution as the largest single-donor gift NSU had ever received in its 85-year history.

> "To get a $40 million unrestricted gift for an institution of our size is really unheard of" ... "Scott's gift almost doubled our endowment, and since her gift, we've seen an increase in major gifts of over $50,000," said Porter. "When you receive a transformational gift like that, it really is a seal of approval for the institution and leadership. It says to people that you're doing the right thing at the right time. For us, it has really given a green light to other donors."

Corporations, individuals, and foundations have reached out to NSU and become new donors since Scott's donation. That doesn't happen without a leader who can articulate the vision but also operate in the calling to serve more than themselves.

Dr. Javaune Adams-Gaston is but one of several Black women who in the past two decades has increasingly answered the call to lead HBCUs. Adams-Gaston assumed leadership of Norfolk State in 2019, and while not the first woman to do so, she is still the seventh president, among the few in the institution's history. During her first year at NSU, the COVID-19 pandemic created multiple challenges for the nation and the world. President Adams-Gaston worked together with her team to continue to move the institution forward despite the challenges arising from the pan-demic. This led to the university achieving multiple successes.

The goals of access, opportunity, and success for NSU students remained her focus even during these unprecedented times. Under President

Adams-Gaston's management, NSU has successfully achieved the status to appear in *U.S. News & World Report* 2021, Top 20 HBCUs designation.

However, in the recent past, successes at the helm have not translated into Black women's longevity in HBCU presidencies. The August 2014 issue of *HBCU Digest* noted a shift in the male-dominated leadership of HBCUs with the appointment of women presidents at 10 colleges and universities including, but not limited to, North Carolina Central University (NCCU), Florida A&M University, Florida Memorial University, Morehouse School of Medicine, Talladega College, Alabama State University, and University of Maryland Eastern Shore. In 9 of these 10 permanent positions, the woman selected was the first woman to ever serve in the permanent position as president (Lewis, 2017). While this spike from 2011 through 2014 is notable, increasingly, women have been selected to lead HBCUs since the late 1990s, at schools where they would serve as the first woman to lead institutions that have existed for over 100 years.

By 2015, at least nine of the first-time, first Black women presidents at HBCUs had left their positions under duress, having served terms of less than five years. This is in stark contradistinction to traditionally and historically long tenures seen in HBCU presidencies where the notion of a "lifer" in the presidency role is still a reality contemporarily. At the time of this volume, none of those women, featured in the 2014 *Diverse* issues, were still at the selected institution; and many were no longer serving in a presidency at all. Where there have been permanent replacements, those replacements have been men. In many of the scenarios, enrollment was stabilizing, the facilities and grounds were updated, upgraded, or newly constructed, and academic programs were added to or enhanced as a result of the women's leadership. This raises the question as to what are the unique experiences of being the first woman to lead a historically Black institution?

The women targeted for this study were all chosen to lead schools located in North Carolina. Each institution was amid a crisis when they were selected for the number one job on campus: financial, accreditation, reputation, and enrollment, amid other challenges, were all crises at stake among the institutions these women led.

HBCUs are uniquely situated in higher education history as schools in crisis. From their inception, HBCUs have had to do more with less. Many will recall that Mary McLeod Bethune founded the Daytona Beach Literary and Industrial School for Training Negro Girls, which became Bethune Cookman University, with just $1.50. One may not, however, recount that Spelman College was opened in 1881, just nine years before the University of Chicago, an institution with which it shared a major benefactor, the Rockefellers. However, support for these institutions was quite disproportionate (Anderson, 1988).

Contemporarily, given the populations they serve, and the consistent charge to prove their worth and competitiveness, HBCUs tend to have greater institutional stress. With traditional and innovative funding strategies, coupled with changes in federal regulations, much of that weight and accountability is borne by their leadership teams. This increases the probability of HBCUs' need to consistently confront individual institutional crises, as well as the need to select leaders who are well versed in crisis management.

When selected candidates, regardless of gender, are prepared for the prevailing climate, they have the opportunity to consider their own skill level and calling. They are able to determine not only if they are a good fit for the goals of the school, but also if the school and community are a good fit for what they are being asked to do. Thus, to endure the presidential position successfully, Black women need to transcend the challenge of the campus presidency set against a backdrop of potential crises. She must also transcend cultures which foster racialized sexism, especially when it comes to the image of who makes for a good leader (Cole & Guy-Sheftall, 2003). To do so, there is a deeper commitment to the role: There must be a calling (Bower & Wolverton, 2009).

THE CALLING: WHY WOULD ANY BLACK WOMAN WANT THIS JOB?

Merriam-Webster has two relevant definitions of a calling: "a strong inner impulse toward a particular course of action especially when accompanied by conviction of divine influence" and "the vocation or profession in which one customarily engages." Bower and Wolverton (2009) and Cole (1993) delved into the concept of the sense of calling, and the tendency of women in leadership to see beyond doing a job for the sake of doing a job. The idea of calling was framed to suggest that as Black women educating predominantly Black students at HBCUs, some greater responsibility exists beyond just ensuring that students are meeting standards of classroom learning outcomes. The same calling applies to the desire, drive, and commitment to lead HBCUs.

Perhaps, one of the articles I reviewed that most closely matches the exploration of the experiences of the first woman to lead an institution is Turner's (2007) that studied women of color as campus presidents. Here, she interviewed three women who were the first women of color (Mexican, Asian, and Native American) to lead four-year colleges and were not seeking presidencies, but rather looking for senior leadership roles where they could make a significant contribution and impact on a type of institution with which they were connected.

Similarly, none of my study's participants moved through their careers seeking a presidency. In total, three women participated in my study, a narrative design. Two were appointed to public institutions, one to a private institution. Their tenure ranged from four to 15 years. Each was prompted to apply for the presidency/chancellorship by different people—peer, another sitting president, or members of the board at the college itself. Thus, women in both studies were identified by others as having an acumen for successful leadership within them. Each woman talked about a career of commitment to developing students before assuming the role of president.

Focusing on the women in my study, as described in Chapter 6, Browning and Smith's experiences with student development had been at historically Black colleges, but Smith also worked from the sense of calling to develop and expose Black children as young as kindergarteners. Golden specifically noted her record accomplishments with faculty development and enhancing teaching and learning through technology, but her stories were always followed by an example whereby the faculty development served as a launching pad of success, and exposure for Made It Better University (MIBU) students. Thus, the calling develops iteratively over time. It does not emerge after the presidential position is obtained, although the calling, commitment, and connection with the institution can deepen with time. It is one thing to have a vision. But leading faculty and staff who may not be interested in change, or staff who have only had the experience of being at only one institution (e.g., alumni-turned-employee) takes a level of motivation that is generated by more than a generalized drive for personal success. When conducting or considering the selection of Black women to lead these institutions, it's critical to consider how the candidate gives meaning to success and in that context, to consider her professional success rate of achieving in similar environments, within similar populations, in the field of education. The calling was evident in the participants' approach to the work, which created a foundation for how to set and implement a vision.

Calling Drives Vision

Browning, Smith, and Golden's visions drew from a call to Black excellence and student success. This included changes in institutional infrastructure such as new buildings; adding wiring to computer labs that had PCs but not cables or software; increasing scholarship among faculty; creating student organizations; pushing for grants to develop and expand curriculum, programs, athletics, and more. The goal of their visioning process was to position their respective school to address unique needs in the labor market. Their accomplishments in setting and executing that vision, had a level of success that translated to the success and readiness of their students as graduates. Their implementation of and drive to push the vision despite the challenges internal to the university, and its periphery, could be more ascribed to the call toward continuous and sustainable growth, and less about self-gratification or edification.

Each woman interviewed in my study talked not only about leading the development of the curriculum but also about specific opportunities and points of exposure for their students. For example, Golden spoke about "our" successes with upgrading the technology—as she rarely used "I" statements:

> We had some very good students. I'll never forget. One day I had a kid come to school early. I think he must have come to Smith when he was about 16. He was showing some people around in the technology center. He had his little chest stuck out and all. I said, "God, you're awfully

arrogant today." ... He looked me in the eye and he said, "Dr. Golden, this is not arrogance. I'm confident." ... There was an air of confidence that students had. Those computers did more for them than any gadget that you could have ever given them, because it said something [about the caliber of degree they were worthy to receive by attending MIBU].

In addition, the general Southern Association of Colleges and Schools Commission on Colleges accreditation processes, the vision of these women encompassed special accreditation for programs such as education, business, nursing, and social work. Browning gained specialized accreditation for over four academic programs which was not done prior to her arrival. She developed the branding for a bar of excellence in programming and academics named "the Rhino Way"; and she was responsible for the purchase of the sizable bronze rhinoceros, in front of which her successor posed, in his first appearance in the alumni journal after her departure.

Beyond the classroom, each participant provided evidence of how their students learned things outside the classroom that allowed them to progress beyond graduation. For example, Golden shared that her first student government association president who was in the midst of leading a protest during her first 100 days against the changes she was making, went on, after her tutelage to pursue a career in higher education herself. She says of this time, during homecoming:

> Just as I was being announced, getting ready to be announced, the students had a protest. I knew it. I was at UNCF meeting in Dallas, Texas. It was in October. I got on the plane early and came back to MIBU. The students were protesting. Turns out it wasn't about me. It was about what they thought the school was not doing and should be doing, but they weren't expressing it very well. A couple of the kids, one was the editor of the newspaper, and the other was in student government. I talked to them. I had them in my office. I found out what was really going on with them.

According to local news outlets (*citation omitted to protect confidentiality*), she also charged them to "re-read" W. E. B. Du Bois's *The Souls of Black Folk*. "She gently but firmly encouraged them to re-read it, without once referring to the somewhat uncertain financial future for the university" (p. 21). Golden intertwines her recollections of her student encounters with notes of about what those former students are doing in their current-day careers. She says of that meeting amid the protest, "I knew I had to keep raising money. I knew I had to keep working on SACS. I knew that I had to do it all at the same time." Faculty development and scholarship was at a record high with MIBU faculty and students traveling, studying, and presenting internationally at J. F. Oberlin University in Japan, University of Wollongong in Australia, Shaanxi Normal University in China, and University of Bahrain to name a few. She even led the NC Consortium for International and Intercultural Education delegation to Moscow on an observation tour.

They spoke of milestones either in student programming or faculty development in terms of the impact it had on shaping their student populations for life beyond the campus community. Golden shared the establishment of the Center for Information Services, which was "responsible for training faculty in the use of technology in instruction" (*citation omitted to protect confidentiality*). However, in doing so, she also discussed how students were trained to be support staff and staff the computer labs established on campus, positioning them to bypass entry-level helpdesk positions in information technology roles because they had been serving in that capacity sometimes for their whole collegiate career. She talks about providing support for student athletes, inclusive of having a star athlete report to her office weekly as a condition of his being able to play while he strengthened his grades. However, in the narrative, she highlights how that struggling student is now a coach in a high-performing high school in Raleigh, NC.

Another example is when Smith and Golden discussed a 2013 experience where the Saint Monica's University (SMU) student leaders and athletic team student leaders attended a city council meeting. Smith set the scene:

> I took a group of kids to a town meeting where some of the community people were opposing the building of the stadium on our property, and clearly the dialogue was racist. They referred to us as "those people" and "that school" and all of the clichés that go along with racial bias. And I ended up with a group of students who were devastated and undone … And in that one moment we had an opportunity to see both sides of life—

to understand that there were ... people in that neighborhood who were very much proponents ... But there is this segment of the population out there [who are against you], and this segment is [one] you are going to have to move strategically around.

As practitioners of never allowing a good crisis go to waste, these women saw this opportunity as, in Dr. Golden's words "a teachable moment." Dr. Smith expounded,

> We had a teachable moment.... these were athletes ... in tears. And they said to me "Dr. Smith, they don't want us here because we're Black. I said yeah, that's exactly right.... This is why you must always defy the stereotypes". (*Citation omitted to preserve confidentiality*)

Having reinstated football, Smith created a platform to highlight the possibility of high academic achievement for male student athletes, which was evident in the SMU teams who repeatedly were achieving the highest academic awards in the CIAA conference.

Calling is not always or only manifested in seemingly over-dramatized gestures of passion during new student orientation or commencement speeches. One's calling can also be seen or described through the way in which someone goes about doing the work. Each of them described a collaborative and inclusive style throughout their tenure. Holmes (2004) and Lewis (2017) talked about style as a factor in the success of women leaders.

Calling Provides Impetus to Overcome Challenges and Achieve Success

Each woman president in this study shared recollections of their milestones and pivotal points during their tenure. These times were pointed with highs, lows, and stories of real people. The calling is what pushes a president to go beyond just the data points. For example, upon Browning's arrival at Conversion State University (CSU), there was, as mentioned in the previous chapter, a great deal of discovery. Student satisfaction was not the only early hurdle. Having assumed the role in July, student enrollment for that very first fall was also a concern. Dr. Browning discovered applications for admission that had not been processed.

> There was a scare about enrollment. I didn't know this, but the person
> who'd been hired [prior to my arrival] to be in charge of admissions had …
> all these applications … in boxes, and nothing had happened with them.
> We find out at the 11th hour that we are not going to [meet any] an
> enrollment [targets]. That's when I did the recruitment tour. I think I must
> have gone to about twenty places.

She personally went around to areas where recruitment had been successful
in the past, where she had networks, she employed faculty and staff to do the
same at their churches and area churches, and organizations to which they
held membership to ensure a strong enrollment for the fall semester. Browning
did so even beyond the scrutiny of her (White and Black male) peers:

> One of my colleagues, a person at the same level as I said "That's not what
> a chancellor ought to be doing. Chancellors don't recruit. I'm thinking I
> will do whatever I need to do in order to keep this place functioning."

According to official documents from the university archives, her initial
recruitment tour was successful. For example, the CSU 2003–2004 Annual
Report noted record enrollments in Fall 2003 semester, 48 additional new
first-year students from the previous year, with an overall increase in
enrollment [5,329], up .4% from the prior year.

Enrollment and student satisfaction were important to Browning because
she was charged with stabilizing the university, and was selected, she
believed, to continue to build its position in the region. What she learned
revealed even more about the prevailing climate. As a way to combat the
issue and give employees and students a more effective way to communi-
cate that would not compromise the university, she began what Browning
called listening tours on campus. Browning conducted these tours by
going to every department and unit on campus. She would listen to concerns on one condition—for each negative comment or complaint, people
had to share two positive experiences or attributes about CSU.

Another challenge Browning faced was that of fulfilling her calling when
those entrusted with her vision, withheld information from her, or made
decisions beyond their role in the institution to do so. After less than a
month in the role, the true financial status of the university was released,
and she discovered more that she didn't know what she did not know.

In the first month, Browning terminated her head of business and finance. She operated the school with an interim, as the consultant had agreed to stay. She also had to deal with an immediate issue of unpaid wages to faculty who had been teaching summer school. She learned, through an article in the paper, that someone in the business office had not paid summer faculty in accordance with the scheduled pay cycle and had decided to pay them on another day. There was also an issue with the way in which financial aid was being managed from a customer service perspective in terms of efficiencies in the distribution of financial aid checks to students.

> When I first came to Conversion State, the first week I was there, there was an article about how students at Conversion State were complaining about financial aid ... faculty were complaining because they were supposed to get paid for summer school on a certain day ... and a fairly low level staff person had decided checks would come out another day ... I was away at Harvard when this all came out....

As a result, Browning felt that it is important to lay out her expectations right away, in terms of service and student interactions.

> [At] one of my first [staff meetings] my message was "we're here to serve students which means that we need to respect them and treat them well" ... I will never forget I noticed students standing in line for financial aid, those long lines and I [had to say] "you know students are in line, so we're going to provide them with cold water" ... it sounds like a small thing [but I had to make that suggestion] ... [I also didn't understand why they were waiting to give students financial aid checks] because actually data suggested that if they got checks early, they did not take the money and disappear. I had people who became angry with me because I said that we need to get the checks to students more quickly ... [and] that's just not how we do things.

Based on student feedback, it appeared that anecdotally, that message was received by staffs and being felt by students on campus. Another article in the local paper touted the student experience in this way:

> This year also marks the first homecoming for CSU's new chancellor, Dr. Browning, ... As Browning led the parade with the title of grand marshal, several people in the crowd and waving from floats said her leadership has bolstered school pride and brought about noticeable improvements.

"The spirit is out there more this year," said CSU sophomore Tatianna LeCroix, who rode on a float. (*Citation omitted to preserve confidentiality*)

This early news article leaned more toward positive than others. It demonstrated the ways in which the collaborative approach increased her connectivity with her students, which has an immediate impact on the student experience.

In her first 100 days, Golden also experienced a significant challenge from students. She described a student protest led by then-MIBU student government president and the editor of the student newspaper. One of those students himself went on to become an HBCU president. Dr. Golden's calling truly comes alive in her examples shared by her commitment to the developing of everyone on campus. The faculty became more productive because they were beginning to produce; they had national recognition. They had a joint agreement with Al Akhawayn University in Morocco and MGIMO University in Soviet Union.

Beyond addressing student concerns, these women served students by broadening student opportunities to learn. For example, one of the milestones of Browning's tenure was the growth online education. She indicated that it was in large part a way to increase enrollment and better serve nontraditional student population. Post the initial interview, Dr. Browning shared a little-known milestone which was her very significant role in saving the university's programs at the largest U.S. Army installation in the country.

> The university was going to be thrown off the base because the director of the program did not convert to the military's revised way of handling enrollment. At the time I served on a commission at the American Council on Education, and a member with responsibility for education of military-service members telephoned me … My national reputation saved CSU.

Browning's milestones mirror the noted impact her vision had on enrollment. She had a series of milestones around targeted recruitment that included strategic recruitment of Hispanic students and an initiative for nontraditional (adult) students.

Dr. Browning also exercised leadership in the establishment of the partnership with international educational institutions, including "the establishment of a first-rate foreign-language laboratory; and signing memoranda of understandings with seven Asian universities, and hosting

Fulbright Language Teaching Assistants annually." However, in the narrative, she highlights the students who were able to travel through that study-abroad experience, including one young man, who was hired to teach English at a Mongolian university upon graduation.

In a magazine focused on four local women presidents of private four-year universities, Dr. Smith spoke highly of the acknowledgement of her "bringing back football." That decision was both strategic and linked to her passion. In addition to being a draw for male students, it was also a way to demonstrate to Black students they can compete and succeed. Smith spoke about her development of the honors college and student leaders program. In doing so she discussed how those experiences not only had an impact on enrolling a student population which became decreasingly dependent on federal aid, but also reestablished a level of prestige and confidence for the SMU student.

Through pursuing a vision of Black excellence as directed by calling, these women were able to raise institutional profiles, increase enrollments, stabilize finances, and expand the social mobility of their students. Under Dr. Golden's leadership MIBU was awarded the MacArthur Foundation "Genius" Award for her work which improved teaching and learning, faculty productivity, and created a Freshman Academy in which students were grouped by majors and could engage in joint projects with faculty. Moreover, there was increased computerization and connectivity on campus:

> We went live in 1995. [I am credited for turning MIBU into a laptop campus. Getting the software and having the faculty and students trained was a goal but] my vision of technology was not just to do the laptop thing. My vision was, this is what's going to drive teaching. It's a requirement to be able to compete in the world. Students even ran our Training Lab, which was for faculty, staff, students to learn the technology. It was about competing in the 21st century.

The student technical assistant program was also established:

> We trained the students to operate as help desk support on campus. Everybody wanted it because it paid $10/hour. [MIBU] still has it. I knew we would never have enough professionals in computer science to run the computer systems that I wanted.

In her words,

> In 1996, and I always forget to tell this, we received this award. [MacArthur Foundation, typically to between 20 and 30 individuals, working in any field, who have shown "extraordinary originality and dedication in their creative pursuits and a marked capacity for self-direction" and are citizens or residents of the United States.] It gave us visibility with foundations that we had not had before, because they had never given it to a college before ... opened doors because people saw you.

One of the most welcome initiatives Smith began was organizing a Community Day. After removing the barbed wire that constituted the gates around the parameter of Saint Monica's College, it was a way to invite the surrounding neighborhood onto campus. It was a small-scale carnival that included bounce houses, face painting, entertainment and exhibition step shows by the fraternities and sororities on the campus, and free hot dogs, burgers, cotton candy, and frozen ice. The event always took place on a Saturday, and by Monday campus was transformed back for learning. The Higher Education Leadership Foundation institute features a panel of women presidents during the three-day symposium. In the opening introductions for the presidents of Black colleges in Texas, Oklahoma, North Carolina, and Louisiana, all these women talk about the simple things they thought to do, and train their staff to take care of (early on) in order to change the atmosphere of the campus. Upgrades to the grounds and special attention to the appearance at the entrance of campus are part of each introduction. Smith had done the same things—converted a nonworking water fountain to a burgeoning rose garden; allocated funds to service the water fountain outside the library and set a schedule for lighting the water; annually purchased a ring of evergreens; and hosted a departmental decoration contest for each Christmas tree. Those trees were then donated to families in the surrounding community who were unable to purchase and decorate on their own. Smith gave a chance to a woman familiar with maintenance to lead the facilities and grounds, who also proved to appreciate the significance of the campus "looking good." Smith's final departure was weeks prior to the Annual Community Day. That year, for the first time in the event's 12-year history, on the Monday morning following the event, staff and students entered a trash-and-litter covered entrance way on their way onto the yard.

Part of the scrutiny of HBCUs is their relevance, and at the same time their positioning in higher education as institutions who offer accessible education. In order to stabilize these institutions, the leaders have to be able to see beyond today, to put themselves aside and direct teams of people who can prepare HBCU students beyond graduation. Presidents at HBCUs have to possess past experiences using available resources, inclusive of the willingness to access their own networks to graduate a self-aware global citizen who has developed a level of confidence to compete against others from much less privileged upbringing. Graduates' ability to compete adds to the national profile of the institution—the leader has to be one who has that at the forefront of the vision.

Raising the profile of an institution is essential in stabilizing the organization, as it allows for better programming and attraction of resources to meet student needs. Thus, attending to the *institutional profile* is part and parcel of the call. During the newly introduced segment of the NASPA NUFP conference (held on the campus of NCCU in summer of 2019), there was a running theme among participant questions and comments about the perceived constant state of lack at HBCUs. The notion that HBCUs are always hemorrhaging money is reflected in the misconception that because of fewer resources, these institutions are of lesser quality. The availability of resources impacts the ability of any institution to attract competitive leadership, staff, and faculty. During my time in leadership recruiting for positions at three different HBCUs, candidate questions (and declined offers) are often couched in the rational, or candidate experiences that institutions of this type, have limited personnel, and out-of-date facilities. If these perceptions impact the talent acquisition for those who would perform the work, student and donor recruitment also becomes an uphill race to the finish for those who are in charge of leading HBCUs.

Leading as a Black Woman: Commitments, Intrusions, and Sacrifice

To lead from calling takes a commitment which can engender intrusions into one's personal decisions and can require sacrifices. American Council on Education (ACE) studies of the U.S. college presidency over a 36-year span indicate very little change in the presidential career path (Melidona et al., 2023). Most college presidents report moving up through careers in higher education, and this was especially true for women presidents. Where there was growth in the numbers of men from nontraditional routes, women traversed more traditional pathways, which may speak of the acceptance of women at the helm. The 2016 ACE College President's Survey found that women were more likely to be first-time college presidents and tended toward shorter tenures (Gagliardi et al., 2017). Similar analyses for the 2022 edition are ongoing. While there was more gender parity in positions for master's-granting institutions (Melidona et al., 2023), for bachelor's and doctorate-granting institutions, the percentages of women were relatively lower (Gagliardi et al., 2017), although women seem to have made progress in their share of baccalaureate degree institutions since 2016 (Melidona et al., 2023).

Further data collected first in the 2017 Survey and again in the 2022 Survey revealed an updated category that may be considered as an acknowledgment of the sacrifice presently embedded in the role. Across both surveys, women were more likely to report that they altered their career progression to care for a dependent, spouse or partner, or parent. Career alteration in this context was defined as having left a position, worked a part-time or reduced schedule, postponed a job search or promotion, or made other career decisions because of the responsibility to care for others (Melidona et al., 2023).

In the present study, of the three women included, one was divorced, one had been a widow four years prior to her appointment, and one was currently married. The women were either not mothers or had adult children. In this manner these women were able to devote their full attention to the campus community, a community that is circumspectly demanding on a 24/7 basis. There are choices, commitment, and even intrusions for Black women who accepted the role as first-time HBCU presidencies.

For example, consider the explicit language of the contract for then-Alabama State University president Dr. Gwendolyn Boyd, age 58, which regulated who could come visit her home. Dr. Boyd's $300,000 a year employment contract stipulated that as long as Boyd is single and president of the university—and residing in the president's house on campus—she cannot "cohabitate with any person with whom she has a romantic relation." ... "The state is trying to interfere with this woman's personal life," said Raymond D. Cotton, a Washington DC lawyer, who has negotiated more than 300 contracts for university presidents. "Let's say she has someone stay overnight. How are they going to determine whether they are cohabitating or not, or whether or not she has a romantic relationship with that person?" he questioned ABC News (Dimitrova, 2014).

Women within the context of the present study also incurred personal intrusions. For example, Dr. Browning spoke about several ways in which her womanhood was made more of a focus, than her skill set to move to stabilize the CSU and move it into a competitive position. Yet, the media wrote about her clothes and her husband. Initially, during her transition, Browning was introduced to the culture of the community; however, it was less direct. She was introduced to it through a warning from her sister. Amid her response to a question specific to gender, Browning continued to talk about the culture in a way that caused her to have to consider a very personal choice for which she would have to contend:

> My husband is White ... He wasn't planning to come [South with me] ... That wasn't the plan, but [the president of the system] persuaded me to have him come. She said, "You're going to need that support." I think in some ways it was a mistake because my sister warned me that people wouldn't like it. Black people wouldn't like it, and White people wouldn't like it. Also, too, I was the first Black person who joined the ... Country Club.

Similarly, Dr. Golden spoke about her interview process and how her adult daughter had to agree to be her partner at events. Golden was recently divorced at the time of her appointment. Do male candidates have the same requirement? And if so, why would a candidate's ability to get the job done be determined by the availability of a plus one. Golden also spoke about her board member who was determined to have her commit to dating and buying a house. She discussed how her board chair would make a mention of her not having changed her car license plates from an out-of-state tag to a North Carolina tag. Dr. Golden was repeatedly questioned by a woman on her board about the privacy of her dating life and also about her building a home in another state versus choosing to build or purchase locally. To each experience Golden responded with a quick-witted retort to silence this intrusive line of questioning and inappropriate conjectures regarding her personal life.

In addition to personal intrusions, these women are often asked to lead in ways that may even conflict with basic business practices. For the Black women in the study, their decision not to conform, or to at least hold as standard the bar expected and accepted by men, puts an added strain on their ability to meet the goals of their institution. In an industry-related periodical, key points of Dr. Browning's three-year contract were mentioned. What was not mentioned, however, was that part of the transition period which included Browning waiting to receive the written contract because of internal negotiation, about *whether* to offer an actual contract *or not*. This debate and negotiation among the board were taking place for BOTH of the women who were being offered chancellor positions in the system at that time. Interestingly, it was the first woman system president who was pushing for both women to have written contracts. Chancellors being offered written contracts was not typical in the system at that time. As Browning discussed,

> I was hired when a woman was president of the System … When I was hired, a woman [another woman was hired at the same time for another System School]. I would not have come to CSU had I not been offered a contract … I was under the impression that all chancellors got contracts … I had never worked in a system in which chancellors did not have contracts … a particular Black board member who lobbied on my behalf, in addition to the System president was trying to persuade that board to provide this other woman and me with contracts. Now the other woman … was given a contract, and there was board member who said, "I know you're not going to bring in this Black woman and ask her to come without a contract when you just gave this White woman a contract…"

Dr. Smith's recollections include a variety of ways in which her calling and who she was were challenged. She recounted dealing with judgement she was unaccustomed to, including experiences where those in power in her city indicated that no African American had ever risen to the role of leader in the way she did. In pushing that SMU has access to monies and resources that were designated for colleges and universities in the city but had not been accessed before her tenure, Smith touts the unlikely allyship of White businesswomen and philanthropists opening doors and offering support rather than other Black leaders and HBCU-affiliated professionals. One of her most telling experiences is the lack of basic business practice or courtesy which surrounded her last days in the role.

Dr. Smith announced her retirement on April 4, 2014, effective on May 30, 2014; it was a Friday. In an email to her over the same weekend, her board chair informed her last day was to be April 4, 2014; a press conference was held on Monday, April 7, announcing an interim leader. Through that gesture, she discovered it was more important to the male-dominated leadership of the Board to impugn her dignity than to consider the greater impact on the institution. What they had not considered was that the institution was currently in negotiations with the U.S. Department of Education for additional funding to offset the impact of changes to Parent Plus loan, and other Title IV-related policy changes; a consideration that rested largely on Smith's reputation as a trusted steward of educational resources.

In response to an interview question, "What was different or the same about your experiences at [the point of your last 100 days]" Dr. Smith first gave some backstory:

> ...I was told once by a major player in The City—a philanthropic leader, "When you can tell me why should I invest in St. Monica's, then come back and we'll talk about a fundraising initiative" ... Early in my tenure, when I first met him, I could not. [At the end of my tenure] I could literally tell you: student graduate success, facilities, role in economic strength of The City, unique academic programs, etc.... Here's this institution that's fiscally solvent, that has a stable enrollment, that is garnering its place in higher education, where the president is on the White House ... President's White House advisory board, where the kids are doing well, where Fox is giving out scholarships to nobody but kids from St. Monica, and there's just a litany of things that show that this institution had moved from obscurity to really having a place in higher education where people noted

it and where its faculty and staff were beginning to benefit from being employed by Saint Monica University. I think what happened was I got comfortable as in, "Here's the success. Certainly this is enough for us to now move into some level of normalcy."...

Black women in almost any field, have a historical and yet unwritten expectation placed on them to succeed, support, and lead beyond all else. To be the ones to pull it together, to hold it down, and to make it count. The presidents of HBCUs are no different, yet they carry the additional burden of having to actually do it for "the culture." Yet and still, there are stories of Black women who lead these institutions that even the men who lead them may believe to be far-fetched.

Bond (2011) and Kaba (2005) subscribe to the idea that as the Black woman in America has progressed, and made significant gains in status, inclusive of a shift in attaining senior positions in education, those accomplishments appear to be at the expense of Black men. Cole (1993) considered sexism and racism as parallel challenges for Black women, and reflected on experiences where she said the most damaging encounters for Black women occurred through their engagement with Black men. That inference was evident in my findings through descriptors of institutional culture. The literature considered race and gender "institutionally" in a broader context, but it was evident in each of the lived experiences of my study participants, that challenges regarding perception of these women's skills and abilities were raised by Black men within the governance structure. Even more apparent was the challenge to the women's authority that was initiated by men, and in two of the instances, specifically Black men. In some scenarios, possible derailment of Black women in the president's seat came at the expense or detriment of the school. Each participant identified men who were in power, or who wanted to be in power, whose behavior was the alternative of supportive. To provide balance, each woman also talked about how Black men in their lives were also crucial allies and supporters of their success. These women did not see themselves as being in competition with men, as they were most driven by the calling to improve, stabilize, and raise the profile of the institution, far beyond the gratification of raising themselves. Black men in many instances served as allies. Many of the milestones celebrated by these women, were those resulting from true collaborative efforts with men as directors, coaches, vice presidents, and vision-minded board members. It is not always a zero-sum game. The idea that Black women must advance at the expense of Black men is a myth. Moreover, there are men who see the strategic benefit of working with or following a woman who is a visionary or has a genuine commitment to people and students of color (Cole & Guy-Sheftall, 2003).

How They Made a Shift In Spite of What They Faced

In contrast with other researchers who may consider the leadership styles associated with women as the reason they may be more likely to be chosen as leaders amid a crisis, Ryan and Haslam (2006) considered an alternative to the reasons in the upward trend of women in leadership of corporations and government. In this 2007 study, they examined the responses to men and women related to the concept. The themes that emerged in the explanations for the glass cliff categorized in Ryan et al. (2007) are of relevance to the current research on the experiences of women who were the first to lead HBCUs. Those categorical themes include sexism, favoritism, women's expendability, and lack of opportunities, lack of support, gender stereotypes, equality, company factors, and denial of phenomenon. The themes with the highest frequency of response were sexism, gender stereotypes, and lack of opportunities. Responses varied by gender of respondents as well, oftentimes to the extent that primary feedback was gathered from one gender over another. Of interest to this study are the considerations of expandability and scapegoating rationale:

> Related to explanations based on discrimination and in-group favoritism, respondents also argued that women are appointed to glass cliff positions because company decision makers see women as more expendable ... Once more, gender also played a role in such explanations. So while over 13 per cent of women favored expendability and scapegoating as explanations of the glass cliff, no men generated this as a response. (p. 188)

Most significant in Ryan and Haslam's (2009) study is the issue of the complexity in evaluating the existence or influence of a potential glass cliff, particularly when the studies only considered the financial performance of an organization as a determinant of a precarious environment (p. 15). When viewing an organization to be at risk, one must look beyond "risk as operationalized in terms of poor performance but [consider risk also as] defined by a history of failure, a high risk of criticism, and low levels of support or lack of resources" (Ryan & Haslam, 2006). In this vein, the context Ryan and colleagues describe fits the perception of conditions at HBCUs. As one respondent in Ryan's study suggested:

> Women will be placed in glass cliff situations because women are expendable. A glass cliff requires a competent individual, so senior managers will figure which candidates can handle the role. Then they will take out any candidates that they are grooming or care about in order to protect them. Those will often be men, because senior managers are men, and are more likely to mentor younger men than they are to mentor women. So, the candidate pool they are left with will have a large percentage of women—women who are capable, yet expendable because no one is really rooting for their success. (Female middle manager, 35)

Gender stereotypes act as if "women always want to help, and often help the underdog" women "have more skills to balance risk" and they "tend to cope with failure more pragmatically than men." These perceived abilities are epitomized in the comments of another female respondent in Ryan's study when describing the reasons why she thought her mother had been placed in a glass cliff situation: In certain cases, women are thought to inherently possess "soft" skills that make them part manager—part human resource director.

> My mother was given a department of viciously feuding staff members to oversee—a job that no-one in their right mind would take—because, aside from her managerial skills, they felt that she could "smooth things over." Not something a man would be expected to do. (Female professional, 35)

Still another participant in the glass cliff study had this to say about women appointed to lead in precarious positions in industry, or in taking over government positions in challenging districts "Women are perceived to be more competent in crises involving other people and their fate." Though Ryan and Haslam's studies of the glass cliff framework were not applicable in educational settings, the tenets of the study and the findings set a powerful foundation when considering its application in comparison and conflict of a woman's calling to serve schools in crisis, which are designed to change the social mobility of marginalized populations.

The Calling Emerges

What influences the calling in these, and other Black women who lead HBCUs? For each case in my study, participants did not attribute gender as a defining characteristic of life or career goals, at least not until they assumed the presidency. Drs. Golden and Smith both had fathers who encouraged them to be their best selves regardless of their race and gender. In fact, given Dr. Smith's experiences as a young person, her father took the lead in her care during her early development. Her father, a college professor, was the one who went to parent–teacher meetings and did the grocery shopping. He was the one who taught her to question and challenge the societal norms. Dr. Golden's childhood included experiencing and managing the wages for her father's farm from the time she was nine years old. This provided her with a foundation of her aptitude to get things done by building rapport as well as in managing and raising money.

However, in their experiences of being the first Black woman president or chancellor at the respective HBCU in a patriarchal environment, the findings confirm that all three women had a realization that they must contend with the duality of their identity as Black and a woman. Each woman's narrative revealed their awareness of their womanhood in response to one question I reserved for the end of the interview. Each, in her own way, acknowledged how their gender was not something they had ever considered, at least not the same way in which their Blackness had been an element of their identity. The findings related to gender were communicated during the interview and emerged more as lessons for aspiring Black female leaders, as well as realizations about culture in a broader context.

This reflection from Dr. Smith, while specific to her tenure, surmises the sentiment of many of those women who served. Smith found her identity as woman most relevant in her experience during her last 100 days.

I'm not sure that I ever conquered the burden of being African American and female. I don't have a placating, accommodating personality, I'm an advocate ... In much of my professional career, my competence, my articulation skills, my ability to analyze quickly and summarize and take action served as assets. That doesn't mean that I didn't get into trouble along the way, but almost in every other aspect of my career, the language would be, "She's going to tell you what she thinks, but she's smart. She's this. She's that." It's positive. "If you want to get it done, give it to her to do." The 15 years at St. Monica was the first experience that I had where I actually was dealing with people whose reaction to that combination of skills and attributes was vicious; where people were not attacking decisions that were made or the true content of the decision but were personal in their attacks. I'm not sure I recognized being a woman was a REALLY big deal ... had never had to deal with the factor before, or so I thought. I'm not sure I recognized that that had not changed along the way

After prompting, Golden had this to say about her experience in leading MIBU as its first Black woman president:

I learned that you can't do anything, and you cannot move ahead, unless you have the support of the people. Everybody has a different way of getting the support. My way of getting their support was to get engaged with the work. I rolled up my sleeves and helped them do it ... To [heck] with the rest of them ... At first, I didn't [have an awareness about being a woman in the role of president]. To be honest with you, at first I did not. It has been in recent years, that I could see what the problem was of being a woman, and it was colored by my experience at [a PWI in Georgia]. Whereas [there] being Black was the guiding thing. You had more flack because of that than you did because you're a woman. It was so bad either way.

As their gender had not been made a focal point or posed a dilemma in their career prior to assuming their role as campus president of an HBCU in North Carolina, none of the women spent any considerable time during the preparation period to guard against this, a factor that may become a pivotal point in their journey.

The Need for Black Women's Leadership

It is often through the lessons learned, that one gains the greatest insights, and therefore I will share some of those here for ponderance and consideration.

Each of these women did what they were told they were brought to do in their respective colleges. Not unlike the case with the women of focus for this study, where there have been permanent replacements, after their tenure those replacements have been men. In many of the scenarios, enrollment was stabilizing, the facilities were updated, upgraded, or newly constructed, and academic programs were added or enhanced as a result of the woman's leadership. And graduates were experiencing increased social mobility.

The appointment of women in the role of the president at HBCUs is of critical importance. There is an increasingly high number of vacancies over the last few years at these institutions, as long-standing men who are presidents retire, or move on to other career opportunities (de Gregory, 2016; Selig, 2022). Thus, the cultivation and support of women leaders is necessary as a matter of practice. Organizations such as Black Women Collegiate Presidents and Chancellors (BWCPC; BWCPC1@gmail.com) are working toward increasing the preparation and support of Black women to rise to these roles.

A quoted higher education expert says this in the context of why recent openings may be primed for more diverse executive leadership "less-selective and less-well-resourced institutions are more challenging to lead and manage, resulting in less interest from White and male applicants." Lynn Perry Wooten, president of Simmons University in Massachusetts, gives a nod to the rise in women of color being interested in and selected as presidents at an increasing rate:

> Wooten, who has extensively researched crisis leadership, said moments like these present an opportunity to inject diversity and innovation. Wooten is the school's first Black president, and she said that as she was completing her PhD in the '90s, institutions were making a push to invest in diversity. Those students have now grown up to have the age and experience to lead, she said. (*quoted in* Selig, 2022)

THE FUTURE OF BLACK WOMEN'S SENIOR EXECUTIVE ACADEMIC LEADERSHIP

The thing about calling is it does not dissipate as one moves out of one role and assumes another. The Black women who lead HBCUs, continue to train, coach, mentor, and try to guide. This was a very small sampling of the women who answered the call to lead the masses. In June 2022, the collective group of Black women who have now served as presidents and chancellors of HBCUs have formalized a non-profit organization designed to expand their calling and help other women to do the same. According to the press release:

> The purpose of the organization is to provide charitable support, consultation, and activities that transform life destinies especially of vulnerable persons through education, information, community development, and partnership building. Some of the specific endeavors will be to increase the number of well-prepared Black women who are Collegiate Presidents and Chancellors as well as CEOs; provide training and technical assistance and mentoring support for potential and new Black Women Presidents and Chancellors and serve as advocates for Black Women Presidents and Chancellors.

Further supports for Black women presidents at HBCUs are identified by Lederman (2022) including preparatory initiatives with an HBCU-specific focus such as the Higher Education Leadership Foundation's Leadership Institute, as well as the HBCU Executive Leadership Institute, founded by current Clark Atlanta University president, Dr. George T. French, Jr.

CONCLUSION

The women in the study were all presidents during the same period, in the same state. In some instances, each woman, had an opportunity to connect with the other, but in most instances, there was something on the inside that prevented them from leaning on each other in a more intentional way. Each woman reflected on her last 100 days with a reference to timing—Smith spoke of staying too long, Golden spoke of knowing it was time, while Browning admitting to running out of it (time). In more recent years, there has been a rise in podcasts, articles, or even pop culture idioms praising and promoting the benefits of professional and peer mentorship among Black women. Browning and Smith, separately spoke about getting to a point where they saw each other as a resource, but for both, it was well after their first 100 days. Unfortunately, not leaning into this level of vulnerability was not uncommon, as Black "girl" mentorship did not appear as essential during that era. When you were the first, particularly during the tenures of those women who moved into roles in the early 2000s, there were very few examples from which to pull. Black "girl" mentorship may seem to some a missed opportunity by today's standard. One of the main tenets (driving force) for the BWCPC was a decision by the over 30-member roster to fill the gap for the insufficient support of newly minted or current Black women as top college/university leaders. And as a way of true calling, these are the sentiments and attestations from each member who attended the inaugural meeting. Each woman was asked to share, in round robin format, the word or phrase that made meaning of their experience as presidents, and the significance of being present that day:

> When women lead, streams run uphill … Humbled and honored … safe space. Intentional and Intrusive … long-lasting impact … Agents of change … Idea of community and belonging … salutes and prayers … Hope toward the advancement of humankind…Keep looking for the sun…Grateful. … Caring Connections … Dealing with dynamics seen and unseen … Own Your Own—Always look out for yourself, your home, and have your own car … OOOOOH the possibilities. (Personal communication)

For the women of my study, many of their stories have ceased being told. On most campuses, there is intentionally barely a trace, physically, that they were ever there. But it is this calling and their decisions to shift even when it put their career in jeopardy that has made the difference.

These women "went to schools in trouble [and were] care givers to students, communities and constituents." As a parting reflection, these women share, "We have held up half the sky. It will take women leaders to help the sustainable democracy," and our "transformative leadership."

QUESTIONS TO PONDER

1. What is my calling? Is it a calling of service? Where? And to whom?
2. What is the source of inspiration/renewal? What keeps me motivated?
3. Do I have vision for my present leadership role? What am I doing to realize that vision?

4. Who are my partners?
5. How do I know when it is time to transition?

KEY TAKEAWAYS

- Calling comes from within. Center yourself to better understand who you are and your purpose before endeavoring in formal leadership.
- Crises come and go. Preparation is the best defense against the unexpected.
- Celebrate all wins. Create short-term goals and use the momentum from achieving these goals to achieve more wins.
- The support of diverse constituencies is never 100%. Cultivate allies but be aware of shifting agendas.

KEYWORDS

Black women; leadership; historically Black colleges and universities; college presidency; mission; commitment

REFERENCES

Anderson, J. D. (1988). *The education and the rise of Blacks in the New South, 1860–1935.* University of North Carolina Press.

Bond, H. (2011). Black females in higher education at HBCUs: The paradox of success. In C. R. Chambers (Ed.), *Black female undergraduates on campus: Successes and challenges. Diversity in higher education* (Vol. 8, pp. 131–144). Emerald Group Publishing Limited.

Bower, B. L., & Wolverton, M. (2009). *Answering the call: African American women in higher education leadership.* Stylus Publishing, LLC.

Cole, J. B. (1993). *Conversations: Straight talk with America's sister president.* Anchor.

Cole, J. B., & Guy-Sheftall, B. (2003). *Gender talk: The struggle for women's equality in African American communities.* One World.

de Gregory, C. (2016, November 22). Where have all the Black women HBCU presidents gone? And why aren't male presidents getting the same treatment? *HBCUDigest.com.* https://medium.com/hbcu-digest/where-have-all-the-black-women-hbcu-presidents-gone-3346d8146def

Dimitrova, K. (2014, Jan. 10). 'Love clause' appears in contract of college president. *ABC News*. https://abcnews.go.com/US/love-clause-appears-contract-college-president/story?id=21494543

Gagliardi, J. S., Espinosa, L. E., Turk, J. M., & Taylor, M. (2017). *American college president study 2017*. American Council on Education. Washington, DC.

Holmes, S. L. (2004). An overview of African-American college presidents: A game of two-steps forward, one step backward and standing still. *The Journal of Negro Education, 73*(1), 21–39.

Kaba, A. (2005). The gradual shift of wealth and power from African American males to African American females. *Journal of African American Studies, 9*(3), 33–44.

Kelliher, R. (2021, December). How three HBCUs are using MacKenzie Scott's gifts. *Diverse Education*. https://www.diverseeducation.com/institutions/hbcus/article/15286550/how-three-hbcus-are-using-mackenzie-scotts-gifts

Lederman, D. (2022, February). Diversity on the rise among college presidents. *Insider Higher Education*. https://www.insidehighered.com/news/2022/02/14/colleges-have-hired-more-minority-presidents-amid-racial-reckoning

Lewis, N. R. (2017). *Herstory: Exploration of the lived experiences of women who were first to lead an HBCU 1994 to 2014* [Dissertation, East Carolina University, Greenville, NC].

Melidona, D., Cecil, B. G., Cassell, A., & Chessman, H. M. (2023). *The American college president: 2023 edition*. American Council on Education. https://www.acenet.edu/Documents/American-College-President-IX-2023.pdf

Ryan, M., & Haslam, A. (2006). What lies beyond the glass ceiling? The glass cliff and the potential precariousness of women's leadership positions. *Human Resource Management International Digest*.

Ryan, M. K., & Alexander Haslam, S. (2009). Glass cliffs are not so easily scaled: On the precariousness of female CEOs' positions. *British Journal of Management, 20*(1), 13–16. https://doi.org/10.1111/j.1467-8551.2008.00598.x

Ryan, M. K., Alexander Haslam, S., & Postmes, T. (2007). Reactions to the glass cliff: Gender differences in the explanations for the precariousness of women's leadership positions. *Journal of Organizational Change Management, 20*(2), 182–197. https://doi.org/10.1108/09534810710724748

Ryan, M. K., Haslam, S. A., Hersby, M., & Bongiorno, R. (2006). *Think crisis—Think female: Glass cliffs and contextual variation in the think manager—Think male stereotype*. University of Exeter.

Selig, K. (2022, July 7). With a large number of college presidents stepping down, vacancies may open door for more diverse leaders. *The Boston Globe*, https://

www.bostonglobe.com/2022/07/05/metro/with-large-number-college-presi-
dents-stepping-down-it-could-be-perfect-time-diversify/

Turner, C. S.V. (2007). Pathways to the presidency: Biographical sketches of
women of color firsts. *Harvard Educational Review*, 77(1), 1–38.

Afterword

Kassie Freeman, PhD

When reading and reflecting on the *Black Women's Pathways to Executive Academic Leadership: Lessons From Lived Experiences* in this book, especially highlighted from their lessons and lived experiences, both good and sad feelings become intertwined. On the positive side, the good feeling, there is no denying that Black women bring an added dimension to the academy and, really, to any organizational leadership. Their leadership and voices carry a perspective and nuance that capture their lived experiences and will, understandably, be different from any other cultural group. That is why when Anna Julia Cooper as cited in the introduction of this book states, "When and where I enter … then and there the whole Negro race enters with me," it so perfectly indicates the interconnectedness of cultural experiences, how they become a symbol/metaphor for individuals of their cultural group, and also the way their actions are judged based on their lived experiences.

However, it is important to unpack and explore what Anna Julia Copper's statement means at a deeper level as it relates to Black women leaders even today. Although the book explores some of the Black women's lived experiences as it relates to pathways in the academy, it can be argued in some aspects it stereotypes or limits the vastness and richness of what Black women's leadership has meant and can mean—that is the sadness. On the other hand, if Anna Julia Cooper's statement is unpacked or reviewed in new and different ways, it captures a boldness and pride that often lacks in describing Black women's leadership and the pathways to their leadership possibilities.

First, when describing the characteristics of Black women leadership, there tends to be a confusion between soft versus hard skills. Black women leaders are often described almost like "mothering," as caring and nurturing—all great and worthwhile but that can tend to undermine their knowledge and expertise. When Anna Julia Cooper states, "When and where I enter," she is describing her pride in her race/culture, readiness, and preparation to take on challenges, that can be unmatched with any group or individuals she encounters. Therefore, although nurturing is certainly a characteristic that Black women leaders possess, their skillset, knowledge, and expertise cannot be underestimated.

Next, another area of sadness often describing Black women leadership tends to focus on the challenges and obstacles to leadership in the academy. While this is entirely appropriate and necessary, it tends to de-emphasize the ways Black women have already broken barriers and expanded beyond expectations. Highlighting some of these examples will provide much more upliftment, particularly for future women leaders. This book is advancing this important cause and it sets a course for the importance of including more voices across institution types. However, there is much more room for examples that captures the boldness and brashness from Anna Julia Cooper's statement, "When and where I enter..." There should be much more of those examples.

This book opens the door and can and should lead to more possibilities for Black women leadership in the academy. From this important book, here are takeaways in thinking and possibilities—broadening the definition of academic executive leadership; providing new and different narratives; and beginning different conversations about how, who, and what should increase Black women leaders in the academy.

BROADENING THE DEFINITION OF ACADEMIC EXECUTIVE LEADERSHIP

For starters, the definition of academic executive leadership can and should be broadened. The very fact that there is a need to have a necessary volume such as this that is inclusive of women leaders across institution types, that is, historically Black colleges and universities

(HBCUs) and community colleges, already sets up a hierarchy and block-age in pathways for women leaders. The fact that leadership skills and expertise gained at these institution types are often devalued, and already limit a huge number of women of color and their leadership possibilities for upward mobility, is troubling.

In addition to academic leadership being more inclusive at different institution types, it is also important to broaden the possibilities to begin focusing on skills and expertise in building women of color way below the levels of Provosts and Presidents—really should begin at the student levels. If the intent is truly to build pathways for academic leadership, the paradigms and models need to be conceived and developed for earlier pipelines.

Why is this important? If data are true according to the information published by United Negro College Fund (Herder, 2021), "62% of students at HBCUs are women, yet only about a quarter of HBCU presidents are women" (p. 4). Similarly to women in leadership roles at HBCUs, Ramsey (2003) in a much earlier presentation described African American women as, "still engaged in an on-going struggle with the insidious, double discrimination of racism and sexism" (p. 1). Not much has changed since that description. However, beginning the pipeline at the level of women students will pay much more dividend. This book suggests that as one important takeaway.

PROVIDING NEW AND DIFFERENT NARRATIVES

Another important takeaway from this book is that more voices and different narratives need not only to be told but also be written. If a wider range of voices is not captured, how can new and different pathways be effectively created? For example, how will scholarship on building pathways be inclusive of voices of someone like President Artis, president of Benedict College, who discussed how a member of her board focused on her looks and how that introduction "diminished me" (Herder, 2021, p. 3). As she indicated, that statement limited the value of her accomplishments. In a different way, the immediate past president of Spelman College, President Campbell, discussed "The Consequences of not—is that you are not able to bring your whole self into the room" (Herder, 2021, p. 5).

These are examples of narratives and perspectives necessary for search committees, institutions, and boards. It is hugely important to share stories/narratives from the current and past women leaders, indicating new and different pathways—challenges that can be addressed. A significant takeaway from this book is that it captures narratives from women of color across different institution types, provides a venue for building new and different pathways for many women, utilizing a wider array of women in leadership roles.

BEGINNING NEW CONVERSATIONS—HOW AND WHO SHOULD ADDRESS INCREASING PATHWAYS FOR WOMEN OF COLOR IN LEADERSHIP

Even with all the lessons learned and recommendations for enhancing pathways to academic leadership covered here, a question that will need much more attention going forward is, how and who should address building pathways to increase the number of women in leadership? Should it be the institutions or should it continue to be on the shoulders of the women of color?

Obviously, institutions of all types must play an important role. As demonstrated in this book, there are women of color leadership vacuums across all institution types. As highlighted here, institutions must address culture, climate of institutions while being proactive in creative new and different approaches. As highlighted throughout this volume, that will necessitate listening to and including a much broader range of voices.

One thing is for certain, while it is critical to include women of color in leadership roles, the sole responsibility of increasing academic pathways for other women leaders cannot and should not be placed on their shoulders. Certainly, as mentioned throughout this volume and in most volumes on women leadership, mentoring is crucial in creating opportunities and pipelines for future women. However, if the goal is to create environments and opportunities that are fair equitable, that will require societal and institutional support. However, once students enter higher education institutions, regardless of type, community college, HBCU, or predominately White institution, they have the opportunity and responsibility to provide new and different models to build pathways for all students.

One of the significant takeaways from this book is that it already addresses "how" to increase leadership pathways for women of color. It is all the more significant in that it is inclusive of women's voices across institution types, inclusive of institutions that are often limited and undervalued, that is, community college and HBCUs. That makes this volume an important contribution to the academy and the larger society.

WHERE TO NEXT … WHEN AND WHERE I ENTER?

Kudos to the authors of this volume. As someone who has led across institution types and have benefited from insights and mentoring from leaders, this is a volume that I highly suggest. This is an important beginning to often-overlooked and under-researched area in the wider society and the academy.

Listening to the stories and lived experiences of the women leaders of color in this book is inspiring. While mentorship is hugely important for creating pathways for future women leaders of color, my own upward mobility attests to that, having benefited from guidance and mentorship from two of the premier leaders of higher education, Dr. Johnnetta Cole and Dr. Ruth Simmons, and also from impactful White male President of Bowdoin College, Dr. Barry Mills. Their mentorship led to me being the first Dean of academic advancement at Bowdoin College, president of the nation's only HBCU system, the Southern University System, and now founder of a nonprofit, the African Diaspora Consortium that works in partnership with Teachers College, Columbia University, Tuskegee University, and the University of Notre Dame.

Based on my personal experiences, mentorship when being explored needs to be expanded to be inclusive of a wide range of individuals and the cross-pollination of institutional experiences in opening pathways for women of color. Certainly, the role of institutions in creating concrete opportunities for women should be of a much greater depth focusing on scholarship. Even more so, future scholarship needs to highlight women's knowledge and leadership expertise, not just highlighting nurturing as a leadership characteristic, that was so brilliantly captured by Anna Julia Cooper in her statement, "When and where I enter..."

REFERENCES

Herder, L. (2021, October 12). What woman want: Leadership at HBCUs. *Diverse Issues in Higher Education.* https://www.diverseeducation.com/institutions/hbcus/article/15279799/woman-in-leadership-at-hbcus

Ramsey, D. M. (2003). *African American women community college administrators: The legacy of being Black and female* [Conference session]. Eighth Annual National Conference, POCPWI, 2003, Vol. 31. https://digitalcommons.unl.edu/pocpwi8/31

Appendix: Resources for Academic Leaders

Black Women Collegiate Presidents and Chancellors

PRESS RELEASE

Our Legacy Builds the Future

It is a pleasure to announce that Black Women Collegiate Presidents and Chancellors (BWCPC), a powerhouse voice organized for the greater good, was established on June 21, 2022, for sharing professional expertise and support by providing training and technical assistance, mentoring, networking, as well as providing scholarships and funding support of charitable endeavors. Members of the 501c3 organization will serve as unified bridge builders and as a collective voice for good in the marketplace for influencing educational issues, policies, and practices of a culturally diverse perspective. The purpose of the organization is to provide charitable support, consultation, and activities that transform life destinies especially of vulnerable persons through education, information, community development, and partnership building. Some of the specific endeavors will be:

- Increase the number of well-prepared Black women who are Collegiate Presidents and Chancellors as well as CEOs
- Provide training and technical assistance and mentoring support for potential and new Black Women Presidents and Chancellors
- Serve as advocates for Black Women Presidents and Chancellors
- Provide scholarships and funding support of charitable educational causes and activities

Charter Members: Dr. Roslyn Clark Artis, Dr. Gwendolyn Boyd, Dr. Kemba Chambers, Dr. Johnnetta Betsch Cole, Dr. LaTonia Collins Smith, Dr. Phyllis Worthy Dawkins, Dr. Karrie Dixon, Dr. Cheryl Davenport Dozier, Dr. Vernell Bennett-Fairs, Dr. Regina Favors, Dr. Rochelle Ford, Dr. Algeania Warren Freeman, Dr. Glenda Glover, Dr. Cynthia Hammond, Dr. Beverly Hogan, Dr. Marvalene Hughes, Dr. Cheryl Evans Jones, Dr. Shirley A.R. Lewis, Dr. Julianne Malveaux, Dr. Elmira Mangum, Dr. Carolyn Meyers, Dr. Charlotte Morris, Dr. Glenda Price, Dr. Trudie Kibbe Reed, Dr. Lily McNair-Roberts, Dr. Patricia Sims, Dr. Gloria Scott, Dr. Dianne Boardley Suber, Dr. Thelma Thompson, and Dr. Dorothy Cowser Yancy.

Founders: Dr. Johnnetta Betsch Cole, Dr. Algeania Warren Freeman, Dr. Glenda Price, Dr. Trudie Kibbe Reed, and Dr. Dorothy Cowser Yancy.

For additional information, please contact: BWCPC1@gmail.com

Building Skills for Executive Academic Leadership
- The Leadership Competency Framework (B. D. Ruben), https://www.researchgate.net/publication/333075961_An_Overview_of_the_Leaders hip_Competency_Framework
- DISC—Knowledge of Self and Others, https://www.discprofile.com/what-is-disc
- Reflective Practice, https://www.forbes.com/sites/forbescoachescouncil/2021/12/22/seven-tips-for-designing-a-leadership-self-reflection-practice/?sh=2a4849bc1ea0

Pathways to the Presidency Resources
- Abdul-Alim, J. (2017, November 6). Chief diversity officers transitioning to the presidency. *Diverse Issues in Higher Education.* https://www.diverseeducation.com/home/article/15101613/chief-diversity-officers-transitioning-to-the-presidency
- Beardsley, S. C. (2017). Higher calling: The rise of nontraditional leaders in academia. University of Virginia Press.
- Bowen, W. G., & Shapiro, H. T. (Eds.). (1998). *Universities and their leadership.* Princeton University Press.
- Bower, B. L., & Wolverton, M. (2009). Answering the call: African American women in higher education leadership. Stylus Publishing, LLC.
- DeLoitte's Center for Higher Education Excellence, https://www2.deloitte.com/content/dam/insights/us/articles/3861_Pathways-to-the-university-presidency/DUP_Pathways-to-the-university-presidency.pdf
- Holmes, S. L. (2004). An overview of African American college presidents: A game of two steps forward, one step backward, and standing still. *Journal of Negro Education, 73*(1), 21–39.
- Holmes, S. L. (2008). Narrated voices of African American women in academe. *Journal of Thought, 43*(3–4), 101–124.
- Jones, T. B., Dawkins, L. S., McClinton, M. M., & Glover, M. H. (2012). *Pathways to higher education administration for African American women.* Sterling, Stylus.
- Martin, Q. (2018). Chief student affairs officers: Transforming pathways to the presidency. *Journal of Research on the College President, 2*(1). https://doi.org/10.54119/jrcp.2018.205

- McCarthy, C. (2017). Discover how a student affairs professional became a college president. *Student Affairs Today*, 20(8), 12.
- Risacher, J. (2004). The extent to which four-year college presidents who previously served as senior student affairs officers report having the characteristics of effective presidents. *NASPA Journal*, 41(3), 436–451.
- Viernes Turner, C. S. (2007). Pathways to the presidency: Biographical sketches of women of color firsts. *Harvard Educational Review*, 77(1), 1–38.
- Whitney, K. M. (2022, August 24). The 4 stages of a presidential lifecycle. *The Chronicle of Higher Education*. https://www.chronicle.com/article/the-4-stages-of-a-presidential-life-cycle

Preparing Your Leadership Package

Resume Templates, https://www.greatsampleresume.com/resume/examples/education/college-president, https://www.qwikresume.com/resume-samples/campus-president/

Writing Diversity Statements

- Higher Education Recruitment Consortium, https://www.hercjobs.org/write-your-diversity-statement-in-four-steps/
- Inside Higher Ed, https://www.insidehighered.com/advice/2016/06/10/how-write-effective-diversity-statement-essay

Writing Cover Letters

- The Balance Careers, https://www.thebalancecareers.com/cover-letter-example-higher-education-communications-2060189
- Inside Higher Ed, https://www.insidehighered.com/advice/2009/05/13/how-candidates-can-stand-out-good-way

Executive Coaching Resources

- Inside Higher Ed, https://www.insidehighered.com/advice/2021/04/20/seven-advantages-executive-coaches-can-provide-college-presidents-opinion
- *Diverse Issues in Higher Education*, https://www.diverseeducation.com/opinion/article/15306152/choosing-an-executive-leadership-coach-what-matters

Index

www.ingramcontent.com/pod-product-compliance
Lightning Source LLC
Chambersburg PA
CBHW062128020426
42335CB00013B/1135